THE CONTEMPORARY
PEASANTRY IN MEXICO

THE CONTEMPORARY PEASANTRY IN MEXICO

A Class Analysis

Ann Lucas de Rouffignac

PRAEGER SPECIAL STUDIES • PRAEGER SCIENTIFIC

New York • Philadelphia • Eastbourne, UK
Toronto • Hong Kong • Tokyo • Sydney

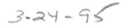

Library of Congress Cataloging in Publication Data

De Rouffignac, Ann Elizabeth Lucas.
    The contemporary peasantry in Mexico.

    Bibliography: p.
    Includes index.
    1. Peasantry--Mexico.   2. Agricultural laborers--
Mexico.   3. Agriculture and state--Mexico.   I. Title.
HD326.D38   1985   305.5′63   85-6317
ISBN 0-03-071868-6 (alk. paper)

Published in 1985 by Praeger Publishers
CBS Educational and Professional Publishing, a Division of CBS Inc.
521 Fifth Avenue, New York, NY 10175 USA

© 1985 by Praeger Publishers

56789 052 987654321

Printed in the United States of America on acid-free paper

INTERNATIONAL OFFICES

Orders from outside the United States should be sent to the appropriate address listed below. Orders from areas not listed below should be placed through CBS International Publishing, 383 Madison Ave., New York, NY 10175 USA

Australia, New Zealand
Holt Saunders, Pty, Ltd., 9 Waltham St., Artarmon, N.S.W. 2064, Sydney, Australia

Canada
Holt, Rinehart & Winston of Canada, 55 Horner Ave., Toronto, Ontario, Canada M8Z 4X6

Europe, the Middle East, & Africa
Holt Saunders, Ltd., 1 St. Anne's Road, Eastbourne, East Sussex, England BN21 3UN

Japan
Holt Saunders, Ltd., Ichibancho Central Building, 22-1 Ichibancho, 3rd Floor, Chiyodaku, Tokyo, Japan

Hong Kong, Southeast Asia
Holt Saunders Asia, Ltd., 10 Fl, Intercontinental Plaza, 94 Granville Road, Tsim Sha Tsui East, Kowloon, Hong Kong

Manuscript submissions should be sent to the Editorial Director, Praeger Publishers, 521 Fifth Avenue, New York, NY 10175 USA

To

Philippe, Rémy, and Caroline

ACKNOWLEDGMENTS

This project was essentially the final result of discussion, guidance, and encouragement from three persons. It is impossible to thank everyone who had a contribution to the project. I mention these three, without whom I would never have finished such an undertaking.

I cannot begin to pay back my debt of gratitude to Gustavo Esteva. It is rare that a person of his position in Mexico will readily receive a foreign student in his office, take her endeavor seriously, and even open his personal files for the foreigner's use. I ran into many other experts in Mexico not so willing to share or help-- only dominate and manipulate. Without his knowledge of the situation in rural Mexico and his access to otherwise unobtainable data, this project would never have been completed. A simple thank you seems inadequate.

Harry Cleaver's theoretical expertise helped me put order into the confusion that often surrounds a study of class relations in the Mexican countryside. Since my project was only one among several he was actively working on at the time, I thank him for the time and attention he so readily gave me when I needed it. However, I am solely responsible for any errors found within.

Finally, I thank my husband, Eric (and the children, who put up with a lot because of Mama's work), whose encouragement and support were the most essential of all.

A. de R., October 1984

CONTENTS

GLOSSARY

Amparo: a stay of the legal process until the legality of the action can be considered by a judge. In agrarian matters, amparos are usually invoked against presidential grants of land.

ANAGSA: La Aseguradora Nacional Agrícola y Ganadera S.A. (National Agricultural and Ranching Insurance Co.), a state agency.

Avío: short-term credit for cultivation. It covers direct production costs only, usually only partially.

BANRURAL: Banco Nacional de Crédito Rural (National Bank for Agricultural Credit), a state agency.

Cacique: the local agent who represents and operates the dominating structures. He is often an intermediary between campesinos and capital.

CAM: Consejo Agrarista Mexicano. An independent peasant organization active during the 1970s. It is thought to be controlled by the PRI.

Campesinos: peasants whose productive activity is intimately related formally or informally to the requirements of working the land; have their own autonomous productive organization; generally maintain strong community structures, with informal organizations based on social and cultural relationshps. The peasantry forms a sector of the working class.

Cargos: ceremonial positions whose occupants are responsible for important duties and services to the community. Associated with Indian communities.

CCI: Central Campesina Independiente. One of the large peasant organizations.

CIOAC: Central Independiente de Obreros Agrícolas y Campesinas (Independent Organization of Agricultural Workers and Peasants).

Comerciantes locales: merchants established in the peasant communities who buy the crops in the fields. They may be landowners, authorities in the community, municipal owners of stores, etc.

Comisariado de bienes comunales: a council, the authority in an Indian community, formally elected by the comuneros according to terms stipulated by law.

Comisariado ejidal: a council with the maximum authority of an ejido, formally elected by ejidatarios. Includes president, secretary, treasurer, sometimes auxiliary secretaries. It handles credit, commercialization, and other duties for the ejido.

Compra al tiempo: an arrangement between a lender and a peasant. The lender apportions money for seeds and other inputs on condition that at harvest the crop is sold to him, usually at one half of the current price.

Comunero: member of an Indian community officially recognized as a legal socioeconomic entity.

CNC: Confederacion Nacional Campesina (National Peasant Confederation). The largest government-controlled peasant organization.

CONASUPO: Compania Nacional de Subsistencias Populares (National Company for Popular Subsistence).

Consejo de vigilancia: a council above the comisariado ejidal in authority. Links with local authorities, usually has president, secretary, and treasurer.

Ejidatario: member of an ejido.

Ejidatarios or campesinos con derechos a salvo: sons of ejidatarios who have the legal right to a parcel of land but are as yet landless.

Ejido: a specific form of land tenure, stipulated by law, in which an individual member has the right to the exploitation of a specific plot of land. The right is not equivalent to ownership of the land. It consists of direct use of the land. The ejidatario cannot sell, rent, or mortgage the plot.

Finca: rural landed estate.

Ganadero: large cattle rancher.

Guardias blancas: armed paramilitary groups employed by powerful landowners, ranchers, and politicians who repress, intimidate, or murder any individual, group, or organization that threatens the existing sociopolitical economic structure.

Hacendado: owner of a large agricultural property with characteristics of the nineteenth-century hacienda-- power, wealth, and considerable influence over local political and economic affairs.

Indígenas acasillados: Indians and their families who live on a landowner's estate and work for the landowner.

INI: Instituto Nacional Indigenista (National Indian Institute).

IMMECAFE: Instituto Mexicano de Café (Mexican Coffee Institute, a state agency).

Jornal: a monetary payment (sometimes in kind) for a day's work on the land.

Jornaleros: temporary or permanent agricultural laborers.

La Merced: the central wholesale market for foodstuffs of Mexico, located in the heart of Mexico City.

Latifundio: a large agricultural estate generally owned and operated by one family. Although still prevalent in Mexico, this form of land tenure is ostensibly against the law. The presence of latifundios is a constant cause of peasant struggle. Latifundios in Mexico vary from being very modern in their approach to agriculture to still using inefficient methods.

Latifundista: large landowner of a latifundio, wielding considerable economic and political power.

Maquila: a fee. When associated with peasant agriculture, maquilas indicate that the peasant has paid someone else or an agency to use a certain machine or tool; or contracts them to perform a certain task which the peasant or group of ejidatarios is unable to do.

Medieros: campesinos who cultivate other people's land and must give the owner half of the harvest obtained.

Minifundistas: peasants who own or cultivate a small plot of land with only their and their family's labor.

Municipio libre: political and administrative area that forms the basis of the legal structure of federal power in Mexico. Vaguely equivalent to a county.

Nixtamal: fermented maize in a mixture of water and lime; a preliminary stage for the production of the masa (dough) for tortillas.

Obreros agrícolas: salaried agricultural workers.

Pacto de Ocampo: agreement formulated in 1975 between the leaders of the main national peasant organizations for the joint defense of their interests.

PEMEX: Petróleos Mexicanos (government enterprise responsible for production and marketing of the oil in Mexico).

Peónes: workers on haciendas and sometimes on fincas.

Prestanombre: someone who lends his name to a landowner so that the latter can continue to own and exploit more land than legally allowed by placing the illegal land in the name of the prestanombre.

PRI: Partido Revolucionario Institucional (Revolutionary Institutional Party).

PRONASE: Productora Nacional de Semillas (National Seed Producing Co., a state agency).

SAHOP: Secretaría de Asentamientos Humanos y Obras Públicas (Secretary of Human Affairs and Public Works).

SARH: Secretaria de Agricultura y Recursos Hidráulicos (Secretary of Agriculture and Water Resources).

SRA: Secretaría de Reforma Agraria (Secretary of Agrarian Reform).

TABAMEX: Tabacos Mexicanos. State agency responsible for tobacco production.

Tequio: the tradition of communal work. When peasants give their tequio it means they volunteer one workday for projects for common benefit.

Tienda de raya: a type of company store where peons' salary is used to pay real or fictitious debts with the hacendado. The peons receive credit at the store with which they buy consumer items, ending up in an endless situation of debt. Very common during the Porfirato; today only found in remote zones.

UGOCM: Unión General de Obreros y Campesinos de México (General Union of Mexican Workers and Peasants).

INTRODUCTION

In Mexico, conflicts among the peasantry, large landowners, and the state are neither new nor only to be found in history books. They are constant. Today, conflicts rage for control over resources--especially land and water. In fact, at times, the state has been obliged to intervene militarily in a countryside become a battlefield.[1]

Large groups of peasants have invaded lands[2] in such diverse states as Hidalgo, Oaxaca, Vera Cruz, Chiapas, Sinaloa, San Luis Potosí, and Puebla. These conflicts are the direct outgrowth of many problems in Mexican development. During the 1970s, for example, actual decreases in food production caused unprecedented levels of food imports.[3] Despite these imports, an estimated 21 million Mexicans continue to suffer from outright malnutrition.[4] In the face of this problem, policy makers have been forced to reassess their attitudes toward the peasantry and the agricultural sector.[5] They have increasingly recognized that the industrialization model of growth and development applied in Mexico for the last four decades[6] is bankrupt.[7]

During the last decade in Mexico, the centuries-old issues of peasant unrest, conflicts over land tenure, and agricultural production have once more moved to the center of the political stage. On this stage one group of actors-- business people and state officials with interests in commercial agriculture--have sought policies to increase output within the present social structure. Another group--peasants--are fighting to change that structure and to gain more control over their lives as well as obtain higher output. In what follows I will not focus on the efforts by the state to help promote agricultural growth, that is, the various political and economic alternatives presently being set forth.[8] Instead, my subject is the Mexican peasantry and its position within Mexican capitalism.

Instead of the usual Marxist analysis of the peasantry as the remainder of some earlier social formation who are suppressed and exploited by the dominant capitalist structure, I focus on how peasants have survived, have struggled, and have refused to be eliminated. Not only do they stand their ground but they often take the initiative against the capitalist system. The peasant up- heavals of the twentieth century began with the 1910 Mexi- can revolution, continued with the Russian and Chinese revolutions, and have included Bolivian, Cuban, and many other agrarian revolutions. I argue from one specific case (Mexico) why these events should lead us to recognize that the peasantry is an integral part of today's working class.

Three basic propositions of the orthodox Marxist tradition are contradicted. Proposition 1: capital is all- powerful in the economic sphere. Rather, the present cap- italist system is a class relation whose economic aspects are also political. The working class develops the power to force capital to redefine itself. It is the development of that power that constitutes revolutionary potential. Proposition 2: peasants are simply survivors from a pre- vious mode of production and can be largely ignored. In- stead, peasants are an integral part of the working class. Proposition 3: peasants are universally disappearing into the ranks of the urban or rural proletariat. On the con- trary, they constitute a unique and growing political force in Mexico.

These assertions about the peasantry are explained in Chapters 1 and 2. Chapter 1 presents and criticizes some of the major orthodox Marxist interpretations of the peasantry so that a new Marxist interpretation I call the "social capital" perspective can be proposed as an alter- native. The concept of an "unwaged" sector of the work- ing class in the specific case of the peasantry is elabo- rated. Chapter 2 is a look at crucial issues concerning the peasantry and the Mexican Marxists' debate about their status; questions such as, Who are the peasants? What about proletarianization? What role if any do peas- ants play in social change? These questions are consid- ered by analyzing what the most prominent Mexican spokes- men have to say on the subject. The ideas developed in Chapters 1 and 2 are then used to examine concrete rela- tions between the peasantry and capital in Mexico in Chapter 3. The various ways that the peasantry is in- cluded within capitalist reproduction are analyzed. This establishes how the peasant class is a working class-in- itself. Chapter 4 illustrates from contemporary peasant struggles in Mexico (late 1970s) that the peasantry not only is a class-in-itself but also forms a class-for-itself.

The ways peasants have disrupted capitalist accumulation and the positive processes in which peasants have been using their community organizations to struggle for their own forms of development are analyzed. Included is a discussion on the viability of the vía campesina as a path for self-development.

The purpose of this investigation is to encourage political parties and sympathetic policy makers to reassess policies and attitudes toward the peasantry as a sector of the working class. My conclusions are not intended to be taken as definitive, but they should stimulate further research and analysis on the role of the peasantry in social change.

NOTES

1. As the crisis increases, peasant mobilization increases. Clashes between the groups who fight for control of the productive resources claim some victim every day. (Gustavo Esteva, La Batalla en el México Rural [Mexico: Siglo XXI, 1980], p. 18). One important source of discontent that gives rise to much of the violence and protest is peasant loss of lands to the large landowners. It is impossible to note here all the incidents of landowners illegally usurping peasant land. But peasants are constantly proclaiming their losses and intentions to get their lands back in the national press (for example, a letter to the editor of Uno Mas Uno, August 1, 1979, from peasants of Igualapa, Guerrero; statements by the Indian representatives at their conference, July 25, 1979; peasants from Tuxtepéc, Oaxaca, demand that their lands be returned after latifundistas stole them under the protection of the government. Excelsior, April 19, 1979).

2. Hidalgo--officials of the secretary of agrarian reform indicated that in 1977 there were 365 invasions. In Huejutla, Hidalgo, alone that year there were 49 invasions. Uno Mas Uno, May 31, 1979; Oaxaca--peasants invaded 5,000 hectares in Tuxtepéc, Oaxaca. Excelsior, October 11, 1978; Ten thousand peasants entered lands in Juchitán, Oaxaca. Punto Crítico, January 1979; Vera Cruz--peasants from the Campamento Tierra y Libertad invaded lands in the municipio of Carrillo Puerto in 1974. They still occupy the lands despite kidnappings, jailings, and destruction of crops by surrounding landowners. Uno Mas Uno,

June 29, 1979; Sinaloa--there have been invasions in the
municipios of El Fuerte, Salvador, Alvarado, Ahome,
Culiacán, and El Valle de Carrizo since 1976. Excelsior,
April 19, 1978; San Luis Potosí--campesinos from the
Campamento Tierra y Libertad in the Huasteca Potosina
have a long history of invading lands since 1973. More
recently, they invaded lands in La Lima, La Subida, Benito
Juarez, Otates, La Caldera, San Pedro, and San Antonio in
San Luis Potosí. Punto Crítico, April 10, 1978; Puebla--
in the sierra of northern Puebla campesinos associated
with the Unión Campesina Independiente have invaded more
than 20 different pieces of land in the last two years.
Uno Mas Uno, July 11, 1979.

      3. In 1980, 25 percent of the food consumed in
Mexico was imported (Esteva, La Batalla, p. 17).

      4. Report from Instituto Nacional de Nutrición 1980,
in "Programa de Participación Inmediata del Sector Agropecuario en el Sistema Alimentario Mexicano," by BANRURAL
and ANAGSA, April 1980.

      5. The new Ley Federal de Desarrollo Agropecuario
(1980) represents sweeping efforts by the SARH to increase
agricultural production by legalizing direct interference
with the existing land tenure and agricultural production.
The program specifies that all agricultural producers of
each zone shall follow the plans elaborated by the SARH,
which indicate crops for each zone and the timing of the
agricultural tasks. If it is deemed necessary, the municipios can declare lands idle and distribute them to who-
ever has the resources and ability to make them productive.

      This is a powerful instrument that can redistribute
lands from the peasants, who are without "resources," to
the rich, who are supposed to be capable of making the
lands produce.

      Regarding the ejidatarios and comuneros, the law
proposes contracts (see Chapter 3, section on contract farming, for further discussion) between the peasants and a
state enterprise called PRONAGRA (Promotera Nacional para
la Producción de Granos Alimenticios). The contracts
("Contractos de Asociación") will specify technically and
financially all of the tasks, costs, and value of production
that the peasants produce. PRONAGRA will keep all accounts, will obtain crop insurance in its name, as well as
credit, which it will disperse. The peasants, whether
ejidatarios or comuneros, will receive minimum income for
their work. (Confidential document signed by the Dirección

General de Distritos y Unidades de Temporal, SARH, June 5, 1980). Further details from the new laws are not necessary to relate here in order to show that the state is proposing and implementing policies that drastically affect the peasantry.

6. For a description of the model, see Clark W. Reynolds, The Mexican Economy: Twentieth Century Structure and Growth (New Haven: Yale University Press, 1970).

7. Alejandro Schejtman, "El Agro Mexicano y Sus Intérpretes," Nexos 4 (March 1981):37.

8. See note 5. Arturo Warman, in Y Venimos a Contradecir: Los Campesinos de Morelos y el Estado Nacional (Mexico: CISINAH, Ediciones de la Casa Chata, 1976), makes an excellent effort at characterizing the relations between the state and the peasantry. Unfortunately, he viewed the peasants as purely victims or dupes of the state. "In the last instance the State does this: it establishes the general conditions for the plunder of the peasantry" (p. 334). "The essential contradiction is that the State carries out the domination of the industrial capitalist system of the peasant mode of production that sustains it" (p. 336). Later, Warman changed radically his opinion about the helplessness of the peasants. (See Chapter 2 for this discussion.)

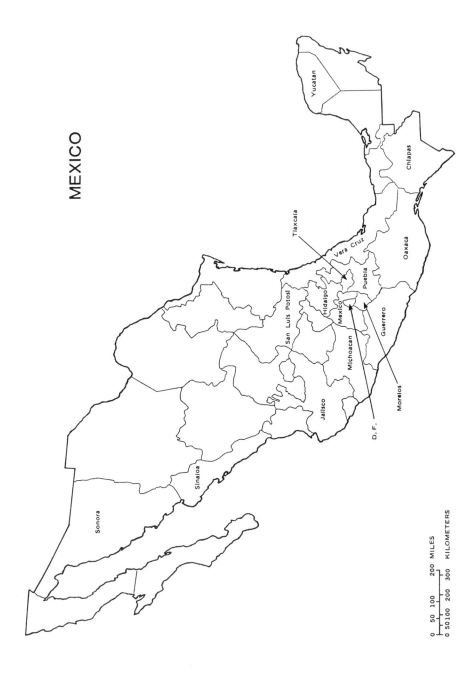

MEXICO

Yucatan

Chiapas

Tlaxcala

Vera Cruz

Oaxaca

Puebla

San Luis Potosi

Hidalgo

Mexico

Guerrero

Morelos

Michoacan

Jalisco

D. F.

Sinaloa

Sonora

0   50 100   200 MILES

0 50100 200   300   KILOMETERS

1

MARXIST PERSPECTIVES ON THE PEASANTRY

KARL MARX

Marx's scattered analyses of the peasantry have generated contradictory interpretations about their relation to the capitalist mode of production and even more controversy over the peasants' role in the overthrow of capital. His various interpreters over the years have either deified his work or ascribed such events as the Stalinist massacres of peasants directly to him.[1] This discussion is not intended to ferret out Marx's final word on peasants. Instead, Marx is studied to see how his ideas and categories could contribute toward understanding contemporary analysis of peasant class struggle. Nevertheless, since Marx has profoundly influenced theorists and consequently policy, it is necessary to expose the basics of many of these theoretical ideas.

In several places, Marx assigns the peasantry to a separate petty mode of production.[2] Marx describes the petty mode of production as flourishing when the laborer is the private owner of his own means of production set in action by himself--the peasant. This mode of production presupposes parceling of the soil and scattering of the other means of production.[3]

In the section on ground rent of Capital, volume 3, Marx continues to specify in more detail the category of peasant proprietorship. The peasant proprietors are the free owners of lands. Most of their produce is consumed directly as means of subsistence by the peasants themselves. The rest, if any, is sold as commodities on the market.

In other references to the peasantry as belonging to a separate mode of production, Marx comments on the social

1

relations within the production process. Claiming that small-holding peasants live in similar conditions, Marx sees that the peasantry forms a class in that they share the same economic conditions of existence.[4] Since they also may be exploited as a class by the bourgeoisie, Marx implies that peasants form a class-in-itself. But Marx asserts that the peasantry "do not enter into manifold relations with one another."[5] Their mode of production isolates them from one another. There is no community, no national bond, no political organization. From these conclusions, it follows that peasants do not form a class-for-itself; thus, they are incapable of enforcing class interests in their own name. "They cannot represent themselves; they wind up being 'represented.'"[6] Consequently, one may conclude that Marx assigned the peasantry to a separate mode of production given their isolation, their lack of class interests, and their inability to lead class struggle.

However, Marx did not emphasize the uniqueness or importance of a peasant mode of production or the study of the peasantry for its own sake. Most of his comments and observations about the peasantry were directed at how capital and the peasantry articulated and conflicted with each other. He was convinced that the influence and impact of capitalism doomed the petty mode of production to disintegration.

Marx states that in order to have capitalism the historical conditions of "free" labor or the separation of free labor from the objective conditions or means and material of labor must exist or be in the process of forming. "Money and commodities are no more capital than the means of production or subsistence. They must be transformed into capital, which means that the various commodity possessors must come face to face with free laborers. . . ."[7] This means that what existed before capital—petty peasant land ownership, feudal landlords, church properties, state properties, etc.—must be broken up.[8] Capitalist production emerged from the dissolution of feudal landownership. In several instances, Marx notes the necessity of dissolving the relations of production where a laborer is at the same time a free petty landowner or free peasant.[9]

This process, called the dissolution of the peasantry, is realized in a variety of manners. First, according to Marx, the peasant mode of production leads to the increasing parcelization and breaking up of agricultural entities through inheritance laws. Agricultural production becomes more inefficient and yields less for the immediate producers, who often fall prey to usury.[10]   Eventually,

> [the] peasant cedes to the capitalist--in-
> terest on mortgages, ground rent, the whole
> net profit and even part of his wages. The
> peasant becomes an Irish tenant farmer
> under the pretense of being a private pro-
> prietor.   The process is accelerated by
> burden of taxes, court costs over litigation
> on land titles, etc.[11]

At the same time, small peasant production cannot compete with the scale of modern agriculture and industry. Thus, the peasants and small handicraft men "sink gradu- ally into the proletariat."[12]   However, while the majority of small peasant producers are being hurled into the ranks of the proletariat, some peasant producers are forming the class of capitalist farmers.[13]   These farmers are enriched by the agricultural revolution just as speedily as it impov- erishes the mass of the agricultural society.   Concentrating the lands of previous peasant owners, they are able to modernize, produce more, and hire more workers, and thus breed their own capital.[14]
The internal dissolution of the peasantry as de- scribed was only one path toward the formation of the rural proletariat.   The other way, the forcible expropria- tion of the peasantry, is described in detail in volume 1, part 8, "The So-Called Primitive Accumulation."   Both pro- cesses occur simultaneously.   Marx goes into some depth about the initial formation of the working class and capi- talist class, using the example of England as a classic case.   Marx clearly describes the process as being violent and forced.   "Primitive accumulation is nothing else than the historical process of divorcing the producer from the means of production."[15]   The expropriation of the agricul- tural producer of the peasant from the soil is the basis of the whole process.[16]   Peasants were driven from feudal estates and the lands were usurped for sheep walks and later for deer forests.[17]   Parliament passed the Acts for Enclosures of Commons in the eighteenth century, which de- creed that landlords could expropriate the common land of the peasantry (communal lands) as their own private prop- erty.   In the nineteenth century the "clearing of estates," where peasants were literally driven off the land, their

houses and villages burned, completed the destruction of the peasantry.[18]

Political Role of the Peasantry

Marx also analyzes the peasantry in the real historical setting of The Class Struggles in France 1848-1850. In this work, the peculiarities of peasant mode of production or the longer-term tendency toward proletarianization are only peripherally mentioned. His principal concern is how the struggle unfolds between the workers and capital. There are parts of this political essay where peasants are on center stage.

The revolution of 1848, which brought to France a provisional republican government supposedly run by and for the proletariat, announced itself to the rural peasant population by the imposition of a new tax on them. Accordingly, they pictured the Paris proletariat as spend-thrifts at their expense.[19] Marx saw that these taxes exploited the peasantry and alienated them from the proletariat. They were the source of peasant reactionary support for Louis Bonaparte. When the peasants voted in Bonaparte, they were voting down their own exploitation and voting in a promise of no more taxes. But soon Bonaparte also trampled upon the peasants by imposing a new wine tax. The "reactionary" peasants took back their support from Bonaparte by presenting thousands of signed petitions. The French peasant, as Marx relates, began learning political language through actual experience.[20] The peasants took various actions against Bonaparte to defend themselves against further exploitation.

Marx's analysis of the peasant struggle with capital shows how the peasantry began siding with the proletariat. The two groups were driven together in open antagonism with capital. At one point, Marx points out that the exploitation of the peasant is only "different in form from the exploitation of the industrial proletariat. The exploiter is the same capital. . . ."[21] Although Marx still concludes that the French peasants were incapable of revolutionary initiative, the process by which he analyzed the history and circumstances surrounding the peasant actions is useful to us as a lesson in analysis.

Historical Materialism and the Peasant Community

In Marx's discussion of the primitive accumulation, he clearly states that he is analyzing the history of the birth of capitalism in England only. He calls it the classic case. We know that analysts following Marx tried to convert Marx's analysis of capitalism in England into a general historical sequence that all countries must experience. We will look at these historical materialists, such as Engels, Lenin, and Stalin, in the rest of this chapter and what their interpretation meant to the analysis of the peasantry. In later writings and letters, Marx emphasizes that he never intended his theory about the development of capitalism in England to be generalized.

In 1877, Marx wrote a reply to an article written by Nicolai Mikhailovsky, published in the Russian journal Otechnestvenniye Zapiski. Mikhailovsky stated that in Marx's view, in order to obtain socialism, Russia had to pass through a capitalist stage, destroying peasant society along the way. With regard to peasant society and communal property, Marx replied, "If Russia continues to move in the path followed up to 1861, it will lose the finest occasion that history has ever offered a people not to undergo all the sudden turns of fortune of the capitalist system."[22] Regarding the generalization of his history of capitalism, Marx replied that Mikhailovsky had changed his original sketch of the origin of capitalism in Western Europe into a "historical-philosophical theory of Universal Progress fatally imposed on all peoples, regardless of the historical circumstances in which they find themselves. . . ."

Confusion about Marx's theory of history and where the peasantry fit in continued. Four years later, in February 1881, Marx received a letter from Vera Zasulich asking for explicit ideas about the future of the village community in Russia and on the historical necessity of all countries passing through the stage of capitalist production.[23] Marx expended some effort in drafting a reply. Actually he wrote four drafts, sending only the shortest and possibly most vague of the four. In one of the drafts, Marx expounds on the village community, its vitality, and possibilities for development.

It [Russian community] occupies a unique situation without precedent in history. In all Europe it is the only one which still

forms an organic structure, predominating
in the rural life of an immense empire.
The communal ownership of the soil offers
it a natural basis for collective appropriation, and its historical environment, the
contemporaneous existence of capitalist production lends it all the ready made material conditions of cooperative labor, organized on a vast scale. The community
can adopt the positive achievements elaborated by the capitalist system without having to undergo its hardships. . . . [I]t
can become the direct point of origin of
the economic system towards which modern
society develops and it can cast off its
old skin without first committing suicide.[24]

The passage is significant not only because it denies the unilineal development of all societies, but it
brings forth the dynamism of the peasant village community;
the real possibilities of a postcapitalist society developing
from the roots of the peasant community. Marx denies the
necessity of a capitalist stage of development and the necessity of the destruction of the peasantry. The letters
are some of the first observations stating that the peasant
community indeed offers alternative possibilities for the
development of society. This observation is particularly
relevant for the analysis of the peasantry and their agrarian conflicts in Mexico.

When we look at Marx's various writings that concerned the peasantry, several key issues emerge that de-
serve further discussion. Marx identifies a separate
peasant mode of production and begins to specify its relations of production. Unfortunately, this task is taken
up by later Marxists as the "key" issue surrounding the
peasantry, diverting much analytical energy away from the
study of peasant class actions. The interpretation of history (historical materialism) that society develops along a
single line, which Marx himself denied, is an issue never
quite laid to rest. We will see this interpretation of history revived in later interpreters of Marx, such as Engels,
Lenin, Stalin, and others. This misconception of Marx's
ideas on history has a direct bearing on the future and
well-being of the peasantry. The proposed sequence of
development automatically predicts the elimination of pre-

vious modes of production and, therefore, the elimination by dissolution and proletarianization of the peasantry. This leads us to another crucial problem--proletarianization of the peasantry. Although in most of Marx's writings he prophesizes doom for the peasantry as a class, he does not claim it must happen for all societies for all times. The extent and degree of proletarianization is a question still pondered today in Mexico.

FRIEDRICH ENGELS

What follows is a brief statement of the essentials of Engels's materialist conception of history. It is necessary in order to understand the basis for other "Marxist" ideas about peasants.

In part 1 of The German Ideology (1846), Marx and Engels lay out the fundamentals of historical materialism.

> Our conception of history depends on our ability to expound the real process of production starting out from the simple material production of life and to comprehend the form of intercourse connected with this and created by this as the basis of all history . . . from this starting point to explain the whole mass of different theoretical products and forms of consciousness, religion, philosophy, ethics.[25]

Engels later builds these fragments from The German Ideology and Marx's Preface to A Contribution to the Critique of Political Economy (1858) into a very detailed interpretive approach to all of history. Engels is more explicit on what he means by historical materialism in "Socialism: Utopian and Scientific" (1880).

> All past history with the exception of its primitive stages was the history of class struggles. These warring classes of society are always the products of the modes of production and of exchange of the economic conditions of the time. . . . Economic structure of society always furnishes the real basis starting from which we can

alone work out the ultimate explanation of the whole superstructure of juridical and political institutions as well as religious and philosophical.[26]

Consequently, the task of historical materialists is to investigate these relations, i.e., economic conditions of production and exchange in order to illuminate the whole development of society.

The ultimate cause of movement in society, according to Engels, results from changes in the economic conditions of production and the human social relations associated with them.[27] The premise that Engels used in his reasoning was "the necessary condition for any society is that men should associate to produce their material means of subsistence."[28] Engels does more than just consult Marx's Preface to A Contribution to the Critique. He actually transforms Marx's statement that "the broad outlines of Asiatic, ancient, feudal, and modern bourgeois modes of production can be designated as progressive epochs in the economic formation of society" into a rigorous linear progression of modes of production. "The capitalist mode of production can be shown to be inevitable in a historical sequence and for a definite period of history as well as the inevitability of its downfall."[29]

Engels's interpretation of history as a linear sequence of modes of production is also seen in his writings on the social and political changes that were occurring in Russia in the late nineteenth century. In a letter to Danielson (Nicolaio-on) on October 17, 1893, Engels specifically states that

it is not possible to develop a higher social form out of primitive agrarian communism unless that form was already in existence in another country so as to serve as a model. Russia had no choice but this: either to develop the commune into a form of production from which it was separated by a number of historical stages an impossible task or else to develope into capitalism what remained to her but the latter choice [sic].[30]

We see that Engels insisted on a thorough bourgeois revolution in Russia despite its heavy human costs.[31]

   Although Marx and Engels began with a shared theoretical statement on history, The German Ideology, their
specific interpretations of historical situations are clearly
different. On the very same issue of development of capitalism in Russia versus the development based on the peasant commune, Marx, unlike Engels, believed that the commune was a culturally vital base upon which to build a
new socialist society. Further, Marx firmly opposed a unilineal interpretation of his ideas on history, made clear
in a letter to Nicolai Mikhailovsky written at the end of
1877.[32]

   Engels did observe and document peasant political
activity. In 1850, he wrote his most thorough treatment
of the peasantry in The Peasant War in Germany. The
purpose of the work was to explain that the 1848 revolution in Germany failed for the same reasons that the
sixteenth-century peasant rebellions failed. Engels wanted
to demonstrate that any revolution would fail that had a
strong petit bourgeois element, i.e., peasants, without the
leadership of a strong proletariat class.

   Engels narrates in detail the history of the peasant
mobilizations, the leaders, victories, and defeats as well
as their demands.[33] After 30 years of struggle, Engels
recounts how an all-out armed struggle defeated the peasants, whom he describes as being not much more than an
undisciplined, ill-equipped mob with no military strategy
whatsoever.[34] Yet from Engels's own description, we can
see how the peasants remained organized, resisted severe
repression, and even spread their influence geographically
for over 30 years. Despite this incredible mass peasant
movement, Engels clings to his idea that peasants can only
be freed from their misery when land is transformed into
social property and cultivated on a common basis by workers. Peasant salvation will come about only through the
introduction of bourgeois conditions and subsequent proletariat overthrow of capitalism.[35]

   But Engels's formalistic argument does not convince
me that this particular peasant rebellion failed simply because the protagonists were peasants. After all, struggles
by the proletariat likewise fail. The reasons for success
or failure of working-class struggles must be sought in
analysis of the strategies employed and of the relative

power of each class at the time. Struggles are not doomed
a priori according to sector of the working class. Engels
remains emphatic that the peasantry cannot contribute to
the revolution or to the transition to socialism because of
their attachment to private property and their peculiar
social relations. The peasant is labeled a survivor of a
past mode of production (the feudalist mode of production),
doomed to disappear. The inevitable disappearance of the
peasantry and their petit bourgeois attitudes toward revolution are ideas that surface again in a much more vivid
and concrete form in the works of Lenin and Stalin.

V. I. LENIN

Using his own studies and the fragments written by
Marx on the peasantry, Lenin proceeded to develop his own
theoretical position on the peasantry and capital. In
Russia, Lenin saw that the path of transition from the old
landlord feudalist economy to wage labor was being forged
by revolution. Once feudalism was destroyed, the new society of free small peasant farmers would then be dissolved,
according to Lenin, by a process he termed the "differentiation" of the peasantry.[36] Differentiation emerges from
the contradictory socioeconomic relations among the peasantry. As commodity producers, they are subject to the
vagaries of the market and at the mercy of finance and
merchant capital. Lenin referred the reader to the section
"Genesis of Capitalist Ground Rent" in Capital, volume 3,
for details of how the old peasantry becomes a class of
capitalist farmers or rural proletariat.[37]
During the differentiation of the peasantry, there
necessarily exist various types of peasants before their
final dissolution. Lenin classified various groups of peasantry to identify sectors that were potential allies to the
proletariat in the revolution to overthrow capital. The
agricultural wage workers (ex-peasants) make up the rural
proletariat, a part of the working class, to be in alliance
with, but completely guided by, the urban or industrial
proletariat. Lenin also included in the rural proletariat
those peasants who still have a small allotment of land
but are forced to sell their labor power part time to survive. The middle peasants were considered by Lenin as
potential inevitable members of the proletariat. "The middle peasants having the least developed commodity produc-

tion who produce for their own survival, and do not hire wage labor, live constantly on the edge of being swept into the ranks of the proletariat." Peasants who hire wage labor are classified as capitalists.

For Lenin, only the "industrialized proletariat is capable of conducting a steadfast and mass struggle against autocracy."[38] Peasant movements directed against feudal landlords that strive for land and liberty can lead to an improvement in their condition, even an overthrow of feudalist conditions, but not an end to capitalism. After the nonworking class struggle to overthrow feudalism, true proletarian class struggle must be brought to the countryside. One of the principal tasks of the party was to explain to the rural workers that its interests are irreconcilably opposed to those of the peasant bourgeoisie.[39]

Once the Bolsheviks were in power in Russia, Lenin had to deal with the peasantry. By definition, Lenin had excluded the peasantry (excepting the rural proletariat proper) from the working class and from the socialist revolution. Instead, they were petit bourgeois with inferior methods of production holding back the victory and domination of the dictatorship of the proletariat. Lenin described the peasantry:

> This group is used to farming each for
> himself. They are proprietors because
> they are in possession of food products.
> He produces more food than he needs for
> himself. So, with surplus grain, he be-
> comes the exploiter of the hungry worker.
> The contradiction is a peasant who lives
> by his own labor as one who has borne
> the yoke of capitalism sides with the work-
> er. But the peasant proprietor regards
> his surplus grain as property which he
> can sell freely.[40]

Lenin's answer to the "peasant problem" was to squeeze and exploit them. The peasants would not receive goods nor money but must begin by "lending" the workers grain at fixed prices.[41]

Concomitantly, the state policy toward small peasant farming was to replace it by large state collective farms, assuming the technical superiority of the latter. However, Lenin was forced to admit that the peasants responded to

these state policies of exploitation by frequent manifesta-
tions and complete rejection of the state farms. In fact,
the work commune became a call to fight communism. The
peasants tried to resist the policies that sought to drive
them into communes by force.[42]

In 1921, Lenin softened his policy toward the peasantry when he recognized that alienating the peasantry,
the majority of the country, would mean risking and probably losing proletarian control of the country.[43] Seeking
to prove to the peasantry that the party now wished to
help them instead of ruin them, Lenin called a halt to the
grain appropriations, substituting in its stead a lighter
tax in kind.[44]

Lenin relied almost exclusively on the category of
the wage to identify social structure in the countryside
and consequently to base revolutionary strategy. Waged
workers who developed the highest class contradictions
would develop class consciousness--form a class-for-itself.
Peasants, unwaged, did not form a class-for-itself. Revolution would be organized and directed by the urban industrial proletariat. The rural proletariat (ex-peasants)
was identified as an ally but incapable of organizing
working-class strategy. Consequently, revolution would be
brought from the cities to the countryside.

In the next section, we will see that for Mao revolution was brought from the countryside to the cities.
Peasants were revolutionaries. On this point, he departed
from Lenin, but Mao retained the requirement that overall
strategy and direction be entrusted to the urban industrial
proletariat.

MAO TSE-TUNG

Mao discovered the peasantry, their problems, their
struggles, and their revolutionary potential through direct
experience. Prior to this experience, however, he did con-
template a scheme of class structure in the Chinese countryside. In the essay "Analysis of the Classes in Chinese
Society" (1926), Mao designated five classes in Chinese society. The criteria included a vague definition of relations of production, economic status, and corresponding
political tendencies.

The first class, the landlord and comprador class,
had the most reactionary relations of production in China.

They were considered an extremely counterrevolutionary group. The second class, the middle bourgeoisie, were representative of capitalist relations of production within China. They favored an overthrow of imperialism but fiercely opposed proletariat domination of the revolution. The third class, the petite bourgeoisie, included lower-level civil servants, professionals, and three types of owner peasants: those who had some surplus money and accumulated capital; those who were economically self-supporting but were oppressed and exploited by the land-lords and bourgeoisie and had to work harder each year to make ends meet--they never opposed the revolution but hesitated to join it; and those owner peasants whose standard of living was falling--they, he judged, were very important to the revolution and formed the left wing of the petite bourgeoisie. The fourth class, the semiproletariat, consisted of five categories: (1) the semiowner peasants-- those peasants who worked partly on their own land and partly on rented land; (2) the poor peasants who owned no land, usually the tenant peasants, and were exploited by the landlords and sometimes forced to sell their labor power part of the year; (3) the small handicraft people who owned some means of production but were forced to sell their labor power part of the year; (4) the shop as-sistants--employees of shops and stores, who were constant-ly impoverished by inflation; and (5) the peddlers, who were extremely poor and unable to feed and clothe them-selves. They, he felt, were highly receptive to revolution. The fifth class, the proletariat, included the industrial proletariat, other service workers such as coolies, dockers, and sewage carters, and the rural proletariat, who had neither land nor implements.

Within this classification, we can see how Mao split the peasantry between the categories of petite bourgeoisie, semiproletariat, and proletariat according to their relation to land. Although peasants, who had extremely low eco-nomic status (with the exception of the owner-peasants, who accumulated capital), were exploited by the landlord and bourgeoisie classes, they were awarded only the status of "friends" of the revolution. By definition, they were neither the "vanguard" nor the "leading force" of the revo-lution but possible allies.

However, Mao went beyond such sociological categori-zation when he made his investigation of Hunan and his subsequent analyses of peasant reality. Finding that the peasants had effectively organized themselves into "peasant associations," Mao judged the peasant upsurge in Hunan to be more than just a haphazard uprising. It was an event--a colossal event, with the most profound implications for the future of China.[45]

> In a very short time several hundred million peasants in China's central, southern and northern provinces will rise like a tornado. . . . All revolutionary parties and all revolutionary comrades will stand before them to be tested, to be accepted or rejected as they decide. To march at their head and lead them? Or to stand in their way and oppose them? Every Chinese is free to choose, but events will force you to make the choice quickly.[46]

Thus, Mao recognized immediately that peasants were revolutionaries, making revolution with or without him and with or without the industrial proletariat.

Nevertheless, Mao asserted that the peasantry must be led by the proletariat or by outside intellectuals (like himself). Whether this came from a careful study of Lenin or from a simple observation that the peasantry led by him, or by the proletariat, could be guided or at least influenced, cannot be determined here. The point is Mao sought to take charge of the peasant movement rather than have the peasant movement take charge of the nation. His writings are replete with references to the necessity of proletariat leadership of the peasantry.[47]

Mao deemed the leadership of the proletariat essential because the proletariat had the highest sense of social consciousness and they also had the best ability to organize.[48]

Mao called the peasantry, the proletariat's most reliable ally, the "motive force" or the "main contingent" of the revolution. He credited the poor peasants with accomplishing revolutionary tasks that had been left unresolved for years.[49] Mao was one of the first Marxists to recognize that peasants are capable of autonomous struggle and coordinated revolutionary action. With the defeat of the landlords' domination, these peasant associations he found formed in Hunan were becoming the sole organ of authority in the countryside.[50]

Like Lenin, Mao insisted that the revolution the peasantry was making was not a proletarian socialist revolution but was rather bourgeois democratic. He saw the peasant revolution as a stage of transition between the abolition of colonial, semicolonial, and semifeudal society and the establishment of socialist society. Mao called this revolution a "new democratic" revolution because he saw it as part of the world proletarian socialist revolution--socialist because it opposed <u>foreign</u> capitalist intervention but democratic because it does not destroy capitalism. The new democratic revolution would clear the way for capitalism because the two obstacles to its development, colonialism and feudalism, would be destroyed. At the same time, it would retain the small peasant economy and those sections of capitalism that were capable of contributing to the antiimperialist, antifeudal struggle. However, Mao reassured his fellow Communists that the establishment of capitalism would create the prerequisites for socialism through the increased importance of the proletariat and the Communist Party, the creation of a state sector of the economy owned by the democratic republic, and the emergence of a cooperative sector owned by the working people.[51]

Mao's analysis of and attitude toward the peasantry certainly was a dramatic change from Lenin's, which regarded all but the rural proletariat as enemies of the revolution. Yet, given his very Leninist belief in the centrality of the proletariat, it is not clear if Mao's attitude toward the peasantry was genuinely friendly or only opportunistic. History shows that Mao's grasp of the revolutionary tendencies of the peasantry was fundamental to his ability to become the central figure in the revolution. Mao clearly realized that the revolutionary force of the peasants was essential to overthrow feudalism, semifeudalism, and imperialism during a long, protracted guerilla war. However, as subsequent history has made clear, once it came to constructing socialism, the Maoist state would seek to reorganize the peasantry according to its own designs and desires for accumulation.[52]

Mao was a Marxist founding his own school of thought. But it is difficult to see the direct influence that Marx may have had upon Mao's thinking about the peasantry. The Marxian concept of a petty mode of production or some separate peasant precapitalist mode of production is absent in Mao. Where Mao analyzes the peasantry he spends little time on their particular relations of production or on their methods and goals of production. Furthermore, Mao used a variety of criteria not used by Marx to classify the peasantry into categories. Mao's use of economic status and property relations stands out in contrast to Marx and Lenin. Mao did follow Marx in applying political attitudes and activities as criteria for distinguishing peasant classes and recognizing allies of the revolution.

Some authors have carelessly claimed that Mao was a "Leninist."[53] It is true that, like Lenin, Mao trusted the proletariat to lead the peasantry in revolution and to have the highest social consciousness. Likewise, he was clearly prepared to exploit the peasantry for socialist accumulation. However, Mao's political attitude toward the peasants was much more flexible than Lenin's. Peasants in Mao's system were not firmly entrenched into one enemy category but spread loosely among three large social classes, making it theoretically simple for Mao to shift policies according to his particular political goal at the moment. We also know that at another moment he was prepared to reorganize peasants into large collectivized farms with or without the peasants' blessing and enthusiasm. Mao actually changed his theory (edited and rewrote essays) to fit particular political goals in particular periods.[54]

Mao's political ideas concerning revolution and the role of the peasantry have had considerable influence throughout the part of the Third World where foreign capitalist interests have conflicted with large rebellious peasant populations. His "Road to Socialism" and use of guerilla warfare were major ideological and strategical components of Third World peasant upheavals in the 1960s. The historical fact of a Chinese revolution being born in the countryside and brought to surround the cities has had a lasting impact. He remains one of the first Marxists to recognize the autonomous organization and struggle of peasants.

MODE-OF-PRODUCTION ANALYSIS
AND THE PEASANTRY

Communist Historical Materialism

Communist Marxists based their theoretical ideas mostly on Marx's brief but now famous overview of history in the Preface to <u>A Contribution to the Critique of Political Economy</u>.[55]   Historical materialism, as developed by Engels, Lenin, and Stalin, has a long history of being used as a weapon against the peasants.

One of the clearest statements of historical materialism was written by Stalin.   In a pamphlet of some 40 pages, he further simplifies Engels's version of historical materialism into a rigid unilinear stages theory of history applicable to all societies.   He sums up his discussion of how society develops:

> In conformity with the change and development of the productive forces of society in the course of history, men's relations of production also changed and developed. Five main types of relations of production are known to history: primitive, communal, slave, feudal, capitalist, and socialist.[56]

Stalin asks the question what force determines the character of the social system and the development of society from one system to another.   "The force, historical materialism holds, is the method of procuring the means of life necessary for human existence, the mode of production of material values. . . ."[57]   We have the answer, according to Stalin, why a given social system is replaced precisely by such and such a new system--the slave system succeeded by the feudal system and feudal system by the capitalist system and so on.

Stalin blatantly ignored (or was unaware) of Marx's writings on the Russian commune.   Instead, Stalin created a dogma, labeled it Marxist, and used it to justify getting rid of peasant society.   He conveniently used his interpretation of Marxism-Leninism for his own political ends.   It justified beautifully the containment or repression of worker struggles.   Since in socialism, by definition, "the relations of production are in harmony with the forces of production," there can be no contradictions; class struggle was defined out of existence.   According to this interpretation of Marx, it was only when the material productive forces of society come into conflict with the existing relations of production that an era of social revolution would begin. Since socialism is defined by the harmony between the relations of production and the forces of production, then political turmoil can only be counterrevolutionary and deserving of repression. Historical materialism in its Stalinist version became the theoretical vindication for oppressing working-class struggles in the Soviet Union and later in much of Eastern Europe.

Understanding the peasantry to be a disintegrating class with their destruction inevitable, Stalinists had the theoretical justification to go ahead with force in their efforts at "socialist primitive accumulation." It is not necessary to go into the details of how many peasants died during the application of the Stalinist version of Marxism. Stalinist policies expedited socialist accumulation in the USSR at the expense of the peasantry.

Since the revelations of the horrors of collectivization, historical materialism as elaborated by Engels and Lenin and then simplified and applied by Stalin has not been as influential or popular among more recent analyses of the peasantry in the Marxist tradition. Historical materialism has been reformulated in a variety of ways by various authors. These reformulations of historical materialism constitute what I call "mode-of-production analysis." This general approach has grown in popularity among political economists and anthropologists studying the peasantry in contemporary societies of many countries.

Historical Materialism: The Structuralism
of Marta Harnecker

Drawing on the theoretical work of such structuralist Marxists as Louis Althusser, Nicos Poulantzas, and Etienne Balibar, Marta Harnecker has sought to apply a renovated version of historical materialism to Latin America and to the question of the peasantry she analyzes.[58] Instead of investigating the ideas of the authors on whom she draws-- an investigation that would be one step removed from the study of the peasantry--I will simply sketch her particular application of those ideas to the subject at hand.[59]

She analyzes the organization of the mode of production into different structures (economic, political, and ideological) whose internal dynamics and interaction determine the development of the "laws of action" of that society.[60] Thus, a specific combination of various structures, where one (not always the economic structure) dominates the others, constitutes the theoretical structure of a particular mode of production. The dominant structure

plays the fundamental role in the reproduction of a determined mode.[61] In capitalism, reproduction of the society
is assured by the internal laws of the economic structure,
for example, those of accumulation and rising organic composition of capital. However, in any actual society one
encounters various relations of production[62] that coexist
and combine but where one dominates and influences the
other. Thus, she studies the "social formation," which is
the historically determined social reality of a particular
society. The main analytical task at hand becomes the
diagnosis of what type of relations of production exist,
coexist, and combine.

Harnecker derives the social classes and their relations from the relations of production associated with the
modes of production.[63] She considers the most important
relation of production to be the relation of ownership and
nonownership of the means of production—identifying ownership with effective possession. In her mode-of-production
analysis this means the definition of social class is based
on economic criteria outside the more complex relations of
political practice.

Using this framework, she has neatly classified the
peasantry as belonging to some precapitalist mode of production. Assigning the peasantry to this separate mode of
production excludes them from capital. From her point of
view, the peasants seek only to maintain themselves and
their families and not to create value from their property.
Further, the private appropriation of a land parcel allows
the peasants ownership of their own labor power.

Since social class relations are assumed to derive
from the relations of production (the separation or exclusion
of workers from the means of production), peasants who
are small commodity producers who control their own means
of production and product of their labor cannot, by definition, be considered members of the proletariat within the
capitalist mode of production.[64] Peasants are, therefore,
seen as impotent, incapable of realizing true socialist
revolution. She sees peasant struggles as "spontaneous,"
isolated, and motivated by petit bourgeois desires for
wealth and property. The peasant mode of production,
she argues, eventually disintegrates as it joins with the
dominant capitalist mode of production. One part becomes
rich enough to join the petit bourgeois while the majority
are continuously pauperized into joining the ranks of the
rural proletariat.

She believes that the proletariat, those workers stripped of means of production and doing productive work, that is, creating surplus value through direct production, are the only ones who struggle for the overthrow of capital.[65] Unfortunately, she provides no analysis of the historical process of struggle, where the content and direction of the strategy of both classes unfolds and reacts to one another.

From my point of view, at any one moment of time the struggle for land, higher salaries, or better prices of output may be appropriate demands if, when gained, they give the peasant sector of the working class more power (i.e., more material foundation) to further build its struggle against capital. Every gain, no matter how seemingly insignificant, may provide the working class the means to struggle more intensely. What we must see is rather how the partial struggles contribute to the overall undermining of capital and together constitute the struggle. Harnecker, stuck within her set of structural categories, gives us no theoretical tools to see or analyze this.

It is true, as Harnecker argues, that capital will try to use working-class demands to its advantage. For example, when the peasants demand land, capital will often attempt to use land reform as a means to stabilize and control the peasantry. Capital may also advance credit, seeds, etc., to try to increase and control production. But what she fails to grasp is that (1) such tactics by capital are often responses to the growth of working-class initiatives and power, and (2) they often fail. Peasants frequently respond to such capitalist tactics by refusing to cooperate, or by taking the resources capital makes available and using them for their own purposes.

This kind of mode-of-production analysis, with all its emphasis on concepts, laws, and theory and none on historical reality, has become very popular for analyzing the peasantry, particularly in Latin America. The political ramifications of this type of approach (denial of working-class status for the peasantry) and consequent practice (ignoring or outright repression of peasant struggles) differ little from those of the older Communist historical materialism, as already discussed. Yet, commonly, those who employ this framework do not frankly admit what this theory means politically to the peasants.

In all, far too many historical materialists such as Harnecker think they have found the key to concrete societal differences without ever considering the problem of class struggle. The absence or even denial of class struggle is apparent in the studies by many anthropologists who have adopted some variety of the structuralist formulation of mode of production.[66]

Mode-of-Production Analysis and
the Debate in Latin America

The revival of Marxist analysis of mode of production as initiated by Harnecker provided a new stimulus to the specific debate over the nature of agricultural society in Latin America. With the "new" analysis, the myriad of production structures in agrarian society could be rigorously distinguished, described, and categorized. This approach offered a more flexible alternative to the orthodox (Stalinist) Marxists' discredited tendency to dismiss today's peasants in Latin America as a part of the feudalist mode of production.

The discussion of Latin America has been centered on the question of which mode or modes of production are present: feudal, precapitalist, capitalist, or some social formation involving the articulation of several modes. These exercises in identifying modes of production, stages of development, social formations, and relations of production carry with them corollary strategies for eventual working-class liberation. The peasantry is directly involved one way or another in each of these strategies.

The debate in Latin America actually gained momentum when the questions about underdevelopment and dependency became serious.[67] Mainstream Marxists still believed that the peasantry disappears with the onset of capitalist industrialization and modernization; therefore, the lack of development and presence of the peasantry must be the result of retarding old forms of production. In other words, underdevelopment was the result of remaining feudal relations of production. These Marxists advised socialists to seek alliance with the national bourgeoisie in order to break with feudal stagnation.[68]

On the other side, André Gunder Frank argued that the backwardness of Latin American society resulted not from feudalism but from the expansion of the world capitalist system. It was capitalist development that produced the exploitation of the underdeveloped. Capital itself linked metropolitan and peripheral countries, advanced and backward regions, city and countryside, and modern and backward agriculture.[69]   Frank went on to say that the peasant sector is not feudalist or isolated but intimately related and exploited by urban and international capitalist society through economic, commercial, political, and social relations.[70]   Frank emphatically denied that the bourgeois capitalist revolution remains to be made.   Instead, he advocated a strategy of peasant-worker alliance in overthrowing dependent capitalism.[71]   Frank argued that there were no more peasants in the traditional sense of independent, self-reliant, cultivators.   Today's peasants constitute the rural proletariat, an exploited source of labor, regardless of whether they are still on the land or among the urban and rural unemployed.

The Marxists I have called mode-of-production analysts entered into the debate over the nature of Latin American society and concomitant political strategy for the oppressed classes.   It was, they announced, simply a matter of putting aside the loose analysis of Frank, with his concepts of extracted surplus exploitation, and then determining the mode of production.[72]   This, they thought, would designate the social classes, including the relations of the peasantry to capital.   Ernesto Laclau, perhaps the clearest representative of this group, denied in one sentence both the views of orthodox Communist Marxists and Frank's dependent capitalist thesis.   "Both approaches designate feudalism or capitalism in the sphere of commodity exchange and not in the sphere of production so the link with the market becomes a decisive criterion for distinguishing between the forms of society--but feudalism or capitalism are modes of production."[73]   Laclau blasts away at Frank, accusing him of dispensing with relations of production to come up with a wide definition of capitalism that includes all different exploitative situations.   For Frank all these different direct producers assign their produce to the market, work for the benefit of others, and are deprived of the economic surplus they create.   The fundamental economic contradiction is exploiters versus exploited.   Laclau asserts that this is not the Marxist conception of capitalism.   "For Marx capitalism was a mode of production."[74]

Fernandez and Ocampo agree with Laclau that the concept of mode of production is the key to resolving the debate.[75]   But they use the concept in an even more

dogmatic manner to advance the old Communist thesis that
Latin America is feudalistic. "The backbone of Marxist
social theory is that the critic arrives by way of the theory of successive modes of production at a correct analysis
of classes in a concrete situation."[76] Fernandez and Ocampo
interpret Marx similarly to Stalin and Engels, with a few
more quotes from Marx and a little more obscure vocabulary.
They claim that Marx's goal was to determine fundamental
features of capitalism and to demonstrate that it was a
historical mode of production that arose in a determinate
(sic) historical moment.[77] This, for them, means a straight-
forward process of analyzing the degree of capitalist development in agriculture by looking at forms of ground rent.
Fernandez and Ocampo's analysis of land tenure in Latin
America concludes that there are feudal forms of ground
rent present and, therefore, agricultural society is semifeudal and extremely backward.[78] They measured the degree of feudal backwardness three ways: first, they
checked the characteristics of the social divisions of labor;
second, they asked to what extent is the surplus product
extracted by industrial profit or by primitive forms; third,
they thought that to have the capitalist mode of production
in agriculture, workers must not have any activity other
than food production. Their conclusion is that Latin
American agricultural society is precapitalist, albeit in a
state of transition.[79]

By describing the variety of production structures
in Latin America these mode-of-production analysts think
they have resolved the problem of identifying Latin American agrarian society as simply feudalist or capitalist.[80]
What they offer is a more authoritative evaluation based
on the identification of several modes, how they mesh with
one another, how one dominates the others, to conclude
that Latin America is in a stage of transition where precapitalist modes of production are still present. Adeptly
manipulating the terminology does not hide the fact that
all this analysis is useless. What is really being said is
that Latin American society is hard to classify into the
neat schemes of historical materialism. Hence, the label
of transition. There is very little concern with the real
struggle that is occurring in front of these writers' own
eyes. Blinded by their approach, they are forever trapped
in a labyrinth of structures. Sometimes they actually see
peasant movements, but they can only ask how they fit
into some formalistic articulation of modes of production.

SOCIAL CAPITAL

In contrast to the Marxist approaches presented and analyzed above, I will present an alternative perspective sometimes call "social capital" or "worker's autonomy."[81] The Italian theoreticians[82] who wrote during the working-class struggles in Italy during the 1960s and 1970s drew on a number of international Marxist sources for their theoretical underpinnings.[83] Many of their ideas were based on a careful study of earlier "workerist" writings. In essence these writings emphasized the self-activity or autonomy of the working class. As opposed to the dominance and role of capital, they concentrated on the initiative of the rank and file within working-class struggle.[84] Thus, a new analytical focus was directed toward studying the working class itself, not just capital.

From that point of departure, Mario Tronti developed the concept of social capital or social factory in two seminal essays, "The Factory and Society" (in Quaderni Rossi #2) and "Capital's Plan" (in Quaderni Rossi 1963). Tronti studied parts 1 and 3 of volume 2 of Capital and brought out the ways in which Marx's concept of accumulation of total capital was accumulation of social capital, which included the reproduction within it of the capitalist class on the one hand and of the working class on the other.[85]

> The work day in the production of social
> capital is divided between a constant part
> and a variable part of capital: between
> production-reproduction of constant capital
> and production-reproduction of variable
> capital. . . . The social work day func-
> tions directly within the process of produc-
> tion of social capital. . . . The social
> work day produces, reproduces, and accu-
> mulates new capital; it produces, repro-
> duces, and accumulates new labor power.[86]

Tronti saw that the process of accumulation of total social capital is the process of accumulation of the classes. Therefore, circulation and reproduction of capital includes reproduction of the classes and class relation. If the social work day produces, reproduces, and accumulates new capital and new labor power, then the working class must be redefined to include those doing the work of producing and reproducing labor power. Workers are not only those producing value in the factory but must now include those working in the social factory reproducing the labor power. Tronti's concept of the social factory provided the basis for understanding and including other groups' struggles (such as students, women, the unemployed, and, as we will see, the peasants) within the overall Marxist analysis of working-class struggle against capital.[87]

Redirecting their thinking toward the working class made these Italian Marxists realize fundamentally that capital is not a thing but the class relation itself. Thus, the working class has a dynamic role, forcing, at times, capital to redefine itself and develop along new lines. We must rethink class struggle this time from the workers' point of view. Consequently, we study and analyze class struggle to discover how workers develop new organizations to represent their interests. We look at how workers create new unities between different sectors of the class when before there were divisions and hierarchies. Finally, we look at how class struggle circulates regionally, nationally, and internationally as the struggle becomes generalized to other sectors of the working class.[88] Generalization of class struggle to other sectors is the circulation of struggle.

The social capital focus not only redirects our analysis toward the activity of the working class but redefines the working class itself. Mariarosa Dalla Costa and Selma James not only grasped the significance of Tronti's work on the social factory but went beyond Tronti to emphasize that the work done in reproduction was done by women and was unwaged. Dalla Costa developed the beginning of a new analysis of the working class in her article "Women and the Subversion of the Community."[89]

Focusing on the key category of the wage, she recognized that the wage or lack of a wage hid not only unpaid work done in the factory but unpaid work done outside it as well. The family is a center of social production, not just consumption. The woman is at home producing labor power as a commodity within the social factory. But because her work is unwaged it appears to be a personal service outside of capital within some precapitalist working condition. Dalla Costa showed that women's work is not simply a personal service to men. Women are workers exploited by capital but whose relationship with capital is mediated by men via the wage. Their unwaged

condition has kept them hidden from the usual definition
of the working class. Dalla Costa concluded, therefore,
that the working class must be understood to include unwaged workers as well as waged.

In 1977 Cleaver extended Tronti's work on accumulation of total social capital and James and Dalla Costa's
work on the unwaged by proposing a way to integrate the
reproduction of labor power into the circuits of self-repro-
duction of total social capital. Using the concept of the
circuits of capital as developed by Marx in Chapters 1 to
4 in volume 2 of Capital, Cleaver showed how the relations
between capital and the work of the waged and unwaged
can be specified more clearly.

Initially, Marx outlined the continuous self-reproduc-
tion and interconnected expansion of industrial capital.
The three interrelated circuits, money capital, productive
capital, and commodity capital, are depicted in Figure 1.1.

By looking at the various phases of these circuits,
one can recognize the processes that must take place if the
circuit is to be completed. For example, the continuity
represented in Figure 1.1 presumes the existence of both
labor power and means of production in the necessary proportions the capitalist requires for production. One also
notices that the commodity capital C', which includes the
surplus value produced and appropriated during the production process P, must be sold (C'--M'). In other words,
the surplus value must be realized in order to have the
M', money capital, to buy more commodity capital, MP and
LP, to start the whole process over again. The reproduction of M, P, and C is accounted for in the unity of the
three circuits; but as Cleaver notes, the reproduction of
LP and MP is not.[90] Since the circuit as discussed here
is of an individual capital, the capitalist must buy MP as
the output, C', of another capital, which is still a part
of total social capital. However, the reproduction of labor
power still falls completely outside of individual capitals.
As Marx indicated in volumes 1 and 2, the reproduction of
LP is taken care of separately by the working class
(LP--M--C).

However, we know from Tronti's work on the social
factory that the reproduction of LP is a part of total social capital and we know from James and Dalla Costa that
this work is hidden because it lacks a wage. Therefore,
by integrating the circuit of reproduction of labor power
to the circuit of industrial capital, Cleaver has proposed

FIGURE 1.1

Circuit of Industrial Capital

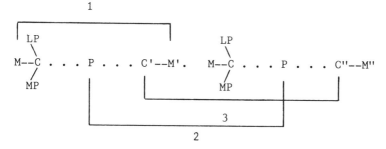

Legend of Symbols Used in Circuits and Discussion

M   Money capital; M_1, M_2 denote separate capitals

C   Commodity capital

LP   Labor power

LP*   New labor power produced by combining purchased means of
        subsistence (MS) and unwaged domestic work during the
        production process P. The asterisk indicates change.

MP   Means of production

MS_1 Means of subsistence produced by peasants

MS_2 Means of subsistence purchased

C'   Commodity capital containing surplus value

M'   Money capital including realized surplus value

P_1 Production of raw unprocessed means of subsistence

P_2 Domestic unwaged work transforming MS (cooking, house-
        work, etc.) into items for direct production of LP

P_3 Production process producing C'

_____   Transaction

. . .   Production process

+   Indicates the combination of the elements immediately
        preceding and following symbol

⟶   Intertwining or connection between two separate circuits
⟵   for a given element

⟷   Indicates same element can be used simultaneously in two
        different but connecting circuits

27

a way to complete the circuit of reproduction of total social capital.

We have looked at the circuit of industrial capital; now let us look at the circuit of reproduction of labor power as follows:

FIGURE 1.2

Circuit of Reproduction of Labor Power

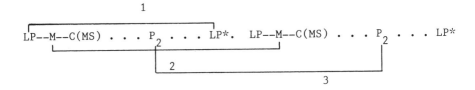

As opposed to Marx's scheme, where wages are just spent on individual consumption, without capitalist interference, Cleaver argues that today consumption of the means of subsistence or C(MS) must be understood to be organized by capital for the purpose of reproducing LP. It has become productive consumption. The work of consumption, P_2, in C(MS) . . . P_2. . . LP*, produces labor power as an output: a commodity to be bought and sold on the capitalist market. In Figure 1.2, circuit 1 is the reproduction of labor power; circuit 2 is the circuit of money invested (wages) in the reproduction of LP; circuit 3 is the reproduction of the productive process itself.[91] LP—M is where the workers sell their LP for a wage that must be equal in value to that of LP. The wage must be sufficient to buy the MS for themselves and unwaged workers in their household, i.e., M—C(MS).

I would like to specify the domestic work process, or housework, cooking, cleaning, child rearing, and house maintenance, to be P_2. This means transforming the purchased means of subsistence from C(MS) into directly consumable items and reproducing LP. P_2 is the productive process that goes on mainly in the home and community. Specifying the productive process of P_2 separately allows us to see clearly the unwaged nature of this work and concomitantly its direct connection with capital. Combining Figure 1.2 with Figure 1.1, as Cleaver proposes, completes the circuit of industrial capital if we assume, as Marx did, that MP is simply C' of another capital with which it intertwines.

FIGURE 1.3

Circuit of Reproduction of Labor Power

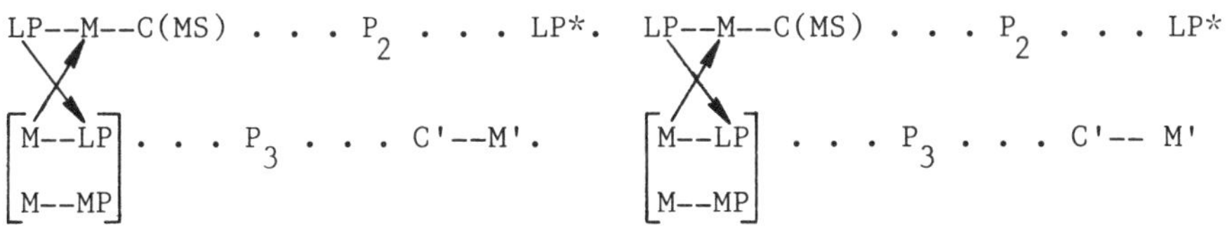

$$LP--M--C(MS) \ . \ . \ . \ P_2 \ . \ . \ . \ LP^*. \qquad LP--M--C(MS) \ . \ . \ . \ P_2 \ . \ . \ . \ LP^*$$

$$\begin{bmatrix} M--LP \\ M--MP \end{bmatrix} \ . \ . \ . \ P_3 \ . \ . \ . \ C'--M'. \qquad \begin{bmatrix} M--LP \\ M--MP \end{bmatrix} \ . \ . \ . \ P_3 \ . \ . \ . \ C'-- \ M'$$

Circuit of Industrial Capital

Extending the analysis of the unwaged to the peasantry, Selma James recognized that the peasantry could be included within the framework of unwaged workers for capital.[92] In her brief but pathbreaking article "Wageless of the World," she saw that the "proletarian character of the laborer on the land, the peasant, landowning or landless, is hidden by the wagelessness of that labor."[93] To be wageless is not necessarily to be outside of the capitalist relation. James explains how the wage or lack of wage comprises the basic division within the working-class hierarchy. But the specifics of the working-class hierarchies and divisions and the unwaged, or of how the peasants work for capital, was left for future work.

From this beginning, Harry Cleaver in 1976 expanded James's work into a more comprehensive view of the peasantry as unwaged workers for capital.[94] He used the concept of the unwaged to show that apparent precapitalist modes of production hide the peasants' real relation with capital. Work, no matter how it is organized, according to Cleaver, has the same usefulness to capital--social control and the production of surplus value.[95] Cleaver exposed the emptiness of mode-of-production analysis.[96]

Cleaver argued that these workers-peasants-members of the reserve army constitute a part of total variable capital and must be maintained, reproduced, and supported by capital. For example, it is sometimes the case that land reform is used by capital to stabilize the peasants on the

land--to keep them working but working at their own reproduction as reserve army, and, to the extent that they
produce an agricultural surplus, contributing to the expansion of capitalist accumulation.[97] "To be wageless is
not to be outside or alongside accumulation, it is to be
part of it. The unwaged must be accumulated right along
with the waged."[98]

Besides the peasantry's unwaged function within
capitalist production, Cleaver stated that the peasantry is
a part of the working class through their struggle against
capital. Peasants by their revolutionary activities have
demanded their rightful place in working-class struggle.
The issue of peasant struggles over land and other related
issues must be reckoned with within the global working-
class struggle against capital and within the framework of
Marxist theory.[99] In other words, the peasantry are members of the working class not only from their unwaged
work of reproducing labor power but from their real struggle against capital. The realization that peasant struggle
(even over land) is working-class struggle potentially disrupting capitalist accumulation shatters the orthodox Marxist image of the petit bourgeois reactionary peasant.

But class struggle is not just negative or destructive
of capital. The concept of people's self-valorization,[100]
as developed by Toni Negri, shows the positive or constructive side. Negri departed from the emphasis on the
social worker or how the worker is subsumed under capital in all spheres of the "social factory." He looked at
how workers pursued the immediate political conditions for
the independence of the proletariat as a deepening of the
concept and experiences of self-valorization. "The process
of valorization is the class's capacity to bring about development which is completely alternative to capitalist
valorization."[101] Self-valorization is the people's definition of self-needs that are outside and autonomous to
capital. Negri explains that the aim or content of self-
valorization is the complete liberation from capitalist production and reproduction, hence refusal of work. The extent of the proletarian's self-valorization is measured by
the reduction of individual and overall labor time sold to
capital and by the increase of socially useful work dedicated to the free reproduction of proletarian society.[102]
The process of people's self-valorization becomes the "power
to withdraw from exchange value and the ability to reappropriate the world of use values."[103] It is against

the subsumption of labor power to capital; it is for the construction of a life separate from capital.

For the analysis of peasant struggle in Mexico, this concept of self-valorization captures the very essence of that struggle. It explains why they struggle for land and not wages. It explains the importance of the peasant community for peasant struggle and for peasant development. The peasant community and the concomitant attachment to land has the potential to allow peasant development of a life separate from and not dominated by capital.

Further, the peasant community with its traditional structures that embody a sense of solidarity gives them an advantage over conventional workers. It is not necessary that they go through the process of becoming an individual unit; being hired independently from others; organizing all the individuals into unions; creating class consciousness. Peasants are already organized and always have been. The community is the basis of their struggle; the basis of their future self-development, which is self-valorization as opposed to capitalist valorization. Using community ties and institutions is not anarchic or a return to the past, but contributes to the overall struggle against the intrusion of capital into their daily lives--that is, contributes to class struggle.

In Chapter 4 I will directly relate the concept of self-valorization to the peasant struggle in Mexico. There is evidence to suggest that these struggles are against subsumption to capital and for creating an existence outside of capital via community structures.

Selma James's perception that peasants are unwaged workers of the working class gets us well past all the other Marxist viewpoints just presented. Lenin, never able to recognize that peasants are also members of the proletariat, labeled the peasantry enemies to Soviet power and the existence of socialism. His answer to the persistence of the peasantry was to exploit and squeeze them until peasant resistance and violence forced him to reconsider state policy. Because peasants did not form part of the basic class relation of capital, according to Lenin, they could not effect a true revolution against capital. By being included in the working class with real working-class demands and struggles (although peculiar to their particular relation with capital), peasants are no longer seen as enemies, are no longer subjects to be exploited or repressed. They are clearly recognized to be workers for capital. Sometimes their work involves direct production of surplus value for capital, and always it involves the unwaged work of reproduction of the labor force when functioning as reserve army.

Peasants are struggling against capital in a variety of ways, all appropriate to their particular self-needs. Peasant struggles for land, better prices, credit, and water are seen by historical materialists such as Balibar, Harnecker, and followers as reformist or economistic. These same struggles are evaluated within the social capital perspective as a part of the overall working-class strategy against capital. Class struggle under social capital is autonomous, organized around self-needs, with no need for the dominance of a party. The social capital focus stresses that the forms of organization change with the structure of the struggle. Recognizing that the organizational needs of working-class strategy change for different times and different situations gives us the flexibility needed to assess the peasant strategies being pursued in struggle. We are not locked into one form of organization or another. A political party or union may be appropriate in one moment of struggle; it may be superseded by another form of organization in other struggles. Finally, the concept of self-valorization reveals the revolutionary nature of peasant struggle within the community and for the land. Looking at all of these Marxist theories on the peasantry is not simply an academic exercise but is necessary to understand the political debate that is taking place in Mexico today. This debate and its eventual interpretation of the issues involved will affect millions of Mexican peasants through government policy and programs. This is justification enough to reexamine some of the Marxist issues already discussed in light of the Mexican debate and juxtapose these to our social capital alternative.

NOTES

1. See, for example, Richard Harris, "Marxism and the Agrarian Question in Latin America," Latin American Perspectives 5 (Fall 1978):6; and David Mitrany, Marx Against the Peasants (London: George Weidenfeld and Nicolson, 1951), pp. 23-28.

2. Karl Marx, Capital (New York: International Publishers, 1967), vol. 1, p. 761; vol. 3, p. 804. All

subsequent references to Capital, unless otherwise noted, are to this edition.

3. Marx, Capital, vol. 1, p. 761.

4. Karl Marx, "The Eighteenth Brumaire of Louis Bonaparte" (1851), in The Marx-Engels Reader, ed. Robert Tucker (New York: Norton, 1972), p. 515.

5. Ibid.

6. Ibid., p. 516.

7. Karl Marx, Pre-Capitalist Economic Formations (New York: International Publishers, 1964), p. 68.

8. Marx, Capital, vol. 3, p. 806.

9. Marx, Pre-Capitalist Economic Formations, p. 104; Marx, Capital, vol. 1, p. 719.

10. Marx, "The Eighteenth Brumaire," p. 577.

11. Karl Marx, The Class Struggles in France 1848-1850 (Moscow: Progress Publishers, 1972), pp. 109-10.

12. Karl Marx, "Manifesto of the Communist Party," in The Marx-Engels Reader, ed. Robert Tucker (New York: Norton, 1972), p. 342.

13. See Capital, vol. 3, pp. 797-800.

14. Marx, Capital, vol. 1, pp. 742-43.

15. Ibid., p. 714.

16. Ibid., p. 716.

17. Ibid., p. 719.

18. Ibid., p. 724.

19. Marx, Class Struggles in France, p. 42.

20. Ibid., p. 112.

21. Ibid., p. 111.

22. Karl Marx, letter to Mikhailovsky, first published in May 1884, in The Russian Menace to Europe, ed. Paul Blackstock and Bert Hoselitz (Glencoe, Ill.: Free Press, 1952), pp. 216-18.

23. Ibid., p. 217.

24. Marx to Zasulich, 1881, one of the four drafts quoted in The Russian Menace, pp. 221-22.

25. Karl Marx and Friedrich Engels, The German Ideology (New York: International Publishers, 1947), p. 28.

26. Friedrich Engels, "Socialism: Utopian and Scientific," in The Marx-Engels Reader, ed. Robert Tucker (New York: Norton, 1972), p. 621.

27. Ibid., p. 622.

28. Engels, "Speech at the Graveside of Marx," in Marx-Engels Reader, p. 603.

29. Friedrich Engels, AntiDuhring (New York: International Publishers, 1970), p. 33.

30. Karl Marx and Friedrich Engels, Correspondence 1846-1895: A Selection with Commentary and Notes (New York: International Publishers, 1935), p. 513.

31. See Engels to Danielson (Nicolai-on), February 24, 1893, in Karl Marx and Friedrich Engels, Correspondence 1846-1895.

32. Marx to the editor of the Notes on the Fatherland, end of 1877 in Karl Marx and Friedrich Engels, Correspondence 1846-1895, p. 353.

33. Friedrich Engels, The Peasant War in Germany, ed. Leonard Krieger (Chicago: University of Chicago Press, 1967), p. 301.

34. Ibid., pp. 106-7.

35. Ibid., p. 10.

36. V. I. Lenin, The Development of Capitalism in Russia (1899), in Collected Works, vol. 3 (Moscow: Progress Publishers, 1972), p. 33.

37. Ibid., p. 172.

38. V. I. Lenin, "Workers Party and the Peasantry" (1901), in Alliance of the Working Class and the Peasantry (Moscow: Progress Publishers, 1971), p. 15.

39. V. I. Lenin, "Revision of the Agrarian Programme of the Workers Party" (March 1906), in Alliance, p. 132.

40. V. I. Lenin, "Speech Delivered at the First All Russia Conference on Party Work in the Countryside" (November 18, 1919), in Alliance, p. 309.

41. Ibid., p. 311.

42. V. I. Lenin, "Speech Delivered at the First Congress of Agricultural Communes and Agricultural Cartels" (December 4, 1919), in Alliance, p. 317.

43. V. I. Lenin, "Report on the Tactics of the R.C.P. Delivered at the Third Congress of the Communist International" (July 5, 1921), in Alliance, p. 359.

44. V. I. Lenin, "Political Report of the Central Committee of the R.C.P. Delivered at the 11th Congress of the R.C.P." (March 27, 1922), in Alliance, p. 365.

45. Mao Tse-Tung, "Report on an Investigation of the Peasant Movement in Hunan" (1927), in Selected Works, vol. 1 (Peking: Foreign Language Press, 1967), p. 23.

46. Ibid., p. 24.

47. Mao, "A Report of the Front Committee to the Central Committee of the Party" (April 5, 1929), in Stuart Schram, The Political Thought of Mao Tse-Tung (New York: Praeger, 1976), p. 259.

48. "Social consciousness," according to Mao, is the ability to form strategy, designate goals, recognize "friends" and allies and identify enemies--to grasp the overall picture of the revolution. Mao, "The Chinese Revolution and the Chinese Communist Party" (December 1939), in Selected Works, vol. 2, p. 325.

49. Mao, "Report on an Investigation in Hunan," p. 27.

50. Mao, original draft of "Report on an Investigation in Hunan," quoted in Schram, The Political Thought, p. 254.

51. Mao, "The Chinese Revolution," pp. 329-30.

52. See for example, A. Doak Barnett, Communist China: The Early Years, 1949-55 (New York: Praeger, 1968); Raya Dunayevskaya, Marxism and Freedom (London: Pluto Press, 1975); John G. Gurley, Challengers to Capitalism (San Francisco: San Francisco Book Company, 1976); Maurice Meisner, Mao's China: A History of the People's Republic (New York: Free Press, 1977); and E. L. Wheelwright and Bruce McFarlane, The Chinese Road to Socialism (New York: Monthly Review Press, 1970), p. 33.

53. See Schram, Political Thought, p. 15.

54. Ibid., p. 250.

55. Karl Marx, Preface to A Contribution to the Critique of Political Economy (Moscow: Progress Publishers, 1970), pp. 19-23.

56. Joseph Stalin, Dialectical and Historical Materialism (1940) (New York: International Publishers, 1977), p. 34.

57. Ibid., pp. 26-27.

58. Marta Harnecker, a principal student of Althusser in the Ecole Normale de Paris, spread her interpretation of his theories throughout Latin America with her book Los Conceptos Elementales del Materialismo Histórico (Mexico: Siglo XXI, 1969). This work, which could be called the Latin American handbook for historical materialism, has gone through 37 editions.

59. The theoretical foundation for mode-of-production analysis comes from Louis Althusser, For Marx (London: New Left Books, 1977); Louis Althusser and Etienne Balibar, Reading Capital (London: New Left Books, 1977); and Nicos Poulantzas, Political Power and Social Classes (London: New Left Books, 1975).

60. Harnecker, Los Conceptos, p. 139.

61. Ibid., p. 141.

62. Cornforth gives one definition of relations of production as the usual relations into which people enter in the process of production and disposal of the product, and of which they become conscious as property relations. Maurice Cornforth, Historical Materialism (New York: International Publishers, 1977), p. 39.

63. Harnecker, Los Conceptos, p. 170.

64. Peasants may possess the land and a few implements but do not control the source of fertilizer, seeds, credit, irrigation, or transportation to and from market. Whether peasants are truly owners of means of production is not so clear-cut.

65. Harnecker, Los Conceptos, p. 175.

66. Three of the most widely read in Mexico include Claude Meillassoux, Mujeres, Graneros y Capitales (Mexico: Siglo XXI, 1977); Pierre Philippe Rey, Las Alianzas de Clases (Mexico: Siglo XXI, 1976); and Claude Servolín, "Aspectos Económicos de la Absorción de la Agricultura en el Modo de Producción Capitalista," Cuadernos Agrarios 2 (April–June 1976):105–26.

67. There is a whole literature associated with the "theory" of dependency. I am not considering the dependency issue nor including its major proponents.

68. Ernesto Laclau, "Feudalism and Capitalism in Latin America," New Left Review 67 (May–June 1971):19.

69. André Gunder Frank, "Not Feudalism--Capitalism," Monthly Review (December 1963):470.

70. Ibid., p. 471.

71. Ibid., p. 476.

72. For a critique of Frank in our perspective, see Harry Cleaver, "The Internationalization of Capital and the Mode of Production in Agriculture," Economic and Political Weekly, March 27, 1976, pp. A2–16.

73. Laclau, "Feudalism and Capitalism," p. 20.

74. Ibid., p. 25.

75. Fernandez and Ocampo, "Latin American Revolution: A Theory of Imperialism Not Dependence," in Latin American Perspectives (1976), p. 39.

76. Ibid.

77. Ibid., p. 40.

78. Ibid., p. 45.

79. Ibid., p. 43.

80. See, for example, Andrew Pearse's discussion of feudal techniques in Latin America, "Agrarian Change Trends in Latin America," in Agrarian Problems and Peasant

Movements in Latin America, ed. Rodolfo Stavenhagen
(Garden City, N.Y.: Doubleday, 1970), pp. 11-40; and
Ernest Feder, The Rape of the Peasantry (Garden City,
N.Y.: Doubleday, 1971).

81.   There is not a thorough history written on "Auto-
nomania." The most complete history to date was written by
Harry Cleaver in his introduction to Reading Capital Politically (Austin: University of Texas Press, 1979), pp. 51-
66. Other summaries include "Autonomy: A Brief Chronol-
ogy," in Working Class Autonomy and the Crisis (London:
Red Notes and CSE Books, 1979); Peter Bell's "Notes on the
History of the Perspective" (London, October 20, 1977, unpublished); and Sergio Bologna, "The Tribe of Moles: Class
Composition and the Party System in Italy," in Working
Class Autonomy and the Crisis, pp. 67-91.

82.   The most important Italians in this perspective
who developed ideas and concepts most adaptable to our
purposes include Romano Alquati, Sergio Bologna, Toni
Negri, Raniero Panzieri, and Mario Tronti.

83.   One important influence came from a splinter
group of the Trotskyite movement of the 1940s in the United
States. This group called itself the Johnson-Forest tendency. Another influence derived from a similar group in
France who split with the 4th International. They formed
a journal, Socialisme ou Barbarie (1949-1965).

84.   See, for example, C. L. R. James, State Capitalism and World Revolution (Detroit: Facing Reality Publishing Committee, 1950); and Phil Romano and Raya Dunayevskaya, The American Worker (Detroit: Facing Reality
Company, 1946).

85.   Mario Tronti, "Social Capital," Telos 17 (Fall
1973):98.

86.   Ibid., p. 101.

87.   Cleaver, Reading Capital, p. 1.

88.   Introduction to Zerowork 1 (December 1975):4.

89.   Mariarosa Dalla Costa and Selma James, The
Power of Women and the Subversion of the Community
(Bristol, England: Falling Wall Press, 1972).

90.   Harry Cleaver, "Malaria, the Politics of Public
Health and the International Crisis," Review of Radical
Political Economics 9 (Spring 1977):97.

91.   Ibid.

92.   Selma James, Sex, Race and Class (Bristol,
England: Falling Wall Press, 1975), p. 19.

93. Selma James, "Wageless of the World," in All Work and No Pay: Women, Housework, and the Wages Due, ed. Wendy Edmond and Suzie Fleming (Bristol, England: Falling Wall Press, 1975), p. 27.

94. Cleaver, "The Internationalization of Capital," pp. A2-16.

95. Ibid., p. A-10.

96. See earlier section on mode-of-production analysis; Cleaver, "The Internationalization of Capital"; and Cleaver, Introduction to Reading Capital Politically.

97. Cleaver, "Malaria, the Politics of Public Health," pp. 81-103.

98. Cleaver, "Internationalization," p. A-10.

99. Harry Cleaver, "Food, Famine and the International Crisis," Zerowork 2 (Fall 1977):11.

100. Toni Negri, "Capitalist Domination and Working Class Sabotage," in Working Class Autonomy and the Crisis, p. 96.

101. Ibid., p. 118.

102. Ibid., p. 126.

103. Ibid., p. 101.

2

THE DEBATE IN MEXICO OVER THE PEASANTRY AND CAPITALISM

Almost all investigators of agrarian problems in the Mexican countryside have participated in the current debate on the peasantry. Participation is not by choice; it is mandatory. To be taken seriously as a student of the problems in the countryside one is expected to answer the following questions: Who are the peasants? What are their needs? How long will they be there? What are they struggling for? It sounds simple, but since the ambiguous treatment of the peasantry by Marx, through their blatant exploitation and repression by Stalin, to contemporary rural insurgencies, reams of paper have been blackened with fierce polemic over the peasantry. Today in Mexico the debate goes on and the prose is as passionate as ever.

In what follows, I will look at how the major battle lines have been drawn over certain issues, especially at the conflicts between the opposing camps of campesinistas and descampesinistas. Although I have divided the participants in the debate into two groups[1] this does not mean that representatives of the respective groups have identical ideas about all issues. Within each group there is considerable discussion, argument, and mutual criticism. While this makes blanket characterizations risky, I venture to say that the one issue that unites each group is the role of peasants in the development of Mexico. The descampesinistas in general see peasants either as a doomed class or as secondary protagonists in any project of building a future society. At most, they argue, peasants will ally with the industrial and urban proletariat and help them make socialism. The campesinistas, on the other hand, are decidedly pro-peasant. Peasants exist, will continue to exist, and will have a say in Mexican agricultural development. The peasant role in the creation of a new society is sometimes called the vía campesina. The content of the vía campesina, its meaning for the peasantry as a class, and its meaning for the rest of the country are debated, but it is the accepted framework for discussion for campesinistas. The descampesinistas take up the banner of industrial workers or the "pure" proletariat. The campesinistas try to see things from the peasant point of view. We will first consider the descampesinistas' view of how the peasantry fits into the class structure of the countryside.

DESCAMPESINISTAS

Class Structure

Roger Bartra[2] assigns the peasantry a class status based on his contention that they belong to a distinct non-capitalist mode of production. This mode he calls the "simple mercantile" mode of production--a mode constituted of small commodity producers who own their means of production. Since peasants within this separate mode of production, Bartra says, are subjected to mechanisms of exploitation distinct from the proletariat, he argues that the peasants are only formally subsumed to capital. Therefore, they cannot belong to the proletariat class, which is defined by real subsumption to capital. The peasant class, according to Bartra's definition, is thus restricted to only those small landed peasants who do not sell their labor power. The peasants who may still have land but must also sell their labor power even part time belong to the semiproletariat. Those workers completely separate from the means of production who sell labor power full time (real subsumption to capital) are considered rural proletariat.

Bartra says that peasants are only formally subsumed to capital through the market and exchange. This is ironic, since using the wage to define the working class is using a particular form of market exchange. He does not examine the content of the economic and social relations that peasants endure with capital (though unwaged) exploited production itself. If capital shapes the structure of production, then we have real subsumption of the peasantry to capital, regardless of the form of the

extortion of surplus value. In Peasant Linkages with Capitalism in Commerce and Production in Chapter 3, I thor-
oughly analyze this matter of formal and real subsumption,
evaluating the concepts in light of actual peasant relationships with capitalism in Mexico.

Fernando Rello[3] claims that his colleague Bartra essentially misuses Marxist theory. Rello claims that Bartra
confuses the forms of production with modes of production.
In other words, Rello does not see the simple peasant economy as a separate mode of production but as a specific
form. He writes that peasant independent direct producers
are not petit bourgeois, despite their property ownership,
but members of a peasant form of production. The form of
production, according to Rello, is defined as a specific
social relation of production. Forms of production can
contain elements that pertain to precapitalist modes of
production but coexist with the capitalist mode of production. For the peasantry there would be many different
forms of production, such as sharecropping, different types
of rental arrangements, the small peasant parcel, arti-
sanry, independent producers associated with capitalist
enterprises or the state, and so on.[4]

He also attacks Bartra for applying specific categories derived from Marx for the analysis of capitalism
(such as rent, profit, wage) to the peasant mode of production or the articulation of the two modes. In good
Marxist tradition, Rello insists that if there were indeed a
separate peasant mode of production, its analysis requires
new categories expressing the specific relations of the
peasant economy. Despite these points of disagreement,
both Bartra and Rello agree on the political conclusion
that the revolutionary character of the peasantry is limited by their condition as owners of the means of production. (The issue of the revolutionary character of the
peasantry will be discussed subsequently.)

In general, Rello argues that the task at hand is
to determine the functions that the peasant economy (peasant forms of production) play in the accumulation of capital and the possibilities of survival within the capitalist
mode of production. In other words, he proposes that
(1) one study how the peasantry aids capitalist accumulation; and (2) one look at how the peasantry manages to
survive given their pathetic worsening situation. On the
other hand, I propose we analyze the linkages between
capitalism and the peasantry to illuminate where such

linkages can be broken. This is a positive pro-peasant stance. The economic and social structure of the country-side is not accepted as is. Instead, the social capital perspective allows us to look at the survival of the peasantry in terms of their development toward satisfying their own self-defined needs; toward creating their own self-defined society. In short, it is a view of the social structure of the countryside from the peasant perspective.

Francisco Gómez Jara identifies three major social classes based primarily on whether the landowner hires waged labor or not.[5] The bourgeoisie includes all capital-ists and petty bourgeois (including ejidatarios) who have individual plots of more than five hectares and who hire waged labor. For Gómez Jara, the Mexican agricultural proletariat has all the sectors that Lenin identified in Development of Capitalism in Russia (see Chapter 1): the strict rural proletariat, semiproletariat (have some land and work for a wage), subproletariat, and lumpenprole-tariat. The peasant class is those peasants who have land but hire no salaried labor. The peasant class in-cludes Indian communities with communal lands who use cooperative labor and who also sell labor power occasion-ally. His criterion for separating peasants from proletariat is the wage relation. However, this criterion does not seem to apply to the differentiation between the worker who works the land cooperatively and does work for a wage and the worker who works the land individually and also works for a wage. The former he calls a peasant and the latter a semiproletariat. Yet both are waged. In addition, he has arbitrarily tossed all ejidatarios or peasants who work more than five hectares of land and hire waged labor into the petit bourgeois. Thus, his petite bourgeoisie in-cludes such ejidatarios (with five hectares of land regard-less of quality) who may hire other peasants to help out with the harvest regardless of the concrete social relations between the peasant doing the hiring and the one hired, regardless of whether a surplus is generated for accumu-lation. Again, we have a classification scheme based on the form of exploitation rather than on its content. I will seriously challenge this position in Chapter 3.

Luisa Paré postulates a similar class structure: the bourgeoisie, the peasantry, and the proletariat.[6] How-ever, she segments these classes into separate sectors, using a quantifiable criterion of what percentage of gross income is derived from the wage. In other words, those peasants who still sustain themselves basically on the land but may sell labor power from time to time are members of the peasant class. Those peasants who work the land but receive more of their income from salaried work are members of the semiproletariat. The semiproletariat has a dual nature—peasant and salaried worker.[7] There is little real difference between Lenin and Paré on the class structure in the countryside. Those who live solely by the sale of labor power are pure proletariat.

However, Paré has recognized that peasants under contract producing raw material for capital (sugar cane, cotton, henequen, tobacco, etc.) should not be included in the peasant class associated with a precapitalist mode of production. They are integrated into capitalism as direct producers.[8] Despite this lucid insight, she hastens to deny that they are proletariat, because they sell capital an agricultural commodity rather than labor power. Trapped by the category of the wage as the only way to define capitalist class relations, she creates still another class within a class, proletarios a domicilio, to solve the problem of what to do with these peasant direct producers subsumed (formally) to capital. She sees the parallel between workers paid piece wages and these peasant producers she calls "home proletariats." But manipulating terminology does not get us anywhere. She insists that features such as presence or absence of the wage relation or percentage of income derived from the wage imply important ideological differences among the classes and class sectors she has named.[9] Paré claims that the majority of the peasants who work the land but get most of their subsistence from the wage are not members of the peasant class, bourgeois, or proletariat; they are semiproletariat.

Ricardo Pozas identifies two major social classes for the Mexican countryside: the bourgeoisie, those who own the means of production; and the proletariat, those who must work for a wage.[10] The small- and medium-sized family agricultural units and peasants who use family labor and a small amount of salaried are petit bourgeois. Only those peasants who are owners of small land parcels and who work temporarily as jornaleros are classified within the proletariat specifically as semiproletariat.[11] Even though Indians are distinguished by their retention of "remnants of the past," Pozas says this does not mean they are outside the capitalist mode of production but are exploited as proletariat. He denies the existence of a peasant class or separate peasant mode of production.[12]

The Speed of Proletarianization

Proletaristas

Those descampesinistas who believe that the peasantry are being transformed into proletariat and are thus a disappearing class are called proletaristas. The process called proletarianization or dissolution of the peasantry was defined in Chapter 1 to mean the process by which the bulk of the peasantry is transformed into wage workers while a few become small capitalist farmers.[13]

Because the descampesinistas have almost unanimously classified the bulk of the peasantry as semiproletariat, they emphasize the process of proletarianization of the peasantry. They point to the vast number of peasants who still work the land but sell labor power part time as the evidence of this process. They also identify the large migrant rural population that travels throughout the countryside as a true rural proletariat. Within the ranks of the descampesinistas there are divisions over how fast proletarianization is taking place. Opinions vary from Bartra's state of permanent primitive accumulation or subcapitalism to Sergio de la Peña's opinion that the process is almost complete. Bartra defines subcapitalism as the socioeconomic formation formed by the joining of the capitalist and noncapitalist modes of production. He maintains that advanced capitalism never developed in Mexico, and this has retarded the proletarianization of the peasantry. Nevertheless, Bartra says the capitalist mode of production dominates and will inevitably lead to the destruction of the peasant economy. How Bartra can justify adhering to the orthodox prediction of the development of capitalism after demonstrating that the process is clearly different in Mexico is unclear.

According to Sergio de la Peña, the peasantry, a social group, is destined to disappear.[14] In the case of Mexico, he claims that the process of proletarianization of the peasantry in the countryside is almost complete. Proletarianization succeeds in such a way that the peasant forms of organization are destroyed; they are dispossessed of their lands and separated completely from their means

of production.[15] The peasants become integrated into
capitalism as workers or as small capitalists. De la Peña
cites statistics from the censuses of 1910 to 1970, claiming
that, in 1910, peasants (defined as subsistence-oriented
farmers who, with family labor or some waged workers,
obtain a small surplus) represented 70 percent of the economically active population, 28 percent in 1950, and 13
percent in 1970. Most of the ejidatarios, comuneros, and
small minifundistas spend the majority of their time as
salaried workers and have therefore lost their character
as peasants.[16] In so many words, de la Peña sees the
development of capitalism in Mexico as based on private
enterprise, the dissolution of the peasantry encouraged by
indirect exploitation, and the formation of a petite bourgeoisie and proletariat.

Gómez Jara divided Mexico into three regions to describe the process of proletarianization. In the north,
class polarization has led to a well-defined bourgeoisie
and rural proletariat.[17] Unfortunately, Gómez Jara cannot
explain why these "rural proletariat" struggle for land
instead of forming unions and demanding better conditions
of work. He calls this "petit bourgeois" conscience (demand for land) something imposed and reinforced by the
agrarian populist manipulations by the state.[18] It is the
only way that Gómez Jara can explain his way out of
identifying a true rural proletariat in the north that has
peasant demands! He says they have not formed unions
(apparently the form of organization) because of antiunion
repression by the government. No one could deny that the
government and the large capitalists discourage the formation of unions by the jornaleros who work the extensive
fields of cash crops in the north and northwest of Mexico.
But the jornaleros themselves have assessed the situation
very clearly, given the reserve army in the rural sector,
the organic composition of capital, and so on. They judge
that a more propitious strategy is to struggle for land--a
lesson that Gómez Jara could stand to learn.[19]

In the central portion of Mexico, Gómez Jara says
the peasant economy is in the process of sub- or semiproletarianization.[20] In other words, most peasants work
parcels of land and sell labor part time. I am not certain if he sees this semiproletarianization as an inter-
mediate stage before full proletarianization or as a permanent situation, such as Bartra's subcapitalism. In any
event, the term semiproletariat is convenient for the

descampesinistas when they must explain the peasant demands of this group. By definition the semiproletariat has a dual nature. In the southeast region, the peasant economy is intact, according to Gómez Jara, but linked to the capitalist economy.

Nonproletaristas

Some descampesinistas are not proletaristas, such as Sergio de la Peña or Roger Bartra. Luisa Paré is certain that the peasantry is being destroyed but does not think that all the ex-peasants are joining the ranks of the rural proletariat. She suggests that the capitalist structure of agriculture cannot and will not accommodate so much labor power. In other words, capital only has the capacity and the need to use the rural workers on a temporary basis; hence the rural workers work the land and work for a wage. They are, therefore, semiproletariat instead of rural proletariat. Paré calls the process descampesinización, or the destruction of the peasantry as opposed to proletarianization.[21] Ernest Feder concurs with Paré on the fact that today the destruction of the peasantry does not automatically imply the creation of a rural proletariat.[22] He is very fatalistic, seeing this huge reserve of ex-peasants whose survival and employment is of no consequence to the bourgeois class. Feder forecasts a disaster-type scenario, with the reserve becoming increasingly more unassimilable and difficult for the bourgeois to control. He implies that the peasantry will be destroyed by some sort of calamity or genocide rather than by being absorbed into the proletariat class.

We can see that most of the descampesinistas recognize a peasant class (one exception is Pozas). They tend to separate those peasants who also work for a salary into a semiproletariat class. In general, they (including Pozas) deny that peasants have a working-class nature because they own the means of production and do not earn the majority of their subsistence from the wage. As we shall see, these conclusions about class structure have repercussions on political strategy and the concept of the peasant role in revolution.

Descampesinistas and Peasant Struggle

In general, the process of proletarianization is thought to spell doom for the future of the peasantry as a class. Consequently, the descampesinistas discount any peasant role in constructing an alternative socialist society. Although they do not deny that embittered struggle is taking place today in the countryside, they do deny its revolutionary possibilities. Struggle for land is peasant, not proletarian, in character. Bartra is strident in asserting that peasants have no class consciousness and are thus incapable of directing or maintaining any class struggle.[23]

Rello agrees that the structural difference between the peasantry and the proletariat necessarily defines distinct forms of struggle. Because the peasants, according to Rello, are exploited as disadvantaged owners of the means of production and not as proletariat, they struggle for better prices, more land, lower interest rates, better credits—demands that Rello identifies as nonproletarian. The proletariat struggles for the "correct" revolutionary demands of higher salaries, shorter workdays, and less intensive work. Nevertheless, the two groups may ally under the guidance and tutelage of the proletariat in any given moment to begin a real struggle against capitalism.[24] Rello borrows directly from Mao for his discussion of the peasantry and class struggle. As pointed out in Chapter 1, Mao also welcomed peasants' struggle as long as it was guided and ultimately controlled by the proletariat, who were waging the real struggle against capitalism. I repeat my conclusion from Chapter 1 that great Marxist thinkers such as Mao or Lenin do not necessarily have the answer for the peasantry in Mexico. Applying Maoism or Leninism to the analysis of the Mexican peasantry, as Rello or Bartra tend to do, denies the specificity of today's peasantry (their working-class character, their existence as a class, their struggles), and, more importantly, denies the peasants' right to self-development along the lines of their own choosing.

Gómez Jara likewise identifies peasant struggle for land as useful only to the capitalist class. He says revitalizing the ejido and distributing land are simply state efforts at stabilizing the peasantry and extracting more surplus value from the peasant economy. It is backward, according to Gómez Jara, because the peasants are then not permitted to form unions and struggle for worker benefits![25]

It is true, as argues Gómez Jara, that land once won may be used by capital to coopt and exploit the peasantry.[26] But as will be discussed and illustrated in Chapter 4, land may also be used by the peasants as a basis for more struggle, further disrupting capitalist accumulation. Land is also used by peasants to realize self-needs defined outside of capital. Gómez Jara seems to have forgotten that there are always two sides and two perspectives in the class relation. In his one-sided view, even working-class demands such as salary increases would be judged economistic. After all, salary increases have been used by capital to increase relative surplus value by spurring capital to reorganize production in order to increase productivity. Wage struggles have thus, at times, become an engine of growth for capitalism. Should we then throw out wage struggles as inevitably advantageous to capital? If not, then why discount peasant struggles?

Gómez Jara does not deny that peasant struggles are part of the history of Mexico and are still frequent and intense. But in his analysis of contemporary struggles, he downplays their importance and their contribution to class struggle in general.[27] He calls the peasants "dissident spokesmen" for the bourgeois order that emanated from the 1917 constitution and the agrarian reform laws.[28] The character of the peasant struggle is isolated, improvised, experimental, and nonuniform. The isolation from similar experiences and from revolutionary parties, Gómez Jara argues, has led to a type of organization neither new nor radical: the commune, or the consejo campesino.[29]

Gómez Jara is locked into the Leninist model of revolution. He advocates the necessity of a Marxist party to direct the struggle.[30] He also implies that violent conflict between the social classes on a continental level is the only route toward social change, denying other strategies for struggle, such as electoral or legal struggles. According to Gómez Jara, the armed peasant struggle in Guerrero directed by Jenaro Vazquez and Lucio Cabañas failed not from isolation or lack of circulation to other struggles or from inappropriate strategy (for that moment and that particular struggle) but from North American military intervention and aid. If a handful of helicopters and military advisers could destroy this "revolution" why could not the entire U.S. military-industrial establishment in a decade of all-out war defeat the peasant revolution in Vietnam? The obvious difference between the two struggles was that one had vast grass-roots support and aid from other struggles, and the other was isolated.

Gómez Jara's analysis of peasant struggle, his assertion of the need for the tutelage of the party, his rejection of "peasant" forms of organization, and his denial of all other strategies but armed insurgence is dangerous to the peasants and to workers who want to see their struggle for a better life be successful instead of suicidal. He is an extreme example of the descampesinistas. He has denigrated peasants and peasant struggle except for the armed, all-out smash-the-state variety. His analysis is a stark reminder of how urgent these peasant questions are if we clearly take the peasant perspective.

Although Gómez Jara recognizes the significance of peasant struggle but deals with it inadequately, Sergio de la Peña practically denies it altogether. For de la Peña, the revolutionary potential of the peasantry, which is doomed if not already dissolved, is unreal. The revolutionary potential in the countryside is with those classes exploited directly by capitalism—the jornaleros and the rural proletariat.[31] This view is very short-sighted. Instead, peasants may appear as independent, direct producers but are in fact working for capital, are therefore directly exploited by capital, and are as a result involved in the struggle against that same capital. Further, the peasantry is not disappearing. This argument, explored by some of the campesinistas, will be clarified and supported in Chapter 3.

In sum, where does the descampesinista viewpoint take us? Even though there is no consensus as to specific class character of the peasantry or to the existence or nonexistence of a peasant mode of production or the rate of proletarianization, there is agreement on the political role of the peasantry. Peasant struggles for land and other "peasant demands" are caused by their supposed dual character (proletariat and bourgeois), by their class status of petite bourgeoisie, or by the unfavorable labor market. These struggles, according to descampesinistas, are not revolutionary. In fact, only in an alliance with and directed by the real working class (meaning the urban and rural proletariat) can these struggles contribute to any social change. No matter how sympathetic toward the peasantry some of the authors, such as Paré or Rello, may be, the final analysis comes to the same conclusions: real social change is orchestrated by the proletariat, not the semiproletariat or the peasantry. The descampesinistas, who almost always rely on some variation of the wage

category to define their social classes, are forced to ignore, modify, or reinterpret today's reality of peasant
struggle. Their viewpoint has great difficulty dealing
with the political reality of increasingly intense peasant
struggles. They are forced to argue that the peasant
struggles have no "socialist" content because they do not
express socialist "ideals" or employ traditional forms of
organization, such as unions or parties.

No matter how unique or creative their individual
applications of Marxism-Leninism or Maoism to Mexican
reality, the descampesinista positions suffer from two basic
weaknesses: (1) they focus on the wage form instead of
considering the content of exploitation and political struggle for class identification; (2) as a result, they formally
exclude all social classes but the urban industrial proletariat from a central role in socialist revolution.

CAMPESINISTAS

Class Structure

The campesinistas are just as divided as the
descampesinistas on issues such as mode of production,
social class, and position in capitalism. However, they
all agree that proletarianization of the peasantry has not
occurred to the degre or in the manner suggested by the
descampesinistas. Their reasons derive from their definition of peasants, their overwhelming distrust of government
official census statistics, and their emphasis on direct
field investigation. The political issue of how to interpret
peasant struggle today receives varying treatments from
the campesinistas.

Arturo Warman, one of the most widely respected
published campesinistas, says the definition of the peasantry does not depend on the particular tasks performed.[32]
Warman says a peasant can grow onions, tomatoes, or
sorghum for the market or emigrate to seek the wage as a
bracero and never stop being a peasant.[33] The essence
of being a peasant, according to Warman, is found in the
complexity of the social relations that govern them. Peasants' lives are not organized by the wage even if they do
sell labor power for a wage part of the year or even most
of the year. Their lives are organized by participation
in the community, access to land, belonging to a family,

and noncommercial exchange of goods, services, and labor.[34] In fieldwork in Morelos, Warman found that all of the peasant cultivators of land, including those with formal ownership and those with access to land only through medería, loans, rent, or asociación, at one moment or another often sell their labor power for a wage in very extensive migration circuits.[35]

Entering the labor market does not indicate proletarianization. On the contrary, it is simply one way the peasants seek to reinforce their existence as a peasant class by bringing resources and funds back to the community. Selling labor power is simply one strategy in the struggle to survive as peasants.

Armando Bartra agrees with Warman that quantitative considerations of salary, percentage of income derived from the wage versus the land (Paré's criteria), is not sufficient to call peasants semiproletariat.[36] Although he does not specify a list of fixed social relations that determine the peasant class, he says peasants orient their life around their parcel of land and its requirements. It is their base and starting point. Peasants will work for a salary only to make up a deficit in their subsistence from their parcel of land. They are still peasants: the presence or nonpresence of a wage is secondary.[37] Consequently, jornaleros have peasant demands, then participate in the peasant simple commodity economy, and they are not totally separated from the land. Jornaleros therefore are not proletariat but peasants.

The key issue for Bartra in determining the class nature of the peasantry is thus the connection (not necessarily formal ownership) with the land. This land requirement for the definition of the peasantry is not seen as essential by other campesinistas, such as Gustavo Esteva, who has identified a recampesinización phenomenon that involves some landless peasants who lost or abandoned poor plots to migrate to the cities but maintained their relations with the rural community. These unfortunates include a host of apparent proletarians, who are actually peasants desperately trying and sometimes succeeding to revitalize their attachments to the community and regain lost land.[38]

Other campesinistas, such as Palerm[39] or Stavenhagen,[40] restrict the peasant class to those who participate in the carefully described peasant mode of production. They include those peasants who receive a part-time wage but still participate in their peasant mode of production. Palerm went to great efforts to specify the peasant mode of production and its articulation with capitalism in his article "Sobre la Formula M-D-M y la Articulación del Modo Campesino de Producción al Sistema Capitalista Dominante" (1977). Palerm has the peasant mode of production articulated, with capitalism linked and exploited in the sphere of circulation and in the capitalist labor market. But he maintains that peasant production is formally outside of capital.[41] Stavenhagen also identifies a peasant mode of production outside of capital but linked with it via the market. Campesinistas such as Palerm or Stavenhagen, who work with the mode of production model, identify a peasant class. I certainly would not argue with their definition of peasant class or who they include in it. But I find it unnecessary to theorize a peasant mode of production, to specify who belongs, to detail how it functions, and so on. Such activity is a needless distraction from the analysis of peasant participation in social change.

The crux of the matter is how this social class interacts with the capitalist system--not what you call it theoretically. As opposed to emphasizing the articulation of modes or forms, I emphasize links and conflicts with capital to understand the peasant terrain of struggle. Further, I believe that peasant production is not outside capitalism but included within it. Chapter 3 is devoted to explaining and illustrating that proposition.

Stavenhagen and Palerm have the peasant modes of production producing commodities outside of the capitalist system, which are then sold to the system below their value, thus giving capital a surplus. According to this view (based primarily on Rosa Luxemburg's The Accumulation of Capital [1913]), capitalism needs the peasant sector for realization of surplus value and as a source of extra surplus value for accumulation. Therefore, a special relationship has evolved that constantly recreates the peasant sector instead of destroying it. The Luxemburg idea that capital needs modes of production outside of the capitalist system for a capitalist system for a capitalist accumulation has been criticized adequately elsewhere.[42]

Feder[43] thinks he has found the Achilles heel of the campesinista viewpoint by identifying and criticizing this old idea about peasant regeneration and the process of capitalist expansion. He trots out the examples of industrial nations like the United States and Canada, whose

agricultural sectors get along beautifully without an exploited peasant sector.[44] However, Feder has identified
a small group of the campesinistas not representative of
the rest. In fact, most campesinistas would agree with
Feder's criticism of the Luxemburg idea about capitalist
development and its need for a peasant sector.

What they certainly do not agree with are the political conclusions Feder attaches to his critique. He argues
that big finance capital and the campesinistas are on the
same side of the fence, allies so to speak. He claims the
World Bank and Ford Foundation have entered the debate
on the side of the campesinistas because they offer credits
and technology to minifundistas. This alliance with the
financial giants reveals the true identity of the campesinistas! According to Feder, birds of a feather flock together. Because campesinistas and big capital are trying
to save the peasantry, he says they must have identical
goals: exploitation of the peasantry.

The only thing this diatribe reveals is Feder's true
misunderstanding of the nature of class struggle. He cannot see that "aid" from big capital opens a two-way street.
One direction is for more direct capitalist exploitation via
credits (we will look at this in Chapter 3); the other direction is for the peasantry to appropriate this aid and
use it as a basis for gaining strength for their struggle
for autonomy from the system (we will look at this in
Chapter 4).

Proletarianization

The campesinistas maintain that the peasantry as a
class is either stable or growing. We have already seen
how they include the so-called semiproletariat within the
peasant class. Warman has also argued that there are
very few agricultural proletariat who live exclusively by
selling labor power. Even in the northwest, on the large
capitalist farms, peasants who sell labor power regularly
return to their communities to take part in highly complex
relations. There are very few completely permanent workers. Politically, some members of the so-called rural proletariat, the permanent salaried workers, ally with the
capitalist landowners. Because of their total dependency
on the patrónes for their subsistence, they become guardias
blancas on behalf of their patrónes. These proletarians

with no class consciousness are powerful enemies of the temporary peasant workers.[45] Warman therefore argues the obvious point that radical separation from the means of production and total dependence on the wage does not necessarily impart class consciousness to the proletariat. We must look beyond these formal categories of wage and ownership to determine class character.

Continuing his critique of descampesinistas, Warman counters the proletarianization argument with some enlightening observations about their data. Almost always, the proletaristas use data from the agricultural and general population censuses. Subtracting from the total agricultural population those that own land or have legal use of the land (ejidatarios) supposedly gives the members of the agricultural proletariat. First, it is common knowledge that the census data are inaccurate. In fact, in the countryside some experts estimate it to be off as much as 100 percent. I was told by an economist in the office of the president that he personally knows that census takers in Chiapas who recorded the municipal data never left their hotel rooms.[46] Warman quotes Marco Antonio Duran about one of the errors in the agricultural census of 1960. Apparently the area surveyed in three contiguous states was appreciably larger than the known geographic territory of the states.[47] Where did the extra land and presumably people come from? The largest error in the agricultural census occurred in 1970. For political reasons, the census was conducted in January instead of July, as in 1950 and 1960. In January the agricultural activity in the non-irrigated zones where most of the peasants work the land is practically at a standstill. July is the most active period. Almost one million peasants were demographically misplaced between 1960 and 1970 because of the timing of the census.[48] For reasons such as these, the data cannot be trusted; comparisons over time with such differing survey conditions are statistically unsound. An estimate of the agricultural proletariat based on census data should be taken with several grains of salt.

The peasants, according to the campesinistas, resist proletarianization and have instead reinforced their forms of social existence in their communities. In some cases, according to Gustavo Esteva, peasants who had left the land or simply did not have any (sons of ejidatarios, campesinos con derechos a salvo) use the wage as an avenue to obtain land. Meanwhile, they never interrupt their participation in the community and family.[49] Of course, it is undeniable that the bulk of the migrants who end up in the cities seeking the wage are peasants trying to find better economic and social living conditions. However, Esteva contends that given the reality of capitalism today (i.e., growing unemployment and very slowly expanding waged employment), there is a tendency for this process to reverse. After a long period, the migrants frequently leave the cities and return to the countryside to the land once again.[50] This phenomenon of returning to the land and to the community has been called by Esteva recampesinización.[51]

Peasants and Subsumption to Capital

In all, campesinistas identify a peasant social class and reject the thesis of proletarianization of the peasantry. They agree that exploitation of the peasantry occurs through the market but they disagree on the extent of peasant subsumption to capital. Campesinistas are divided over the crucial issue of whether peasants are exploited by capital in the sphere of production. The debate over this is best exemplified by articles of Armando Bartra and Gustavo Esteva.[52]

Bartra thinks he has uncovered the secret to the peasantry's production relations with capital. He says, with Esteva, that it is not sufficient to speak of transfer of value from the peasantry to capital through circulation; but we must examine exploitation in production.[53] Let us briefly follow his argument. Bartra contends that the exploitation of the peasant is realized in the market when the surplus changes hands but the base of exploitation is in the conditions of peasant production, since they do not operate as productive capitalists. They do not engage in exploitation of labor power to produce this product. The peasant's goal of production is only reproduction, not accumulation; the peasant's means of production is not in the form of free capital.[54] What I think Bartra means by "free capital" is that the peasants are not "free" to follow market signals and move their capital (in the form of land, tools, etc.) from one capitalist endeavor to another. The difference between peasant producer and capitalist producers is that the former produces only for the goal of subsistence, not profit.

I interpret Bartra's argument to mean that peasants are exploited as producers because of their noncapitalist methods of production. The exploitation of the peasantry in the sphere of production occurs because they are not capitalists. Bartra thinks he has explained the exploitation of the peasant as being based in production, i.e., peasant methods of production, but realized in the market. It is certainly novel that he sees the cause of exploitation rooted in the peasantry itself. Capital just cannot help itself if it takes advantage of such conditions. Does this mean that with the absence of a peasant mode of production capital would function blissfully, in perfect storybook competition, arriving at some sort of Pareto optimum? I'm sure that Bartra would not take his argument that far. But this is the logical conclusion of such reasoning. Bartra points out that the peasants buy the means of production from capital only if it will permit the peasants to continue subsisting as peasants and is the best alternative for them to satisfy their reproductive needs. Peasants see the purchase of these production goods as a way to guarantee their subsistence and social status as peasants, not as a way to make a profit. Consequently, peasants buy even if the price is systematically maintained above value. The exploitation of the peasants in the market is therefore the fault of the peasants. Bartra actually declares that peasants are not "rational," not cognizant that they are exploited by the terms of trade, and worse yet, do not seem to care as long as subsistence is assured. Therefore, commercial monopoly (acaparamiento), caciques, and so on exist because peasant production allows them to exist! He has far too much faith in competition as the great healer of economic injustice, i.e., if peasants behaved as competitive capitalists, there would be no exploitation of the peasant producers.

I believe that exploitation of the peasant is the same as the exploitation of other workers within capitalism. It is defined by the extraction of surplus labor in the form of a marketable surplus product on which a profit can be earned. The extent of exploitation is explained by the concrete history of the struggle between peasant and capital, by the levels of strength, strategy, and circulation of struggle, and by the degree of political recombination among peasants. It is not explained by the peasant mode or form of reproduction interacting with capital, as Bartra asserts. Bartra has failed to grasp the content of the production relations between the peasantry and capital. He therefore has failed to recognize that the peasant class constitutes one section of the proletariat. Gustavo Esteva develops the following argument, which goes further than Bartra in recognizing this.

Esteva characterizes the recent development and expansion of agrarian capitalism in Mexico as seeking the control of the productive processes instead of direct ownership of the land. He, of course, does not ignore the plantations and agribusiness of all kinds that directly operate huge agricultural exploits. But he sees a tendency toward more contract agriculture, where the direct operation and ownership of land remains in the hands of individuals, such as peasants, but the control of the productive processes is acquired by agribusiness. Where the actual productive processes and internal organization of work are not transformed, labor remains formally subsumed to capital.[55] Since the bulk of the risks associated with production and the work of managing or organizing production is left in the hands of the direct producers, the fiction of a peasant class possessing its own productive factors, operating as an autonomous unit, and exploiting its own members of the community (sometimes via wage labor) is maintained.[56] But Esteva, looking through the myth, sees that these peasants are working for capital in a particular relation of production. The entire peasant unit of production, via mechanisms such as credit, contracts, inputs, and marketing, is subsumed to capital. The reason it appears to be an economic unit relating independently with the capitalist unit is because capital adeptly uses this form of production relations in order to elude paying the social obligations and benefits historically won by the working class.[57] It creates the myth to hide the reality of the production relations from view.

Campesinistas and Peasant Struggle

The last issue of the debate between the campesinistas and the descampesinistas is the peasant role in class struggle. Having already looked at the latter's position, we now turn to the campesinistas' argument. Armando Bartra was one of the first Mexican experts on the peasantry to recognize the importance of analyzing recent peasant movements. He noted that while the proletaristas were labeling the majority of the workers in the countryside proletariat or semiproletariat, the struggle was clearly over peasant demands.[58] How could this be explained? He claimed that comprehension of class structure must come from analysis of the recent peasant movement. It was his starting point. Let us look at some of Bartra's contributions to the understanding of peasant struggle.

First, he notes that in general terms the peasant movement takes the initiative. He has advanced quite beyond the usual characterization of pathetic peasants who are exploited but too weak to do anything about it.[59] By looking at the actual struggles, he has seen that the peasant movement has repeatedly obliged the Mexican state to concede to its demands. This position is difficult to reconcile with his other statements about peasant methods of production being the cause of their exploitation in the market.

Bartra identifies land as the main goal of struggle both for peasants and for rural workers with insufficient or no land. He sees the motive of the struggle for land as the desire for more certain subsistence.[60] Esteva agrees that land is the principal motive but adds that autonomy from capital is what the peasantry is really seeking. Bartra sees other motives for peasant struggle, such as better prices, better conditions of production and commercialization, and political control of their local government. He recognizes that peasants are exploited in a variety of ways and therefore adopt a variety of types of struggle.

Although he denigrates the descampesinistas for underestimating, even turning their backs on, the peasant movement,[61] Bartra agrees with his opponents that "the peasant acquires a socialist conscience only with difficulty and by himself cannot offer a strategic alternative to bourgeois society."[62] However, he adds that this is no reason to deny the revolutionary potential of the peasantry against capitalist ownership and control of society. To deny their potential is to deny the function and role of the peasant-worker alliance. Apparently, he sees the revolutionary potential of the peasantry but only so far as a new worker-peasant alliance is formed.

He does not see that peasant struggle as ultimately revolutionary because it leads to life autonomous from capital--disruptive of capital. Peasant struggle should

not be thought of as only help for the workers. I concur
with Esteva's criticism that "the peasant/worker alliance
must not be thought of as two groups on a journey where
one group becomes the demolition material for the other to
transform society for them."[63] Bartra talks about peasant
struggle having no socialist content. He states that agriculture cannot, by its nature, be socialized. What does
this mean? Bartra seems to suggest that rural society can
only be organized along some "socialist" line or the way
it actually is; both possibilities he rejects. He seems to
discount the potential of the peasant movement to create
alternative organizations for agriculture in the countryside.

Studying the concrete history of peasant struggles
in Mexico, Bartra reveals a deep concern and commitment
to the peasantry.[64] I include him in the campesinistas
because he is, in the end, propeasant. However, it seems
inconsistent that he should parrot the Marxist–Leninist
position on peasant struggle while never really relating
his theoretical position to the concrete history he describes
in detail. I am reminded of Engels and his vivid historical accounts of peasant insurgence and his ubiquitous
denial of their significance to working–class struggle. I
venture to say that Bartra ends up tacking the Marxist-
Leninist position onto his analysis simply because he has
denied working–class status to the peasantry. As I have
pointed out, he does not recognize the hidden production
relations between the peasantry and capitalism.

Arturo Warman sees recent peasant struggle in
Mexico not as a sum of individual petitions for a piece of
land but as a class movement. "Peasants are struggling
for a space to continue producing and existing as a group
as the most numerous social class of the country." But
Warman also recognizes that the peasantry is not just
reclaiming the past but is demanding the conditions necessary to transform the future.[65] It is on this issue of the
constructive potential of peasant struggle that Esteva and
Warman part company from Bartra. Esteva and Warman
emphasize that we must heed the solutions proposed by the
peasants as well as those being created by waged workers.
The peasants themselves are creating a variety of new options for development of society.[66]

These options for development and struggle by the
peasantry create a hotly debated issue surrounding the
vía campesina. The vía campesina is an alternative road
to postcapitalist development in the countryside. In other

words, it denies that there is one form of social organization called socialism. As peasants struggle, as peasants transform society, they offer one or perhaps several roads beyond capital, which can be called the vía campesina.

Gustavo Esteva is perhaps the most adamant advocate of the vía campesina. In his research and fieldwork on how peasants are organizing and struggling for resources, for their lives, and for their own society, he has sought to demonstrate with concrete cases that indeed the vía campesina must be seriously considered.[67] Esteva has seen how the peasantry as a class can adopt social organizations of their own to advance a process of modernization that adjusts to their necessities. As he says, "Peasants first must gain control over resources, dedicate themselves to satisfy self-needs, and then develop forms of social (peasant) accumulation." He goes on to point out that politically independent peasants can participate in the project of global transformation. "Peasants would be authentic protagonists via their productive organizations not just followers."

Today the vía campesina is denied both by technocrats in the service of big business and the state and by Marxists in the service of socialist orthodoxy. Both are afraid of losing control over the process of development, of being excluded from a society that may have no room for capitalists or socialists, no room for those who think up ways to extract surplus value for either capitalist or socialist accumulation.

Research, study, and analysis of peasant struggles and their constructive aspects are of first priority. For this reason, the campesinistas who research peasant society and their constant fight to transform it to something new should be applauded. The campesinistas have advanced the analysis of rural social class considerably beyond the taxonomic discussions of Marxist-Leninists, mode-of-production anthropologists, and Mexican descampesinistas. One of their most important contributions is the identification of many peasants otherwise classified as proletarian. I explained how the campesinistas used social and cultural features such as relations with family and community and informal relations with land to sort out the class structure in the countryside. They rejected strictly quantifiable criteria, such as the percentage of income from the wage. They have cleared up why all those so-called proletariats struggle for peasant demands.

Since they recognize a large peasant class in the countryside that is not disappearing, they also recognize that
peasants have a say in the future of Mexico. In fact,
they see that peasants are demanding a say in the development of Mexico by their political actions--their struggles.

Some campesinistas, particularly Esteva and Warman,
seriously consider the possibility that peasants act as
protagonists in creating alternative roads to development,
the via campesina. Another contribution to the peasant
question is their analysis of linkages between the peasantry and capitalism. The campesinistas identify and
specify linkages within the sphere of circulation. However, none of the analysts (with the exception of Esteva)
has seen that peasants have relations of production with
capital hidden beneath the mask of commercial or financial
capital. Esteva understands that peasants under contracts
with capital to produce raw materials are not independent
producers, one capitalist contracting business with another.
The peasant producers are little more than workers for
businesses who employ them. Consequently, Esteva admits
that the peasantry is a social class in formation--a part
of the proletariat.

The social capital focus takes Esteva's analysis of
the peasantry one step further. It explains why even
peasants self-sufficient on the land with no formal wage
must be understood to be included within the working class,
i.e., unwaged peasants producing and reproducing the
working class are workers. It also explains why some
peasants who sell commodities on the market are not just
petit bourgeois but likewise are exploited by capital. The
following chapter will explore these linkages within the
context of contemporary peasant reality in Mexico.

NOTES

1.   There are other groups, mainly representing
orthodox economic perspectives in development. These
non-Marxists will not be considered here. See Alejandro
Schejtman, "El Agro Mexicano y sus Interpretes," Nexos 4
(March 1981):37-47 for a good summary of orthodox perspectives on the peasantry in Mexico.
2.   Roger Bartra is a Marxist scholar, author of
the classic work Estructura Agraria y Clases Sociales en
Mexico (Mexico: Ediciónes ERA, 1974). He is also editor

62 / Contemporary Peasantry in Mexico

of the Communist Party magazine Machete and a professor
of political science at the National University of Mexico
(UNAM).

3. Fernando Rello is a professor of economics in
the Faculty of Economics at the National University of
Mexico (UNAM).

4. Fernando Rello, "Modo de Producción y Clases
Sociales," Cuadernos Políticos 2 (April–June 1976):101.

5. Francisco Gómez Jara is a sociologist with the
National School of Agriculture at Chapingo (Escuela Nacional
de Agricultura de Chapingo). See "La Lucha por la Tierra
Debe Convertirse en Lucha contra el Capital," Críticas de
la Economía Política 5 (October–December 1977):110–77.

6. Luisa Paré is a sociologist with the Institute
of Sociology Research (Instituto de Investigaciones Sociales)
at UNAM. She is the author of El Proletariado Agrícola en
México (Mexico: Siglo XXI, 1977).

7. Ibid., p. 149.
8. Ibid., p. 37.
9. Ibid., p. 49.

10. Ricardo Pozas was one of the first Mexican
social scientists to investigate social classes in rural
Mexico. He is author of the classic work Los Indios en
las Clases Sociales de México (Mexico: Siglo XXI).

11. Ibid., pp. 131–32.
12. Ibid., p. 137.

13. See discussion of the proletarianization of the
peasantry in Chapter 1, sections on Marx, Engels, and
Lenin.

14. Sergio de la Peña is an economist with the
Institute of Sociology Research (Instituto de Investigaciónes
Sociales) at UNAM.

15. Sergio de la Peña et al., Polémica Sobre las
Clases Sociales en el Campo Mexicano (Mexico: Editorial
Macehual, 1979), p. 53.

16. Ibid., p. 56.
17. Gómez Jara, "La Lucha," p. 169.
18. Ibid., p. 170.

19. This point is fully developed in Chapters 3
and 4. Furthermore, Gómez Jara has totally ignored that
peasant life and production on the land have some very
anticapitalist aspects that need to be explored and discussed. I do this in Chapter 4.

20. Gómez Jara, "La Lucha," p. 170.
21. Paré, El Proletariado, p. 31.

22. Ernest Feder, "Campesinistas y Descampesinistas," Comercio Exterior 27 (December 1977):1439–46.
23. Roger Bartra, Estructura, p. 156.
24. Rello, "Modo de Producción," p. 103.
25. Gómez Jara, "La Lucha," p. 161.
26. I spend comparatively more time on Gómez Jara
than the other descampesinistas because he is author of
the now-classic work in Mexico, El Movimiento Campesino
en México (Mexico: Editorial Campesina, 1970). Further,
it is my opinion that he is fairly influential with young
Mexican students of sociology.
27. Gómez Jara, "La Lucha," pp. 171–77.
28. Ibid., p. 172.
29. Ibid., p. 175.
30. Ibid., p. 176.
31. Sergio de la Peña, "De Como Desaparecen las
Clases Campesina y Rentista en el Capitalismo," in Polémica
Sobre las Clases Sociales en el Campo Mexicano, Sergio de
la Peña et al. (Mexico: Editorial Macehual, 1979), p. 59.
32. Arturo Warman is a well-known anthropologist,
now subdirector of the Graduate School of the National
School of Anthropology and History in Mexico City.
33. Arturo Warman, Y Venimos a Contradecir: Los
Campesinos de Morelos y el Estado Nacional (Mexico:
CISINAH, 1976), p. 14.
34. Arturo Warman, "El Problema del Proletariado
Agrícola," in Polémica Sobre las Clases Sociales en el
Campo Mexicano, Sergio de la Peña et al. (Mexico:
Editorial Macehual, 1979), p. 86.
35. Ibid. p. 91.
36. Armando Bartra is one of the chief editors of
the Mexican peasant journal Cuadernos Agrarios. He is
also a member of the economics faculty at UNAM.
37. Armando Bartra, La Explotación del Trabajo
Campesino por el Capital (Mexico: Editorial Macehual,
1979), p. 109.
38. I will more fully develop this controversial
issue of recampesinización when discussing Esteva's
position.
39. The late Ángel Palerm was a professor of
anthropology at the Universidad Ibero-Americana and a
visiting professor at the University of Texas at Austin.
He was a well-published and well-respected anthropologist.

40. Rodolfo Stavenhagen is a well-known sociologist throughout Latin America and Europe. He is currently subdirector of UNESCO in Paris.

41. Ángel Palerm, "Sobre la Fórmula M-D-M y la Articulación del Modo Campesino de Producción al Sistema Capitalista Dominante," Cuadernos de la Casa Chata 5 (1977):8.

42. Paul Sweezy, The Theory of Capitalist Development (New York: Monthly Review Press, 1942).

43. Ernest Feder, professor at the University of Berlin, conducted extensive field investigations in the countryside of Mexico. He participates frequently in the debate about the peasantry in Mexico in the literature.

44. Ernest Feder, "Campesinistas y Descampesinistas," Comercio Exterior 27 (December 1977):1442.

45. Warman, "El Problema," p. 87.

46. Interview, November 9, 1975.

47. Warman, "El Problema," p. 89.

48. Ibid.

49. Gustavo Esteva, La Batalla en el Mexico Rural (Mexico: Siglo XXI, 1980), p. 157.

50. Additional field evidence supporting the hypothesis of recampesinización has been gathered by Jane Margolis in Guanajuato. Her fieldwork in two villages, Magdalena de Araceo and Valle de Santiago, shows that at times 90 percent of the working male population migrates to the United States for long periods, sending back to their family and farms money for investments, etc. Eventually they return, taking up where they left off, never having severed ties with the community despite long absences (sometimes years). Jane Margolis, "El Papel de la Mujer en la Agricultura del Bajío," Iztapalapa 1 (1979): 158-70.

51. Gustavo Esteva, "La Economía Campesina Actual como Opción de Desarrollo," Investigación Económica 38 (January-March 1979):235.

52. Gustavo Esteva is a professor of sociology at UNAM. He is also chairman of the nonprofit research group called Fondo de Cultura Campesina. Interviewed frequently by the major Mexico City newspapers, he is one of the major protagonists in the debate over the peasantry in Mexico.

53. Armando Bartra, La Explotación del Trabajo Campesino por el Capital, p. 87.

54. Ibid., p. 88.

55. Esteva, "La Economía Campesina," p. 237.

56. Esteva, La Batalla, p. 108.

57. Gustavo Esteva, unpublished notes, January 1981.

58. Armando Bartra, "El Ascenso del Movimiento Campesino," in Polémica Sobre las Clases Sociales en el Campo Mexicano, Sergio de la Peña et al. (Mexico: Editorial Macehual, 1979), p. 98.

59. Ibid., p. 100.

60. Ibid., p. 105.

61. Ibid., p. 108.

62. Ibid., p. 111.

63. Gustavo Esteva, intervention at the conference "Encuentro Sobre las Clases Sociales en el Campo Mexicano" (1979), in Polémica Sobre las Clases Sociales en el Campo Mexicano, Sergio de la Peña et al. (Mexico: Editorial Macehual, 1979), p. 119.

64. See Armando Bartra, "Seis Años de Lucha Campesina," Investigación Económica 3 (July–September 1977):157–209; and Armando Bartra, Notas Sobre la Cuestión Campesina México 1970–1976 (Mexico: Editorial Macehual, 1979), pp. 9–20.

65. Arturo Warman, "Frente a la Crisis Política Agraria o Política Agrícola?" Comercio Exterior 28 (June 1978):687.

66. Arturo Warman, "Una Hipótesis que Nace Mas Cerca de los Campesinos que del Poder," Narxhí-Nandhá Revista de Economía Campesina 8/9/10 (September 1978):48.

67. Gustavo Esteva, coordinator and editor of "Informe del Trabajo de Campo y del Estudio Teórico del Sector Rural," recently released results of a research project sponsored by the Fondo de Cultura Campesina, Spring 1981.

3

SOCIAL CAPITAL
AND THE MEXICAN PEASANTRY

This chapter specifies and illustrates the various ways the contemporary peasantry in Mexico is included within capitalist reproduction. Using the social capital focus, we will look behind the petit bourgeois mask placed on the peasantry by the category ownership of the means of production and examine their working-class character. The social capital focus will also help us to see why peasant relations with capital may appear as links between commercial capital and productive capital or as one capitalist dealing with another when we actually have an exploitative relation between workers and capitalists. In addition, we will be able to identify the formal and real subsumption of the peasantry to capital as opposed to segregating the peasant productive unit outside of, but exploited by, capital.

In the first part of the chapter, we will see how peasants work for capital without a wage: (1) reproducing the labor force for the latent reserve army; (2) building social infrastructure; (3) reproducing the waged labor force used in agriculture and lowering the value of labor power; and (4) directly producing surplus value. In the second part of the chapter, we will look at the more formal connections that capital has with the peasantry through commercial and financial arrangements that turn out to involve production relations.

After detailing the peasant links with capital that establish their status as a working class-in-itself, in the next chapter we will examine how and where peasants struggle against these links, thus defining their status as a working class-for-itself.

UNWAGED PEASANT WORK IN MEXICO

First, we must identify and describe the unwaged domestic work that peasants of all kinds are always doing. Then we will look at how this work is work for capital.

The unwaged domestic work process is the production and transformation of the means of subsistence into the form necessary for direct productive consumption (that is, the production and reproduction of labor power). In the case of the subsistence peasant in Mexico, it means producing and transforming almost all of the means of subsistence.

If peasants produce some or most of their means of subsistence, their work includes the gardening required for corn, beans, squash, or chili; the work required to graze goats, cows, or burros; the care of chickens or turkeys and other domestic animals; the making of adobe and thatch for houses, and so on. This work necessary to survive or subsist as a peasant is much more arduous and labor intensive than the unwaged reproductive work of the waged workers, who purchase their means of subsistence almost completely processed by capital. Where the waged industrial worker may have to spend time (unwaged, of course) shopping at a grocery store, cooking the food on a stove of some sort, cleaning and maintaining some sort of housing with implements of varying degrees of labor-saving efficiency, peasants in Mexico grow their own food, or, if they purchase some or all of it, they may still transform the main staple, maize, into tortillas (this is a long process for those making their own nixtomal). For those paying to have it made, making the tortillas still requires a lot of unwaged work for the women going to and from the molino every day, cooking on a fire of their own making, transporting the fuel (charcoal, or leña, which must be gathered sometimes at some distance) herself. For a peasant, water rarely comes out of a tap in the home. It must be transported from the nearest source. Consequently, washing clothes is not done with running tap water, much less in a washing machine, but in a nearby creek or in buckets of water carried to the house.

Most of the unwaged work producing and transforming the means of subsistence in the productive process of producing and reproducing labor power is executed by the peasant woman. The process of production of labor power in the industrial urban societies, as Lourdes Arizpe says, is covered by the various specialized functions of the mother, wife, cook, nursery school teacher, public school teacher, nurse, gardener, and seamstress. In the peasant community, the peasant woman performs all this work.[1]

Peasant unwaged domestic work that produces labor power can be illustrated as a circuit of peasant reproduction of labor power. Subsistence peasants, who produce everything on the land with their own and their family's labor power, can be depicted as follows:

Circuit of Peasant
Reproduction
(Subsistence
Farming):
$$LP \ldots P_1 \ldots MS \ldots P_2 \ldots LP*$$

P_1 is the production of the raw means of subsistence (MS). This work would include the gardening and the work required to graze animals. P_2 is domestic production or transformation of these MS into food, clothing, and housing. P_1 and P_2 are unwaged work producing LP*.

Now that we have recognized the unwaged work done by peasants, we will go on to see how that work is work for capital.

Unwaged Work Produces and Reproduces
the Reserve Army

A common interpretation of "reserve army" denotes a mass of unemployed workers who at any time can be marshaled into working for capital. The presence of such a mass aids capital in keeping wages down and in making available a labor pool from which to draw additional workers should capitalist reorganization or expansion so require. Marx elaborated on this vision of an unemployed mass by specifying three forms of this surplus population: the floating, the latent, and the stagnant. The first category, the floating surplus population, consists of both those workers discharged from industry for technical reasons as the organic composition of capital rises and those workers already "used up" by capital and no longer physically able to work in a different branch.[2] The floating surplus population is those workers who frequently change over from the waged to the unwaged and vice-versa. The second form of surplus population, the latent, consists of agricultural laborers whose wages are reduced to the minimum and those out of a job completely. When capital invades agriculture, displacing peasants from the land (sometimes only partially), its higher organic composition reduces demand for agricultural labor. The principal effect is a lowering of real wages. The latent surplus population primarily involves those peasants tenuously on the land (with or without some wage) who teeter on the brink of pauperism--and are thus potentially available for industrial employment. The third category of surplus population, the stagnant, is those members of the labor army with extremely irregular employment,[3] what we might call today the structurally unemployed. Marx describes three categories of the stagnant reserve army: those able to work but not needed by capital except in times of great prosperity, orphans and pauper children used only rarely, and those physically incapable of working for capital.

Marx's discussion of the reserve army suggests a unidirectional flow of workers into three categories. Peasants, for example, may be forced partially off the land into the latent reserve (differentiation of the peasantry).[4] Eventually, as the organic composition of capital continues to rise and the process of proletarianization of the peasantry is more complete, the peasants, now ex-peasants, move to the urban areas in search of work, becoming part of the floating reserve. Finally, the ex-peasants, members of the floating reserve, who by definition vacillate between employment and unemployment, may become unfit for productive work and wind up in the stagnant reserve.

Classic proletarianization of the peasantry has occurred in Mexico. However, as I suggested in Chapter 2, proletarianization of the Mexican peasantry has not been as complete as some scholars claim. Consider the poor landed peasants (members of the latent reserve) who must seek additional income from day jobs or seasonal work. They strive to subsist off the paltry earnings from their unstable day work and the food they manage to grow on the land.[5] If conditions in the latent reserve become too disastrous for these peasants, they may leave the land completely, migrate to the urban areas, search for work, and thus join the floating reserve.

However, these supposedly new members of the proletariat are more often than not still peasants. They maintain close relations with their original peasant community, family, and land, if not in actuality then in desire.[6]

They are, therefore, not ex-peasants, but peasants. They may be forced into the floating reserve because of the poverty in the countryside, but they work toward returning to the land. As already mentioned in Chapter 2, this process has been called recampesinización. When peasants manage to obtain enough income from waged work in the cities to recover their landed peasant status by paying off debts, acquiring land, or saving enough for essential inputs, proletarianization (peasants flowing out of the latent reserve and permanently into the floating) is reversed. We have instead recampesinización (or peasants moving out of the floating, back to the latent, reserve, and back to the land).[7]

On the other hand, there are ex-peasants who have broken all ties with the community and land and belong to the floating reserve, migrating from place to place in search of work (as well as those peasants permanently in the cities). These are the so-called golondrinas, who are a rural section of the waged proletariat.[8] Unwaged ex-peasants who have no political hope, no financial ability to return to the land, or no interest in doing so belong to the stagnant reserve. The streets of Mexico City are full of pauper children as in Marx's time: fire swallowers, garbage pickers, roving musicians, bead sellers, disabled beggars, and so on. A good proportion are ex-peasants. They are not hired by capital except on the rarest occasions--probably never.

Since the stagnant reserve exerts little direct effect on the hierarchy of wages and the golondrinas of the floating reserve are ex-peasants, I will treat only the peasants who move in and out of the latent and floating reserves. We now turn to the effects of this peasant reserve on the capitalist hierarchy of wages.

In assessing the reserve army and the hierarchy of wages for Latin America, Anibal Quijano, in Populismo, Marginalización y Dependencia (1976), has concluded that the masses of unemployed and underemployed, including peasants, do not function as reserve army in the traditional Marxist sense. In other words, the unemployed reserve army, or "marginalized population," as he calls it, fails to carry out the tasks of (1) depressing salaries of the workers already incorporated into production by the threat of substitution, and (2) being available for capitalist expansion, "the reserve function," since capital no longer requires more workers as it expands.[9]

Nevertheless, in Mexico City, the state government did find it necessary to draw out of the reserve army over 100,000 workers to build the ejes viales (series of rapid transit avenues). Once the job was finished, the president of the Camara Nacional de la Industria de la Construcción, Crescencio Ballesteros, said, "The 100,000 construction workers who constructed the ejes viales must now return to their land."[10] It is not entirely true, as Quijano suggests, that the reserve army no longer fulfills its reserve function.

With respect to substitution, Quijano admits that the marginalized population does depress salaries for those workers in the informal sector--those jobs with the lowest technological and financial level of sophistication.[11] But with respect to the rest of the proletariat, Quijano denies any connection or influence whatsoever from the marginalized population.[12] He has implicitly posited a dual labor market where one set of workers, actually all workers except those doing the most menial tasks, are politically, socially, and technically cut off from the reserve army, in which he lumps all his marginalized population.

This creates an artificial division that obscures important political realities. What we really have is a hierarchy of workers, including unwaged workers on the bottom, where influences from the reserve are mediated but indeed transmitted throughout the hierarchy. Of course, as the number of mediations increases between the bottom and the top of the hierarchy, influences tending to lower salaries or increase discipline are increasingly dampened. Although the influence from the bottom to the top is slight, this is no justification for splitting the workers into only two mutually exclusive groups when there are in fact many strata.

In contemporary Mexican capitalism, no one would suggest that the unemployed or underemployed peasants of the reserve compete directly with the higher-waged industrial proletariat for jobs. It is understood that to some degree certain portions of the proletariat form a worker "aristocracy."[13] They are well organized, well trained, and impervious to outside peasant pressure for jobs. It is doubtful that a peasant with little or no formal education could directly carry out the tasks of workers in petroleum, petrochemical, or electric plants, or in telephone, automobile, and railroad facilities. But this has always been true in every capitalist hierarchy everywhere. In other branches of industry (not just the informal sector, as Quijano asserts), such as food processing,[14] mining, construction, light industry,[15] and some services,[16] the presence of a large mass of peasants looking for jobs has served to keep wages down and interfered with attempts to organize. The immediate effects of the peasant reserve upon the bottom rungs of the wage hierarchy do include downward pressure on wages along with willingness to accept poor working conditions.

Thus, as with the reserve army everywhere, the effect of the peasant masses is felt first as a threat to those on the bottom of the wage hierarchy. Those workers at the bottom are generally unskilled and easily replaced. This is also true for workers a little higher up (in mining, agroindustry, or construction) who are semiskilled but also easily replaced. The direct threat to the bottom level becomes indirect on the next higher level. Workers in construction or in small shops or bus drivers are not worried about peasants immediately stepping into their shoes, but they certainly know that if they lose their jobs, the options on the lower levels are less attractive-- in part, because of the presence of those peasants. Thus, they may toe the line a little more closely. As in all wage hierarchies, the limits on the power of each stratum are formed by the weakness of the lower levels. Only at the top of the hierarchy, where workers and unions control the labor market, is little if any threat experienced from below.[17]

Unwaged Work and Social Control

A further advantage to capital of peasant unwaged domestic labor is the political and social control provided by the peasants themselves who self-manage their own work. Harry Cleaver first recognized that peasant work on small parcels was just another form of piece wages. He pointed out that peasants self-regulate the intensity and quality of the work, knowing that their livelihood or survival depends on those efforts. Capital benefits by having the energy of those peasants diverted from other endeavors, namely struggle, to subsistence activities (work). As I have pointed out before, capital tries to use land as a means to stabilize and maintain the peasantry. Since work is the fundamental method of social control, keeping the peasantry working on the land can provide that control. If this can be accomplished with little or no state capitalist intervention and expense, so much the better; capital's resources are freed for investment elsewhere.[18] Nevertheless, capital does not always succeed in controlling the peasants through unwaged work on the land. All too often, as we shall see, peasant small landownership provides the basis for various struggles that disrupt capitalist accumulation.

In the event that the land resources are too scarce or unproductive to keep peasants employed, the state may step in with additional methods to keep the peasants working. Apart from the traditional state mechanisms of control,[19] we will briefly look at a few such programs taking place in Mexico, some of which involve the unwaged and others involving the waged.

Unwaged Work and Infrastructure

Development programs devised by capital organize the peasants into providing "free" their own social infrastructure, thus accomplishing the dual function of saving capital and serving as social control. The development programs are little more than a mechanism to extract further unwaged work from peasants in addition to their unwaged work providing subsistence on their parcel of land. Their work load for capital is multiplied.

Such a program, the Ejercito del Trabajo, was created by the state of Mexico in 1958. It has mobilized children, young people, and adults who have worked for no pay constructing social infrastructure projects such as roads, drainage systems, schools, and reforestation for water and soil conservation. The people have been organized for work in each community by the presidentes municipales, regional authorities, or someone with political clout over the community, such as the cacique.[20] Since much of the year the peasants in the state of Mexico are supposed to be "underemployed," valuable labor resources otherwise left to their own devices are put to work.

Another "development" program, PIDER, which uses unwaged peasant labor, is a project of the World Bank in collaboration with the Mexican Secretary of Planning and Budget (Programmación y Presupuesto). The project involves investment by the Bank and government in over 86

depressed regions of Mexico. So far, 6,550 rural communities have been involved in the program. The main goal
is to increase the productivity of the peasant farmers by
building infrastructures. The beneficiaries would contribute $20 million worth of material; labor is not included
in the total cost of the project.[21] Evaluation of the benefits of these projects is another matter.[22]

Infrastructure is also constructed at a minimum of
cost by paying peasants less than subsistence wages. The
Secretaría de Asentamientos Humanos y Obras Publicas
(SAHOP) uses peasant labor to build roads and acquire
local raw materials. The wage SAHOP pays for this work
is usually much less than the minimum wage assigned by
law per region.[23] The government also relies on the highly controversial food-for-work programs,[24] called "Raciónes,"
to build transportation and water conservation projects such
as dams or bridges. The SAHOP and food-for-work programs
rely on peasant unwaged domestic labor to make up the
difference between the value of wages paid and actual
value of labor power in each region. This is a crucial
point. Peasant unwaged domestic labor lowers the value
of labor power used in such programs, just as it does in
agriculture.

Unwaged Peasant Work and the Value of
Labor Power Used in Agriculture

At least one half of the economically active rural
population in Mexico divide their time in varying proportions between working a parcel of land (their own or rented)
and working for a wage.[25] Either endeavor alone is insufficient to maintain the peasants and their families. The
history of how and why most of the Mexican peasantry can
no longer be completely self-sufficient on their land would
take us into the heart of the agrarian reform issue and
the model of economic development chosen by Mexico's governing elite. As important as it is, it is not necessary
to relate this history here. I refer the reader to Part I
of Esteva's La Batalla en el Campo Mexicano and also
Arturo Warman's Y Venimos a Contradecir for an excellent
overview and analysis that provide background to the situation today--peasants left with poor land or insufficient
land, as a result of continuous capitalist robbery. This
is what has forced the peasants to sell their labor power

from time to time. Since peasants must sell their labor power anywhere from a week to six months a year (sometimes for years when the peasant is trying to regain or purchase land--recampesinización), this temporary waged condition has a built-in advantage for capital.

By providing their own subsistence at least part of the year, peasants who sell their labor power are paid wages lower than the value of labor power would be in the absence of this domestic work. That is, the wages are not the amount that would be socially necessary to maintain and reproduce the peasants and their families if all means of subsistence had to be bought on the market. The capitalists pay wages for a greatly reduced value of labor power because the peasants work, uncompensated for their own subsistence, the rest of the year. Often, when campesinos migrate temporarily to work during the sowing or harvest, they leave the cultivation of their own land parcels (and therefore a part of their own reproduction) up to the women and children, who continue to work unwaged in their absence.[26] In one case examined by Paré, those peasants who work for capitalists (patrónes) year round are "allowed" by the patrón to return to their own parcel of land two days a week.[27] The boss recognizes that this unwaged work allows him to pay these workers less than the going wage. Thus, those peasants who work permanently for growers but who do not have access to a land parcel for themselves are paid 62 pesos a day in the northwest, while the migrant workers who maintain themselves the rest of the year are paid only 31 pesos.[28]

Another example of peasants who have their own parcels of land but sell their labor power part time are those peasants in Chiapas who work for a wage one to three months each year during the coffee harvest. The pitifully low piecework wages paid these peasants, mostly indígenas, are made possible only because of extensive domestic labor.[29]

Mexican students of the peasantry are very fond of saying that the wages paid the peasants who sell labor power on a temporary basis are below the value of labor power. They claim that the day wages are inferior to the cost of the means of subsistence of the workers and of their families.[30] This is mistaken reasoning. No one would deny that the wages are pitifully low or that the workers have a terrible standard of living, but it is not true that wages must be equal to the costs of subsistence were they to be obtained in the market. They must be sufficient to insure reproduction of the workers and their families. The value of labor power is lower because of the unwaged work. Thus, wages are lower than if there were no unwaged work.[31] But it is not true that wages are less than the value of labor power.

We can schematically illustrate the linkages between peasant part-time waged work, unwaged work on the land, and the circulation of capital. The sale of labor power for a wage by those campesinos is an obvious moment of capital's reproduction. There is a dual circuit of the reproduction of labor power for the peasant. Part of the labor power is sold; part is plowed into P_1 (the unwaged work process of producing MS).

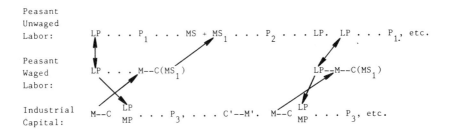

Peasant Unwaged Labor: $LP \ldots P_1 \ldots MS + MS_1 \ldots P_2 \ldots LP. \; LP \ldots P_1$, etc.

Peasant Waged Labor: $LP \ldots M--C(MS_1)$ $\qquad LP--M--C(MS_1)$

Industrial Capital: $M--C \begin{matrix} LP \\ MP \end{matrix} \ldots P_3, \ldots C'--M'. \; M--C \begin{matrix} LP \\ MP \end{matrix} \ldots P_3$, etc.

The peasant circuit thus reproduces labor power by combining unwaged work on the parcel producing means of subsistence ($P_1 \ldots MS$), with the unwaged work processing both the MS_1 purchased with the wage and the MS produced at home ($P_2 \ldots LP$).

There are two linkages illustrated here. First, when peasants buy capitalist commodities ($M--C[MS_1]$), they not only contribute to capital's realization of surplus value, but they may be contributing to an excess surplus value by paying prices higher than market value. Second, when these peasants sell their labor power to capital, as already pointed out, capital benefits by paying wages equivalent to a very low value of labor power. Furthermore, these peasants are forced to sell their labor power only part time. Capital benefits by paying for only the amount of labor power required for the temporary seasonal agricultural jobs. Given the structure of Mexican capital in the countryside, it does not need, nor can it support year round, the quantity of workers that would be available if a true agricultural proletariat were created. On the other hand, the wage earned enables the peasants to continue life as peasants in their community with their own definitions of life. This positive aspect of the wage and how peasants use it for self-valorization will be discussed as a form of struggle in Chapter 4.

Peasant Unwaged Work, Surplus Value, and Capitalists (in Disguise of Feudalism)

Peasant unwaged domestic labor also produces surplus value, which capitalists directly appropriate. The peasant workers who rent lands from owners of the coffee fincas around Simojovel Chiapas provide an interesting example. The peónes work four to five days a week for the landlord as payment for land they live and subsist on. The type of work done for the landlord includes agricultural tasks, clearing new roads, repairing and building fences, and general maintenance of the ranch buildings. In addition, they are expected to run errands for the patrón and his family on Sundays. The women must also take turns helping out in the casa grande under the most servile conditions. These extra tasks, which the peónes take turns doing, could be seen as arrangements characteristic of feudalism. In fact, because the work is unwaged, rent is paid in labor, and the peónes live on the landlord's lands. Mercedes Olivera's investigation identified the "forms of work as characteristic of feudal relations of production in the countryside."32 In some remote fincas, the patrón exercises the right to deflower the virgin daughters of his peónes. Of course, this oppression in its most vile form could formally be identified as feudalist. However, we have an unusual type of feudalism because the relations of production are carried out between the serfs (indígenas acasilladas) and the owner of the coffee finca, who is identified as a capitalist. The author of this recent study cannot deny that the patrónes or owners of the fincas extract surplus value, valorize it, and accumulate capital. Blinded by the trappings of feudalism, Olivera denies working-class status to these peónes.

I see this oppression not as feudalism but as a symptom of the relatively powerful position of the capitalist vis-à-vis the worker. The fact that such disgusting practices take place neither defines the relation as feudalistic or capitalistic. It only proves the relatively weak position of these peasants in this moment. Capitalism does not mean the end of sexism. Perhaps in today's capitalist society sexism is a little less overt than arranged rape between capitalist and peasant, but this is not because feudalism disappeared; it is because the workers have gained more power. (Sexual abuse by employers of female employees has not disappeared everywhere.)

More confusion surfaces when Olivera notes that these peasants who work the coffee harvest three months a year for piece wages are the same peasants who work the rest of the year unwaged doing feudalist type tasks for the same coffee finca owner. Does this mean that the peónes are one day serfs, only the next day to become workers, changing their class nature like a chameleon changes color?

Social capital enables us to see through the particular production and social relations and identify that there are three moments of work taking place here--all three are work for capital by workers:

1. unwaged domestic work on the peasant parcels, which reproduces the labor power (the peónes) used by capital--the patrónes;
2. unwaged work done directly for the patrón, where surplus value is created and appropriated (the cultivation, building of fences);
3. waged work (piece wages) of the coffee harvest three months a year--again, surplus value is extracted.

The complexity of the conditions of labor should not prevent us from seeing that no matter what the form through which the work is imposed, these peasants are members of the proletariat--working for a capitalist.

PEASANT LINKAGES WITH CAPITAL
IN COMMERCE AND PRODUCTION

In the preceding section we looked partly at how peasant unwaged labor functioned for capital in the absence of market or money transactions. Where I discussed the peasants who sell their labor power part time for a wage, this obviously involves production relations and is a direct insertion into capital's reproduction. Although this group of peasants is sometimes the only one recognized as a sector of the working class, I have made a case for the working-class status of all peasants, regardless of land tenure or wage relations.

Now I will discuss a variety of arrangements between the peasantry and capital that confirm more strongly the working-class status of peasants. But more importantly, by clarifying how the peasantry fits into capitalist production and reproduction, we expose how and where the peasantry can rupture capitalist reproduction. In other words, we look carefully at the linkages between the peasantry and capital, illuminating the weaknesses and strengths for the express purpose of evaluating peasant strategy. When we examine peasant struggles in Chapter 4, we will see concretely where peasants have disrupted capital.

The Market

We will begin with the landed subsistence peasants who produce enough for their family's subsistence and sell some surplus to meet other needs. Peasants usually grow maize and beans. We assume that (1) they receive no credit from any source, and (2) they never realize any surplus. Field studies support the latter assumption. In 1978, Pineda found from direct field investigations in the southern part of the state of Mexico that, given the costs of production, the market price of the product, a peasant growing five hectares of maize does not accumulate (or realize) surplus.[33] These peasants produce enough for themselves and at times are able to sell in the market without themselves realizing a surplus.[34]

Before I explain specifically how capital extracts a surplus from commercial relations, let us represent diagrammatically the relations between capital and a peasant family that sells some output on the market.

Merchant
capital

Peasant
reproduc-
tion with
commercial
farming

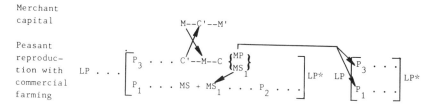

The family divides its labor power between P_1, producing the raw unprocessed MS for its own subsistence, and P_3, the production process producing C', commodities for sale in the market. It is assumed here that no surplus value is realized in the sale. We have C'--M instead of C'--M'.[35] The peasants use the money they receive from the sale to buy both MS_1, additional food to be transformed (P_2) by the domestic unwaged workers for production of LP*, and MP to start the farming process, P_3 and P_1, all over again. The market connections via C'--M are channels for the peasants to reproduce themselves and for capital to extract a surplus from the peasants through unequal exchange. The peasants are often forced by merchant capital, mainly comerciantes locales, to sell their commodities at prices set below value. Peasants acquire the major part of necessary consumer products at high prices from comerciantes locales to complement their subsistence. The comerciantes function partly as buyers of corn and beans and partly as usurers. The peasants lose much of the surplus they generate to them.[36] In addition, as implied above, the terms of trade can be manipulated to be unfavorable to the peasants by inflating the price of commodities the peasants purchase, while holding steady or reducing the price of the commodities the peasants sell in exchange.

To illustrate this circuit, we will assume that the crop sold is a subsistence crop such as maize, which means it is sold either to the government commercial agency, CONASUPO,[37] or to local comerciantes or transportistas, who buy up the crop for resale. CONASUPO estimates that 40 percent of the corn-growing peasants sell to comerciantes locales because they give "advances" in cash. Another 30 percent of the peasants sell to transportistas who come to the fields to buy and then transport the produce. Another 30 percent sell to CONASUPO.[38] I will explain the mechanisms that capital uses either in its state form (CONASUPO) or commercial private form (comerciantes) to extract a surplus from the peasants and therefore involve them in capitalist-worker relations. First, let us look at CONASUPO.

When a peasant sells to CONASUPO there are a number of ways, unofficial, of course, that the agency robs the peasant, thus extracting a surplus. Because CONASUPO has regulations on how pure and clean the crop must be, it has imposed a complicated quality grading system that can cause the peasants to lose up to 16 percent of the market value of their crop.[39] The descuentos can be applied in a very arbitrary fashion. Peasants complain and often refuse to sell to CONASUPO because of the losses due to "quality," etc. A peasant from Tetela del Monte, Morelos, complained that CONASUPO also charged or deducted from the value of the harvest a fee for the use of the scales and costs of costales (gunny sacks), both of which are illegal.[40]

It was also reported in the Bajío that agents from CONASUPO manipulate the scales when weighing the crops. However, this trick is hard to avoid since private acaparadores also rely on this form of cheating to increase profits.

In addition to local commercial arrangements between peasants and commercial capital, the national commercial pricing policy for subsistence crops since 1953 has been one of the most powerful weapons that capital has wielded against the peasantry. By holding the price of corn steady for over ten years while the prices of consumption goods and agricultural inputs rose, the state financed an industrialization program and promoted export industrial agriculture by squeezing the peasantry.[41] Urban wages were kept low (cheap food) at the expense of the peasantry by state intervention in the commercialization of subsistence goods.[42]

Another group of landed subsistence peasants who usually meet their subsistence needs with their parcel of land also relate with capital on unfavorable terms. These peasants, perhaps 40 percent of the corn-producing peasants who do not have an outright surplus but find themselves from time to time in a precarious position, are forced to sell part of their food reserves at disadvantageous prices in order to meet some unexpected emergency--medical expenses, for example. This transaction usually takes place on a local level since it involves small quantities (one or two gunny sacks of maize) and immediate cash needs. The peasants cannot transport maize to other buyers (requiring expensive and time-consuming transportation) or wait for a good price. They must sell right then to the local comerciante for a price set by the latter. Unfortunately, the peasants later must replace this missing reserve in order to survive until the next harvest. They purchase more maize, usually from the same comerciante, at a price higher than they received. In this manner, the landed subsistence peasant is exploited by the voracious capital accumulation of the local commercial capitalists.

Landed subsistence peasants who grow cash crops for sale are also exploited by capital via the commercialization of the crop. The peasants who cultivate coffee in the tropical climate of Chiapas are obliged to sell their coffee beans almost within 48 hours of harvest. The tropical humid conditions that rot the coffee quickly often prevent the peasants from drying it in the sun. These peasants are usually desperate to sell the perishable coffee beans as quickly as possible. Intermediaries purchase the coffee, often at 60 percent of the official price.[43] They use excuses such as spots (manchas) or mold (humedad) to lower the price, as well as their monopsony of the market (28 families control almost 50 percent of the coffee market in Mexico).[44] Intermediaries also buy future coffee harvests from small peasants at 50 percent of the value on delivery. Compra a tiempo (also applied to other crops) is used to extract a surplus from the small peasants, who must submit to such conditions to survive until the end of the harvest.[45]

The government commercial institution for coffee, Instituto Mexicano de Café (INMECAFE) offers an alternative to the peasants that is only marginally better. In 1978-79, INMECAFE purchased 29 percent of total production. Representatives of the institute claim they have insufficient facilities to handle more of the harvest.[46] In fact, it was reported that officials of INMECAFE actually cooperated with unscrupulous intermediaries by telling the peasants that INMECAFE had no money to buy their coffee or that the warehouse was full.[47] Peasants complained that the officials would refer them next door to the private buyer, who always had cash and space for coffee sold below official price.

We continue with the landed subsistence peasants, who, for any number of reasons (not enough land, poor land, no inputs to increase crop yield), usually do not produce enough maize to survive the year round. They enter into an agreement with a prestamista (usurer), who buys the future harvest at one half of the current price (compra a tiempo). CONASUPO estimates that 22 percent of the corn-producing peasants are in this predicament. The prestamistas turn around and sell the peasants the needed items, usually at a price higher than market price, making a profit additional to the 100 percent interest per year they charge for the cash advance.[48] Sometimes the peasants never see the cash. There is a direct transaction of corn for goods, with the prestamista/comerciante keeping the accounts, which the peasant more than likely cannot read. The usurers serve as intermediaries between big business and the peasant. They sell the products of capital to the peasants and channel the surplus created by the peasants on their parcel of land back toward the urban industrial centers.[49] The usurers also channel the surplus they extract in interest to other capitalist investments through financial institutions. It is impossible to follow the surplus via bank statistics documenting regional or rural–urban cash flow, since the prestamistas usually transfer their "earnings" by hand—in suitcases from the rural regions to the capitalist financial centers.[50]

This group of peasants lives constantly on the brink of ruin. They are always in debt or, in the best of cases, breaking even. If one year they manage to produce more than they eat, they pay off their debt; if not, they just increase their debt. Local social relations between peasant and prestamista determine at what point the peasant must resort to temporarily working as a peón or jornalero to pay the usurer. This group of peasants tends to work for a wage only as a last resort, preferring the exploitation of the prestamista's usurous interest rates to working as a jornalero.

Unlanded peasants (peasants who have lost their land or those with derechos a salvo) often enter into arrangements called medieria with local landlords. Although medieria is also engaged in among peasants (see following discussion on credit), here I refer only to relations between peasant and landlord. As a rule, the system works similarly throughout Mexico, with only slight variations from region to region. In the state of Mexico, the landowner generally provides the land and all of the inputs, but only one half of the fertilizer. The mediero, the peasant doing the work, provides the rest of the fertilizer, the implements, and family labor power. At harvest, the landowner receives half of the crop off the top and then discounts from the peasants' half the loan for the fertilizer that the peasant had to purchase. For the state of Mexico, Pineda charges that this arrangement provides for the peasants and their families only a bare subsistence for a part of the year. The mediero must work as a jornalero the rest of the year to insure subsistence.[51]

Peasants who siembra a medias are usually left alone as far as production decisions are concerned. However, the particular crop to be grown is always chosen by the landowner. Their insertion into capitalist reproduction is also obvious in the sphere of circulation. Often, the landowners have a type of tienda de rayas (country store) where, to survive until the harvest, the peasants must purchase means of subsistence at prices established by the landowners. If the peasants ask for one costal of maize, it is customary that they return two costales at harvest. If the peasants instead need cash, they must pay an interest rate of 10 to 20 percent per month.[52]

The different peasant situations that we have discussed involve exploitative relations with capital that lie formally within the sphere of circulation. For Mexico, we uncovered three main mechanisms applied by capital within the sphere of circulation that involve unequal exchange:

1. the terms of trade are manipulated by the state to the detriment of the peasant selling subsistence crops and buying other consumption or production goods;
2. corrupt public officials and private commercial capitalists buy a crop at less than official price or manipulate weight, quality, etc., to lower the price of the crop; and
3. local usurers accumulate at the expense of an immobile peasantry who need cash from time to time.

According to Marx, this is a type of transitional stage en route toward capitalism. There is exploitation from merchant capital and usury but not capitalism or capitalist-worker social relations. Marx distinguishes between merchant capital, usury, formal subsumption, and real subsumption to capital.[53] "Merchant capital commissions a number of immediate producers, then collects their produce and sells it, making them advances in the form of raw materials or even money."[54] Usurers advance raw materials or tools or both to the immediate producer in the form of money. They extort an enormous interest rate from the primary producer but do not intervene in the process of production itself, which proceeds in its traditional fashion. Capital is not yet the direct purchaser of labor or the immediate owner of the process of production. Marx calls these forms the transition to capitalism proper. Formal subsumption of labor to capital is when the capitalist intervenes in the process as its director-manager. There is direct exploitation of the labor of workers and necessarily the valorization of capital that is the manufacture of

surplus value.[55] However, there is no fundamental change
in the labor process. The traditional forms of working
are simply taken over, intensified, made more continuous
or orderly. Surplus labor is exacted but only by increasing absolute surplus value. Capital builds upon and begins within formal subsumption of labor to capital. From
the foundation of formal subsumption of labor to capital,
capitalism proper develops, involving a complete transformation in the productivity of the workers and in the relations between workers and capitalists. Real subsumption
of labor to capital involves direct intervention and reorganization of the labor process, increasingly using relative surplus value strategies as opposed to those for extracting absolute surplus value.
    Although distinguishing among the different forms
of subsumption of labor to capital differentiates among
particular relationships between workers and capital, it
has often blinded Marxists to the substance of the capitalist relationship. Today in all three forms workers are
subsumed to capital in the sense that their labor is annexed and capital valorizes itself. The peculiarities of
merchant capital or usury or formal subsumption are only
strategies adapted in concrete instances. What I am saying is that ultimately real subsumption of labor to capital
may not be in capital's best interest. Capital may not always and everywhere evolve to that point. The Mexican
case demonstrates this well. Peasants, as described in
the above situations, are subsumed to capital, and there
are capitalist-worker relationships present even though in
appearance we have peasants relating with merchant capital only within the sphere of exchange.
    First, most of these peasant situations involved
peasants forced to sell portions, or all, of their crop in
order to secure subsistence goods. The peasant cannot
survive without selling to the capitalist. Self-sufficiency
was not an alternative. These peasants only sold commodities to acquire money to obtain subsistence goods they
could not produce on their own. These poor peasants are
forced to engage in exchange with capital to survive just
like waged workers--only the form of the exchange changes.
Both waged worker and peasant are locked into the same
dependent relationship year after year. Capital controls
or seeks to control both. The difference is what they sell.
The workers sell their only commodity, labor power. The
peasants can sell either their produce or their labor power

or both. Capital manipulates (within the bounds of the class struggle, of course) land use, land availability, inputs, credit, etc., in order to choose the commodity or combination of commodities the peasant sells to capital. For example, if capital has all the waged workers it can productively use and control, then capital will buy produce from the peasants. This strategy produces the relationship of unequal exchange as explained and illustrated previously, which has a twofold purpose: (1) it supplies waged workers with cheap food, keeping the value of labor power as low as possible, thus freeing value for alternative uses; and (2) it perpetuates a dependent relationship between peasant and capital year after year. Capital is assured of a supply of commodities of its choice and assured that peasants are kept working.[56] Capital benefits from the commodity exchange with peasants just as it benefits from workers selling labor power in exchange for food.

When peasants sell a commodity to capital for money, they do so because they must have the money to buy what they lack to survive. But the money they receive is not sufficient to subsist and pay off their debts. They end up destitute and in debt. Just as waged workers must sell their labor power again once the means of subsistence are consumed, ending up right where they started, peasants find themselves in a similar situation at the end of the agricultural cycle. They are forced to plant and sell to capital again to survive. Both peasant and worker are forced into a relationship with capital that is self-perpetuating. The main difference is that one is waged, the other unwaged.

Peasant work (from which capital extracts a surplus), in the form of commodities, is hidden behind the product they sell; hidden by the sphere of circulation; hidden by the peculiarities of this commodity form. Now, as Cleaver has pointed out, the content of the class relations created and maintained by capital is endlessly imposed work.[57] The form of those relations is the commodity form, i.e., exchange. As he argues, the form of the imposition of work on the working class is secondary and not necessarily limited to the money wage. The exchange between worker and capital, through which the former's labor is annexed by the latter, may involve money wages, wages in kind, payment by the hour, payment by the piece, and so on. The examples discussed here support his argument that the labor of the peasant is often annexed by capital through a kind of piece wage. Only in this case the value of labor power is paid in the form of a price on the product within the market instead of a unit wage within the factory. The principle remains the same: workers are paid according to how much they produce, the value of the payment is only equal to or less than the value of the means of subsistence required for the reproduction of the workers' labor power. Marx noted in Chapter 6 of volume 1 of <u>Capital</u> that "the form of wages does not alter their essential nature. One form may be more favorable to capitalist production than the other." We can extend this insight by saying that the form of payment of the value of labor power does not alter its essential nature. One form (wages) may or may not be more favorable to capitalist production than another (market piece rates), depending on circumstances. It is the content of the class relation that is critical, not the form of payment.

Given the structure of capitalism in Mexico today, direct wage labor is often not the best alternative for capitalist development and the control of workers. This is better achieved (from capital's viewpoint) by maintaining the fundamental class relation indirect, mediated. That is, peasants are forced to work for capital by being forced to sell under terms dictated by the latter. Capital benefits by accumulating without assuming any <u>direct</u> control over production. Cash advances from the comerciantes (intermediaries), which keep the peasant in perpetual debt, appear as usury or different variations of merchant capital, but looking beyond the form we find forced work for capital that produces a surplus value for it rather than for the workers--an endless system of work producing endless surplus for capital.

Credit

When peasants receive legal credit, either public or private, the credit not only links the peasants with capital through circulation (commercialization of their products) but in production as well. The degree of capitalist control over the direct process of production ranges from minimal (as with the peasants growing a subsistence crop with credit from BANRURAL) to total control (as with the peasants growing henequen). In what follows, I will uncover progressively more direct links between landed peasant agricultural production and money capital.

About one third of the ejidatarios and minifundistas receive state credit.[58] This lack of state credit forces most of the peasants into the clutches of usurers or local comerciantes, as previously mentioned. Peasants without credit have two more options before abandoning their parcels: to rent the parcel to another producer, who has credit or resources to cultivate the land, or to enter into an arrangement of mediería. Renting involves a strictly monetary arrangement whose prices vary with the quality of land and type of crops. The case of mediería is much more complicated. Arrangements can be made between a peasant who has land but no financing with a peasant who has inputs and land but is physically unable to work; or between a peasant who has both land and inputs but not enough cash to hire workers or is unwilling to do so during harvests.[59]

First we will look at those ejidatarios who have individualized parcels of land within the ejido and are able to obtain credit from the Banco de Credito Rural (BANRURAL). We exclude for the moment those ejidatarios and comuneros who work the land in common.[60] Seventy-three percent of the official state bank credit is given in *avío*,[61] which means material inputs for the cultivation of crops.[62] BANRURAL rarely gives the peasants cash to buy their own choice of seeds, fertilizers, etc. Instead, the credit is extended in commodity form: seeds, fertilizers, insecticides, as well as industrial services, such as rented farm equipment of various types. The commodities provided by the bank are not always valued at the best possible price. Information from ejidatarios in the Valley of Yaqui showed that BANRURAL inputs were always priced higher than those obtainable directly from the supplier.[63] Moreover, the credit in the form of commodities comes with additional strings.

First, credit will only be given to those peasants who pay for crop insurance with La Aseguradora Nacional Agrícola y Ganadera S.A. (ANAGSA), because the guarantee or collateral for the loan is the crop itself.[64] If the crop fails because of a natural disaster (weather, pests), ANAGSA pays off the bank for credit used by the peasants. The peasants receive nothing. This crop insurance is really credit insurance for the bank. Now, here is the point where capital achieves direct control over peasant labor. ANAGSA will not be responsible for the crop unless the peasants follow its directions for the cultivation of the particular crop. The instructions specify how to prepare the land for planting, which seeds, how much seed per hectare, how much insecticide (already selected by the bank), when to plant, when to apply and reapply the assigned fertilizer. The peasant must also submit to frequent field inspections by the bank of ANAGSA inspectors. Official credit is organized so that the essential production decisions are stripped away from the peasant and taken by capital in its form of BANRURAL or other state finance capital organizations, such as ANAGSA.[65] Within this framework, which sets most relevant production techniques, the actual cultivation process is carried out by peasant labor with little day-to-day interference.

In addition to the main staple crops of corn and beans, official credit is granted to the ejidatarios for commercial crops such as sorghum, tomatoes, cotton, and sesame. The BANRURAL has plans for growing each crop-- Plan Maíz, Plan Tomate, Plan Ajonjolí--which specify the desired cultivation techniques to be followed. Often these specifications go against traditional peasant growing techniques. For example, the Plan Maíz forbids the peasants to grow corn and beans together, as is traditionally done. The peasants point out, according to Pineda, that corn shades the beans and that the nitrogen fixation of the frijól gives fertilizer to the corn. Without this "green" fertilizer, inputs of commercial fertilizer must be greater and costlier.

The inputs that BANRURAL acquires for its clients are not any better and sometimes worse than those traditionally employed by the peasants. For example, the so-called semillas mejoradas or improved seeds that the Productora Nacional de Semillas produces for the bank and for direct sale have a coefficient of germination of about 60 to 65 percent. According to one peasant leader, a normal coefficient of germination should be at least 75 to 80 percent.[66] It was shown in a concrete situation on the coast of Jalisco that the yields from fields planted with the improved seeds were not significantly different from those using peasant criollo seeds.[67] The only real difference between the two types of seeds was the cost. Improved seeds, the ones the peasants are forced to buy from the bank, are more expensive. Furthermore, the costs of the fertilizers are higher than the increased yields of the crops, making the use of these expensive inputs not worth it.[68]

Apart from the financing of the inputs and interference in production, the bank is also in charge of marketing. Agricultural credit is defined by the General Law of Rural Credit to include not only financing of the production but marketing and, where applicable, industrialization.[69] This means that the peasants must accept whatever arrangements are made by the bank for the sale of the crop. The bank always extracts payments for the peasants' debt first and then gives anything left over to the peasants. Because the price at which the crop is sold is determined by the bank, a lot of room is left for unsavory maneuvers. For example, one ejido near Los Mochis Sinaloa was extended credit by BANRURAL for the cultivation of cotton. When the price of cotton was very high, the bank paid the ejido only two thirds of that market price. Under a financial arrangement with the bank, the ejido had no choice but to accept the price established by the bank.[70]

Contract Farming

Besides credit from BANRURAL, peasants growing a variety of crops receive credit from other official government institutions, from private wholesalers or commercial capitalists, and from private agribusiness or industrial capital under "contract" agreements. Since Mexican law prohibits industry from directly owning and cultivating land, contract farming is the mechanism widely used to command land and labor and to insure the supply of a specific crop with few risks. The arrangements between direct peasant producers and the institution doing the contracting vary from crop to crop. We will investigate concrete examples from three main types of contracts: (1) contracts offered by private wholesalers, (2) contracts offered by private agribusiness, and (3) contracts offered by official government institutions.

Contracts of all three types always involve specification of quantity, quality, and type of crop, usually the price at which it is to be sold, and varying degrees of control over the actual cultivation. The contract extends "credit" in commodity form of inputs and sometimes cash "credit" for living expenses.[71] The arrangement has become very popular, since peasants, otherwise unable to get credit or ineligible for credit from BANRURAL, can survive with the cash advances and plant their lands. Often peasants who are unable to finance the cultivation of their lands end up abandoning or renting their lands to others and seeking work as jornaleros.

This control of financing or credit for cultivation is used as a tool by capital to control the use of land and labor. When complete control of the land and the production process is required for either technical reasons (the tobacco plant nurseries) or for easier management (Del Monte intensive vegetable farming), capital will restrict the contract arrangement to larger capitalist farmers, who often acquire their land by illegally renting peasant parcels. Apparently, agribusiness prefers (when possible) to arrange contracts between a limited number of producers for a large output rather than numerous contracts with small producers for a limited output. Representatives of Del Monte operating in the Bajío have claimed that the small minifundista does not have the resources to cultivate vegetables.[72] What Del Monte does is to refuse credit to small peasants by requiring the direct producer to contribute a minimum of 10 percent of the cash required for cultivation. This encourages the concentration of rented ejidal lands under one grower. Peasants end up working for a wage on their own land or elsewhere. Since they are excluded from the contract system and credit is not forthcoming from other sources, they give up their land to direct capitalist use. Lack of credit or a contract has also forced peasants to rent their land to capitalists who have contracts with the agribusiness strawberry processing firms in the Zamora region of Michoacán.[73] In other words, contracts are often signed between agribusiness and capitalist growers who rent peasant lands. Since the risks of the illegal act of renting lands and all of the risks associated with cultivation are assumed by the direct producer, this contract arrangement between large capitalist growers and agribusiness is ideal for the latter.

In some cases capital prefers to control completely the agricultural process by directly renting the land itself from the peasant landowners and then contracting the peasant owners and other jornaleros to work their own land!

This practice is not too common in Mexico due to the legal risks involved for capital. However, TABAMEX, the public monopoly that supplies tobacco to the cigarette industry and to the export market, retains total technical and financial control over the cultivation of tobacco seedlings by directly renting peasant lands. The fact that

TABAMEX rents lands is no secret. A government or state enterprise enjoys a certain immunity in these matters. Of course, the land remains in the names of the ejidatarios, and the financing of materials and the cash advances are in the name of the "owner" of the nursery (plantero).[74] Apparently, the ejidatarios engage in business with a financial partner and/or with a technical director. The ejidatarios, however, are owners/direct producers only on paper. The company controls every detail of production, directing every task that the ejidatarios are hired to do on their own land.[75] Despite the fact that the peasants may own the land and may even hire waged laborers to work the land in addition to themselves, it is clear that these peasants are working for TABAMEX, and the jornaleros they may hire are also working for TABAMEX, not for the ejidatarios, who may have technically done the hiring with credit advanced by the company.

Commercial capitalists or acaparadores who want to monopolize the purchase of a certain crop will contract both large growers and peasants to grow the particular crop. In the Bajío, acaparadores strive to capture the soya and sorghum crops by extending credit in cash to buy fertilizers or seeds, to pay workers or to rent machinery, and leave direct cultivation up to the peasants themselves. In this case, direct control over the production process is not required by the commercial capitalists. They make their profits when they buy the crops from the peasants as stipulated in the contract. This is one of the rare contract arrangements where interference is found only in the sphere of circulation. There is only formal subsumption of work under capital.[76]

The relations between the potato-growing peasants of the state of Mexico and the private commercial capitalists of the Merced provide us with yet another example of contract farming between commercial capital and peasants. Ursula Oswald conducted a field examination detailing the arrangements between the peasants and the Merced bodegueros (potato warehouse wholesalers). The peasant receives credit in the form of seed, fertilizer, insecticide, specialized workers who harvest the potatoes, and transportation of the crop to the Merced. The peasant provides land, water, labor, and implements. The value of the harvest is calculated the day of delivery to the Merced at prices that day. After the bodeguero's expenses (the credit) are deducted from the total, what is left over is split fifty-fifty between the peasant and the bodeguero.

There are several mechanisms used by the bodegueros to increase their profits at the expense of the peasant. First, the bodegueros produce their own seeds. Consequently, the prices charged the peasants can be adjusted accordingly. The peasants have no choice but to accept the seeds they are given at the price they are quoted. Second, the peasants do not deduct their expenses like the bodegueros before dividing what is left fifty-fifty. Third, the commercial capitalists decide when the harvest is to take place since they provide the skilled potato harvesters. Nothing prevents them from choosing a day when the price is lowest for potatoes. In that fashion, when they resell the potatoes their profits are even higher (the peasants' income lower). Ursula Oswald estimates that the bodegueros make a 1,414 percent return on the amount of capital they lend, all in about five months.[77]

Contract farming is also prevalent between industrial capital, as represented by the food-processing industries, and the peasants. Exactly how much of agribusiness is involved in contract farming is not readily known (much of agribusiness is transnational).[78] However, evidence suggests that it may be extensive. Alfonso Garzón Santibanez of the CCI estimates that 50 million hectares of the 28,000 hectares of vital lands are controlled by agribusiness (mainly transnational) through contracts. The most notorious companies he mentioned are General Foods, Anderson Clayton, Purina, Del Monte, Nestle, and Coca-Cola.[79] I will cite only two examples, which is all that is necessary here.

Anderson Clayton Company contracts ejidatarios to grow cotton in northwest Mexico for their vegetable oil industry. I was told by the production manager of the vegetable oil division of Anderson Clayton that the main reason for the contract arrangement was to be assured of a guaranteed supply of the raw material: cottonseed.[80] Large companies such as Anderson Clayton have the warehouse and financial capacity to buy large quantities of raw material at the peak harvest time, i.e., when the price is lowest. Since the timing of the harvest is set by the company in the contract, they benefit by paying the producers the lowest possible price.

Another example of contracts between peasants and agroindustry is the peasants who contract to grow barley for the malt industries, which in turn supply the beer breweries.[81] Peasants from the high mountain valleys of

Tlaxcala, Hidalgo, and Puebla grow barley for the monopoly Impulsora Agrícola, which was created by the beer industry to insure and manage the supply of barley. These peasants are forced to grow barley because of unusual climatic conditions in the high valleys, where late rains or early freezes prevent the cultivation of other crops. Year after year, according to Esteva, the peasants have been obligated to the commercial monopoly, which is directly linked to the beer industry, to sell barley. The peasants have consistently sustained net losses.[82]

The contract arrangement is also employed by the government for almost all of the commercial crops it tries to control, from coffee, with the least government control, to tobacco, all of which is controlled by the government.

In the case of coffee, INMECAFE has begun organizing small peasant coffee producers for tighter control over production. They have a usual contract arrangement, where INMECAFE specifies cultivating practices, advances credit, and follows up with field technical assistance (inspectors). The peasants are paid an advance of 750 pesos for each estimated quintal of coffee. When the peasant delivers the harvest the credit (advance) is discounted from the total value of the crop. INMECAFE pays for 80 percent of the total crop at current prices. The balance of the crop is paid in six months at current world prices.[83] On the surface this appears to be a purely commercial arrangement between the direct independent producer and the commodity capitalist (in this case, publicly owned INMECAFE). However, once again the relations between the peasant and capital include more than just commerce; they involve production where the worker's labor is annexed by state capital. The peasants' "advance" is little more than a wage paid for agricultural tasks, tasks specified and supervised by INMECAFE.

The landed peasants who grow sugar cane and receive credit are in a special situation because of the high degree of government intervention in the industry.[84] At present, the state has taken control of the sugar mills, has a financing company, Financiera Nacional Azucarera, the only commercial enterprise, Unión Nacional de Productores de Azucar S.A. de C.V. (UNPASA), and a national commission controlling the industry.[85]

Besides the overwhelming government control of the industry, the factor that differentiates the sugar-cane-growing ejidatarios from the others is that they are obli-

gated by law to plant sugar cane.[86] Compounded with
the government monopoly on finance and commercialization,
the forced cultivation of cane completely subsumes the
peasants to capital. The peasants receive seed and fertilizer from the sugar mills and cash advances on the
promised cane crop for subsistence. The sugar cane is
cut by waged jornaleros who work by the piece or by the
day. The contracting and transporting of the cane and
workers is usually arranged by the sugar mill for the
cañeros. (Sometimes the ejidatarios contract and pay the
jornaleros themselves with the money advanced to them by
the ingenio, which is later discounted when the cane is
sold.)[87] Upon delivery of the cane, the ingenio deducts
the advanced credit, advances for living expenses, and
the salaries of the peónes. What is left over must support the peasants and their families until next planting
season, when they can again receive the advances.[88] From
fieldwork conducted on ejidos surrounding the ingenio, in
Oacalco, Oaxaca, it was found that the peasants growing
cane rarely, if ever, realized a surplus. More often, they
ended up in debt or breaking even.[89]

It does not take much imagination to see that the
ejidatarios cañeros are in the middle of a putting-out system where credit is authorized to insure a constant supply
of a raw material to productive capital, the ingenios, at
prices predetermined and set by the government. More recently, the ingenios have been experimenting with direct
control of production of cane, turning the ejidatarios into
paid laborers on their own land.[90]

The growing of henequen[91] is also subject to direct
control and financing by the official bank. In Yucatán,
where most of the henequen is grown, there is practically
no alternative use for the land. The peasants are in a
situation of either cultivating henequen or nothing at all.
After heavy losses on credit to henequeneros,[92] the Banco
de Crédito Rural Peninsular, with the advice of the president himself, "restructured" the financing of the crop. Previously, ejidatarios were on nóminas, payrolls of the bank.
They received cash weekly, unrelated to productivity. Now
the "unproductive" ejidatarios, youths, old people, the disabled, etc., were removed from the nóminas. Ejidatarios
were to receive payment only after work was completed:
"trabajo hecho--trabajo pagado." The bank thus linked
productivity and salary in a neat package to guarantee
the extraction of relative surplus value. In addition to

this major change in the form of payment, the bank specified exactly, sparing no detail, how the cultivating and
harvesting of the henequen should take place in the "Reglamento de Trabajo Sobre el Cultivo y Explotación de Henequen."[93] The peasant has no alternative but to deliver
the final product, rolls of henequen (pencas por rollas),
to the bank inspectors, who give the peasant a certificate
that can be cashed at the bank. There is no deduction of
credit expenditures, etc., because the "credit" is now a
salary for completed work. Thus, weekly the peasant receives a determined amount of money for the particular
task carried out. The inspector validates that the work
is done according to the reglamento and then pays the
peasant accordingly.[94]

At each stage the peasants are producing surplus
value, which is appropriated through piece wages. The
salaries paid are close to minimum subsistence.[95]

The wages paid the henequenero are calculated exactly to be the very minimum required for reproduction of
labor power. They take into account all of the unwaged
domestic work (as documented by Villanueva) that goes into
reproduction. As I explained earlier, the unwaged work
and low wages do not mean that the wages paid are less
than the value of labor power. It does mean that wages
are considerably lower than they would have been had
there not been the extensive unwaged domestic work representing a considerable savings to capital. The henequen-
growing peasants, "owners of the means of production,"
although formally receiving "credit," are clearly subsumed
under capital. In this case, the "credit" is a wage paid
to the peasants (workers) by the bank (patrón) for specific work controlled in every detail by the patrón. The
petit bourgeois disguise is so thin that the true worker-
capitalist relations are obvious.

One of the clearest examples of peasants subsumed
under capitalism in the spheres of circulation and production is the ejidatarios tabacaleros, or tobacco growers of
Nayarít. These peasants have their own land, conforming
to the legal norms of an ejido, but are contracted by
TABAMEX, the public tobacco enterprise, to grow specific
types and quantities of tobacco. TABAMEX selects the
lands that have the proper technical characteristics for
tobacco cultivation, then proposes a "contract" with the
ejidatarios organized into solidarity groups of producers
(grupos solidarios de producción).[96] Because ejidatarios

cannot use their land as collateral for private credit (they are not "owners" per se of the land), they must be organized in such a fashion that the product of the group's work is the assurance that the debt will be paid. Hence, TABAMEX directly deals with grupos solidarios and not ejidos or ejidatarios.[97]

TABAMEX made contracts with approximately 860 groups, averaging 34 hectares per group, each group consisting of about 14 members.[98]   The contracts are drawn up as the results of discussions between the jefe of each group and TABAMEX as to the amount of credit needed per hectare for each agricultural task.   Each stage in production requires labor (jornales) performed by the ejidatarios, maquilas (see glossary for definition), and material inputs.   Thus, a certain amount of money is stipulated for each task.   The final price of the tobacco that the ejidatarios "sell" to TABAMEX is imposed by the latter in the contract.   TABAMEX agrees to pay for insurance (credit insurance, as previously discussed), provide inputs such as seedlings at a fraction of the real cost (they charge peasants 8 pesos/1,000 plants when the real cost is 39.87/1,000),[99] fertilizers and insecticides at below market price,[100] and also pay the quota for each direct peasant producer to the IMSS or social security.

The peasants, on the other hand, are committed to grow a specific quantity and type of tobacco, the process being directed by TABAMEX, and to deliver and sell it to TABAMEX at the price as stated.   The company has a detailed program for each of the phases of tobacco production.   To insure that the peasants follow instructions, TABAMEX sends teams of specialized personnel who oversee and inspect the work being done in the fields.[101]   Once a week at each productive unit an employee of the company (auxiliar de campo) inspects the work completed, determines the tasks (jornales) to be performed, orders the required inputs, and gives cash for required maquilas.   However, the enterprise counts on the leader of each group to pressure his fellow members into working hard.   It is the leader who receives the cash each week and distributes it to the other members of the group.   By dealing with a leader, TABAMEX simplifies its relations with the direct producers and saves itself administrative costs.   The leader's fee comes out of the salaries to the direct producers, not from TABAMEX.[102]

The credit that the ejidatarios receive is mostly in cash (77.8 percent). The cash is for the payment of the salaries of the workers, themselves and outside workers hired for the harvest, and to pay for maquilas, which include the mechanized preparation of the land, the riegos (irrigation), and transportation of the harvested crop.[103] Of the total credit, 3.4 percent is for subsistence expenses apart from the salary; 22.7 percent is extended in the form of material inputs or services provided by TABAMEX.

The peasants deliver the tobacco to TABAMEX, which then purchases it, minus any defects.[104] The difference between the credit extended and value of the harvest is the final income of the ejidatarios for each group. According to the field investigations by the researchers at CIDER (Centro de Investigaciónes de Desarrollo Rural), the average final income per producer in 1974-75 was 11,881 pesos.[105] There is no question that the 11,000-odd pesos that the peasant receives for the harvest is in no way profits from his agricultural enterprise. This final income is carefully computed by TABAMEX and the cigarette companies to allow just enough money for the peasant producer to subsist during the off-season of June to October. During these months, the lands most suitable for tobacco are flooded or otherwise unusable. Capital guarantees these peasants subsistence to be assured of the lands and labor force next season. Although the final income is presented in the ideological guise of "profit," it is a salary for work--for the seasonal domestic work that produces needed labor power for capital. The final income represents pay for what is usually unwaged domestic work for peasants in Mexico. This time we do not have the absence of a wage that hides the peasants' working-class status; we have the appearance of a profit (the final income), which disguises them as petit bourgeois. The credit extended during the agricultural cycle also confuses the status of the tabacaleros. It appears as credit extended between one business partner to another. Pointing out two aspects of this credit is enough to remove the petit bourgeois label from the tabacaleros completely.

First, 77 percent of the total credit is extended to the ejidatarios in cash strictly for the remuneration of their labor. The "credit" is nothing more than a wage paid to a worker (ejidatario land possessor) for work completed (cultivation of tobacco) for capital (TABAMEX). Second, it is not as if the peasants can freely dispose of the fruits of their labor (the tobacco) as they would choose. It is specifically stated in the contract that the product (a certain type of tobacco) will be delivered to the company for a specified price. TABAMEX is the owner of the product before it is even produced. Furthermore, clarifying the wagelike nature of the credit is the clause in the contract that states that the ejidatarios contracted for tobacco must personally perform all labor unless unusual circumstances (harvest) require the hiring of additional labor.[106] It is a relation of workers to management, not at all like a contract between business and business.

Additional evidence that this credit is in reality a wage comes from the fact that TABAMEX charges no interest. Its principal concern is to guarantee the supply of their raw material, tobacco. The best way to guarantee that supply is by guaranteeing the subsistence and reproduction of the peasants in cash advances without interest. By offering subsistence on favorable terms in return for tobacco, TABAMEX assures its supply of raw material, the land to grow it, and the labor force to tend it.

Although the investigators at CIDER agree that the ejidatarios are not capitalists, they insist that the tobacco-growing ejidatarios are not proletariat either. They cling to the old ideas that because they may buy labor power from time to time and because they possess the means of work (rudimentary implements and the land), this disqualifies them as workers.[107] Even more perplexing, CIDER also claims they are not peasants, defining peasants restrictively as independent agricultural producers who control the productive process and its product--not capitalists, workers, or peasants. CIDER says they are "social agents inserted in a process of vertical integration which places each unit of production as subunits of a complex unity. They are landholders who produce tobacco under conditions of vertical integration."[108] This nondefinition (not capitalists, workers, or peasants) is absurd. It is little more than a description of a highly particular situation that says nothing about how these "social agents" relate to capitalism. The position of CIDER has serious political consequences. If the peasants are not workers then how are we to treat their struggles against TABAMEX? Ignore them? Repress them?

I have demonstrated why we should consider cane-, coffee-, henequen-, and tobacco-growing peasants as workers. We have seen that their landholding status in no way invalidates this assertion. The work process, controlled in every detail by capital, is such that the peasants work for capital on their own land! The credit received in either commodity or cash form is simply capital's guarantee for the production of a certain needed crop. In fact, credit does not free the peasants to produce in the manner they would choose. It is a mechanism that capital uses to insert itself directly into the production process, controlling it and its product for its own use.

We can symbolically represent all of the preceding cases where peasants received credit in commodity form guaranteeing the delivery of a certain output to the lending institution. With the exceptions of the contracts with BANRURAL and commercial capital, the final price was usually stipulated in the contract by the agribusiness. This modern-day putting-out system, where the peasants are given just enough to survive in order to produce and deliver the promised raw material, can be depicted as shown on page 101.

These peasants use their labor power LP plus the means of production provided by the capitalist institution to produce (P_3) commodity C', equal in value to M' but sold back to the company for only M where $M' > M$. The rest has already been explained in other circuits. The "lending" institution extracts a surplus value since $M' - M = S$. It then uses surplus for personal consumption or further capitalist investment. In this manner capital controls agricultural production and the reproduction of the labor force itself.

Including the peasant who hires labor to work within the working class is controversial. As we saw in Chapters 1 and 2, orthodox Marxists always go back to this criterion to disqualify peasants as workers. I believe that in these cases the matter of hiring or not hiring labor is not the crucial factor determining class status. Both the peasant doing the hiring and the peasant being hired are working for capital. For example, laborers hired by tobacco-growing peasants are working for TABAMEX, not for the ejidatarios, even though technically they are hired and paid by the latter. We have a situation of one set of workers mediating (the ejidatarios) between capital (TABAMEX) and the other workers (jornaleros). Both ejidatarios and jornaleros work for TABAMEX. But it appears that the jornaleros work for the ejidatarios. TABAMEX enjoys the advantage of having some of its workers managed

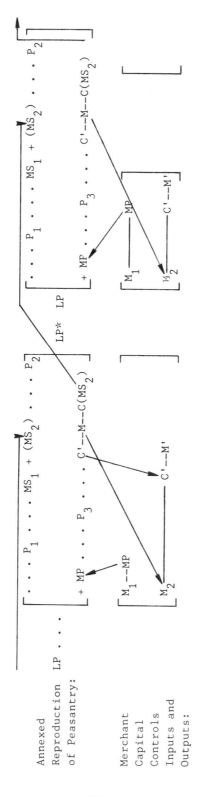

by other workers. Is this so unlike the use of supervisors in a factory? It is typical of how capital uses the wage hierarchy to try and divide worker from worker. The entire peasant unit--ejidatarios and jornaleros alike--is subsumed under capital.

Most of the peasants who occasionally hire wage labor are only doing what is necessary to repay the credit advanced by the bank. They are not extracting a surplus, valorizing it, and therefore accumulating capital. They are only trying to survive. It is the bank that is extracting a surplus from both peasants (the one extended the credit and the one hired to help pay back that credit). In all the situations we have examined, peasants cultivate crops for capital. Consequently, the workers they may hire to help out in that process are also working for capital, not for the other peasants. In one study of peasants hiring other peasants, it was found that peasants work for money in order to have the cash to in turn hire peasants for their own harvest. There is no net gain for either peasant. It is survival--a break-even situation. Individual peasants find themselves in both positions at one time or another. The author of the study says "to hire peónes is not a luxury nor does it signify that one stops working the land himself. On the contrary, it is the normal way to obtain sufficient labor to insure a good harvest."[109]

Peasants are always exploited in the sphere of capitalist circulation. We uncovered the principal links when we discussed the peasants who suffer unequal exchange when they sell their crops (staples or commercial crops) on the market and buy MS and MP. Manipulation of the terms of trade and unsavory policies of intermediaries were the principal mechanisms of unequal exchange. But peasant subsumption to capital is more than just market exploitation within the sphere of circulation. Although often hidden behind the sale of commodities, peasant subsumption to capital invades the sphere of production. Credit in all its forms and variations, from official bank credit to credit extended by private agribusiness, is the means by which capital strives to control and direct the work process, to insure the supply of a product, and ultimately to extract surplus value.

Peasant work in general (except waged jornaleros) is unwaged work, which makes it difficult for most Marxists to recognize their working-class status. Peasants who receive credit in the form of cash for living expenses, such as the cañeros, henequeneros, or tabacaleros, also have somewhat hazy status. The credit makes the peasants appear as business or financial partners of a profit-making enterprise. Although investigators are quick to point out that these peasants are caught up in an exploitative relation with the institution extending the credit, they are less eager to award these peasants proletariat status. The social capital analysis breaks through this confusion, since we are not constrained by the Marxist-Leninist position, which insists that the proletariat must receive a wage and must not hire workers or own means of production, such as land. This analysis allows us to see that the lack of a wage may also define one's working-class status, or for that matter the presence of a credit (an indirect wage) or the selling of commodities can mistakenly label peasants as petit bourgeois. What is common to both the unwaged peasants and waged peasant members of the working class is that the endless work they are forced to provide throughout their lives is done for capital. This work includes unwaged domestic work producing and reproducing the labor force and work done producing commodities on which capital realizes a profit.

NOTES

1. Lourdes Arizpe, quoted by Ludka de Gortari and José del Val, "Mujer Campesina, Parentesco y Explotación," Nueva Antropología 2 (April 1977):5-16.
2. Karl Marx, Capital, vol. 1 (New York: International Publishers, 1967), p. 641.
3. Ibid., p. 643.
4. Differentiation of the peasantry was discussed in Chapters 1 and 2.
5. See unwaged peasant work and the value of labor power in this chapter for discussion on these peasants.
6. Through fieldwork, Larissa Lomnitz documents the close ties that peasants maintain with their communities when they migrate to the cities in search of income. See Larissa Lomnitz, "Supervivencia en una Barriada en la Cuidad de Mexico," Demografía y Economía 7 (1973); and by the same author, Cómo Sobreviven los Marginados? (Mexico: Siglo XXI, 1975).

7. See Marta Romer's field study, Los Mixes de Totontepec en Comunidad, Migración y Desarrollo: Un Proceso Integrado de Cambio Social, Tesis Profesional, INAH, 1979.

8. See Gustavo Esteva, La Batalla en el Mexico Rural (Mexico: Siglo XXI, 1980), pp. 140-41, for discussion.

9. Anibal Quijano and Francisco Weffort, Populismo, Marginalización y Dependencia (Costa Rica: Editorial Universitaria Centro Americana, 1976), pp. 180-81.

10. Uno Mas Uno, July 6, 1979.

11. Quijano, Populismo, p. 192.

12. Ibid., p. 267.

13. The vice-president of the Camara Nacional de la Industria de Transformación said, "Existe una clase privilegiada formada por los petroleros, ferrocarrileros, electricistas, y telefonistas." El Universál, November 22, 1977.

14. Many agroindustries in the countryside employ peasant workers, of whom there is practically an inexhaustible supply. See NACLA, "El Imperialismo en Almibar: La Compania Del Monte en Mexico," Cuadernos Agrarios 6 (May 1978). ("Del Monte se queda en Mexico porque las condiciónes que . . . [hay] una mano de obra barata, sindicatos oficiales cooperativos y subsidios para la exportación.") "El Proletariado Agrícola en la Region de Zamora Michoacán," Cuadernos Agrarios 6 (May 1978):100-1.

15. Devon Peña suggests that female workers in the Border Industrialization Program of Mexico are true mass workers with little skill and easily replaced, making organizational efforts more difficult. From Devon Peña, "Las Maquiladoras: Mexican Women and Class Struggle in the Border Industries," Aztlan 11 (Fall 1980):193, 200.

16. Some services have been almost impossible to organize due to the high substitutability. These would include domestic help, gardeners, dishwashers, and errand boys.

17. Even then there must be some limits on rising wages, but the reserve army may not play the major role.

18. Harry Cleaver, "Malaria, the Politics of Public Health and the International Crisis," Review of Radical Political Economics 9 (Spring 1977):96.

19. Traditional government mechanisms for control of the peasantry include the CNC, the bureaucratic manipulation of SRA, the credit deals, the efforts at collectiviza-

tion. These are but a few of the ways that the state tries to conciliate, control, and take over the peasants and their products. They will be discussed in Chapter 4.

20. For a definition and discussion of caciques, see Esteva, La Batalla, pp. 117-22.

21. World Bank New Release, No. 77/136, June 17, 1977. It is also stated in the news release that the poor peasant farmers whose incomes are estimated by the World Bank authorities to be less than $100 per capita per year are required to provide $7.2 million in cash. The question comes to mind as to how these peasants are to come up with that kind of money. Or are they going to be paying back the World Bank for this "help" over a long period of time?

22. Miguel Pineda, in field work in the state of Mexico, found that the peasants whose lands surrounded the construction projects were eventually forced to sell their lands because they could not afford to change their productive process to complement the new infrastructure or did not choose to. Where the peasants remained, they were subordinated to capital by being forced to accept loans to implement goals set out by the project. Miguel Pineda, "La Subsunción del Trabajo Agrícola al Capital," unpublished draft of master's thesis (1980), courtesy Gustavo Esteva.

23. Ibid., p. 58.

24. See Harry Cleaver, "Food, Famine and the International Crisis," Zerowork 2 (Fall 1977):7-70, for a discussion of food-for-work programs.

25. Esteva, La Batalla, p. 156; and Arturo Warman, "Los Campesinos y la Política," La Cultura en Mexico Suplemento de Siempre! 778 (January 12, 1977):II-IV.

26. Jane Margolis, "El Papel de la Mujer en la Agricultura del Bajío," Iztapalapa 1 (July-December 1979): 161-63.

27. Luisa Paré, El Proletariado Agrícola en Mexico (Mexico: Siglo XXI, 1977), p. 190.

28. NACLA, "Cosecha de Ira: Agroimperialismo en el Noroeste de Mexico," Cuadernos Agrarios 5 (September 1977):8.

29. Uno Mas Uno, February 11, 1980.

30. See, for example, Margarita Rosales Gonzalez, Los Intermediarios Agrícolas y la Economía Campesina (Mexico: INAH, 1979), p. 24.

31. Suppose in the United States the workers had to purchase all of their means of subsistence on the market because there were no unwaged house workers contributing to their maintenance. The value of labor power would be astronomical. The cost of buying those goods and services otherwise provided for by unwaged workers would dramatically increase the value of labor power. But we know that the minimum salary in the United States is not sufficient to have cooks, housekeepers, governesses, gardeners, etc. The same reasoning applies to peasants, the value of labor power, and wages.

32. Mercedes Olivera, "Sobre la Explotación y Opresión de las Mujeres Acasilladas en Chiapas," Cuadernos Agrarios 9 (September 1979):44.

33. Pineda, "Subsunción," p. 19.

34. Gustavo Esteva, "La Experiencia de la Intervención Estatal Reguladora en la Comercialización Agropecuaria de 1970 a 1976," in Mercado y Dependencia, ed. Ursula Oswald (Mexico: Editorial Nueva Imagen, 1979), p. 219.

35. Before this proposition is rejected out of hand, Marxist readers should recall Marx's own discussion of the division of surplus value among capitalists. Although he represents the industrial capitalist's sales as C'--M', we know that in the presence of commercial capital, money-lending capital, and ground rent, the M' realized by the industrialist is actually less than the value C'.

36. Fondo de Cultura Campesina, "Informe del Trabajo de Campo y del Estudio Teórico del Sector Rural" (Mexico: unpublished, 1981), p. 6.

37. See Esteva, "La Experiencia," for a history of CONASUPO.

38. Direct survey by CONASUPO, published in Centro de Investigaciónes Agrarias, Estructura Agraria y Desarrollo Agrícola en Mexico, vol. 1 (Mexico: Fondo de Cultura Económica, 1974).

39. Hector Díaz Polanco, "Estructura de Clases y Comercialización un Caso Mexicano," in Mercado y Dependencia, ed. Ursula Oswald (Mexico: Editorial Nueva Imagen, 1979), p. 158.

40. Interview with peasant published in Voces del Campo 5 (September 1979).

41. Esteva, "La Experiencia," p. 220.

42. See Chapter 2 for discussion on similar policies used in the Soviet Union, known as "Soviet Scissors."

43. Uno Mas Uno, February 11, 1980.

44. Uno Mas Uno, March 9, 1980.

45. Aguillera Gomez, director of INMECAFE, quoted in Uno Mas Uno, March 9, 1980.

46. Uno Mas Uno, March 9, 1980.

47. Peasants say that at night the intermediary resells the coffee to INMECAFE for the official price. The two, I assume, share the spoils. Uno Mas Uno, March 11, 1980.

48. Arturo Warman, Los Campesinos Hijos Predilectos del Regimen (Mexico: Editorial Nuestro Tiempo, 1972), p. 69.

49. Ibid., p. 70.

50. Interview with Angel Palerm in November 1975. Dr. Palerm said that anthropological field studies have found that an incredible amount of surplus, otherwise impossible to trace, was drained by the prestamistas from peasant production to urban finance capitalists.

51. Pineda, "La Subsunción," pp. 26-29. Szekely reports a similar situation for the coast of Jalisco. Miguel Szekely, "La Organización Colectiva para la Producción Rural," Comercio Exterior 27 (December 1977):1472.

52. Pineda, "La Subsunción," pp. 26-29. See also Szekely, "La Organización," p. 1474, for other arrangements of mediería.

53. Marx, Capital, vol. 1, Appendix, "Results of the Immediate Process of Production" (New York: Vintage, 1976), pp. 1019-23.

54. Ibid., p. 1023.

55. Ibid., p. 1019.

56. We know that peasants do not accept this relation contentedly. They struggle for land and inputs to break the grip capital has on their lives.

57. Harry Cleaver, Reading Capital Politically (Austin: University of Texas Press, 1979), p. 74.

58. BANRURAL, January 1981. Mimeograph.

59. Enrique Astorga and Clarisa Hardy, Organización Lucha y Dependencia: La Unión de Ejidos Emiliano Zapata (Mexico: Editorial Nueva Imagen, 1978), pp. 100-1.

60. For a good survey of credit in agriculture, see Gustavo Gordillo, "Estado y Sistema Ejidal," Cuadernos Políticos 21 (July-September 1979):7-24; and by the same author, "El Núcleo Estatal en el Medio Rural: Algunas Consideraciones Sobre el Crédito Agrícola en Mexico," Investigaciones Económica 147 (January-March 1979):199-221.

61. Warman, Hijos Predilectos, p. 78.
62. Gordillo, "Estado y Sistema Ejidal," p. 11.
63. See Chapter 5, discussion of the Coalición.
64. Centro de Investigaciones Agrarias, Estructura Agraria y Desarrollo Agrícola en México (Mexico: Fondo de Cultura Económica, 1974), p. 783.
65. Gordillo, "Estado y Sistema Ejidal," p. 24.
66. Uno Mas Uno, May 19, 1979.
67. Szekely, "La Organización," p. 1479.
68. Warman, Hijos Predilectos, p. 78.
69. Gordillo, "Algunas Consideraciones," p. 207.
70. NACLA, "Cosecha de Ira," p. 80. Through legal channels, these peasants have tried unsuccessfully to reclaim the loss. Subsequently, they have sought financing from foreign private capital.
71. See Ruth Rama, "Empresas Transnacionales y Agricultura Mexicana: El Caso de las Procesadoras de Frutas y Legumbres," Investigación Económica 37 (January 1978):75-117, for more discussion on contract farming in Mexico.
72. NACLA, "La Companía Del Monte en Mexico, Cuadernos Agrarios 6 (May 1978):89.
73. Ernest Feder, El Imperialismo Fresa (Mexico: Editorial Campesina, 1977), pp. 88-89.
74. Jesús Jauregui et al., TABAMEX, Un Caso de Integración Vertical de la Agricultura (Mexico: Editorial Nueva Imagen, 1980), p. 124.
75. For a description of the work process, see ibid., pp. 126-30.
76. Díaz Polanco, "Estructura de Clases," p. 158.
77. Ursula Oswald, "El Monopolio de la Central de Abastos y Sus Efectos en la Sociedad Campesina," in Mercado y Dependencia, ed. Ursula Oswald (Mexico: Editorial Nueva Imagen, 1979), pp. 178-79.
78. See pp. 84-85 of Rama, "Empresas Transnacionales," for a complete list.
79. Uno Mas Uno, February 5, 1980.
80. Interview with Lic. Simón of Anderson Clayton in Mexico City, November 1975.
81. Gustavo Esteva, "Los Campesinos ante el Poder Económico," El Día, November 2, 1980.
82. Ibid.
83. Uno Mas Uno, March 9, 1980.
84. See Esteva, La Batalla, p. 142, for a brief summary. See David Ronfeldt, Atencingo: The Politics of

Agrarian Struggle in a Mexico Ejido (Stanford, Calif.: Stanford University Press, 1973), for a detailed history of the relations between the peasants, the ingenio (sugar mill), and the government.

85. Centro de Investigaciones Agrarias, Estructura Agraria, p. 794.

86. Decree by past president of Mexico, Avila Camacho (September 22, 1943), quoted in Uno Mas Uno, December 24, 1979.

87. Paré, El Proletariado, p. 176.

88. See ibid., pp. 176–81, for more detail on contracts with ejidatarios cañeros.

89. Gisela Espinosa and Roberto Sandoval, "Capital Industrial y Explotación Campesina en Oacalco Morelos," Cuadernos Agrarios 4 (October–December 1976):48.

90. Esteva, La Batalla, p. 173.

91. For a brief history of henequen and its cultivation in Yucatán, see Luís Barjau, "Yucatán Trabajo y Explotación Económica," in Capitalismo y Campesinado en México, ed. Rodolfo Stavenhagen (Mexico: CISINAH, 1976), pp. 163–96.

92. These heavy credit losses are in fact measures of peasant success in the struggle to be discussed in Chapter 4.

93. José J. Gamboa, "El Crédito en el Proceso de Restructuración de la Zona Henequenera Yucateca," Estudios Políticos 4 (July–September 1978):73.

94. Ibid., p. 77.

95. For a detailed description of lifestyle and living standards, see Eric Villanueva Mukul, "Las Condiciones Económicos y Sociales y Políticas del Trabajador Henequenero," Yucatán Historia y Economía 3 (September–October 1977):21–25.

96. Gordillo, "Algunas Consideraciones," p. 207, for background and the legal aspects of credit and solidarity groups.

97. Jauregui et al., TABAMEX, p. 141.

98. For the year 1974–75. Ibid., p. 142.

99. Ibid., p. 134.

100. Due to economies of scale, TABAMEX buys large quantities of specific fertilizers and insecticides at considerable savings. Ibid., p. 267.

101. Ibid., p. 140.

102. Each group has its own particular formula for arriving at the leader's fee. Ibid., p. 146.

103. Ibid., p. 147.

104. For details on discounts, see ibid., p. 237.

105. Ibid., p. 241.

106. Ibid., p. 233.

107. Ibid., p. 334.

108. Ibid.

109. Marielle Pepin-Lehalleur de Martinez, "El Empleo de Trabajo Ajeno por la Unidad Campesina de Producción," in Capitalismo y Campesinado en México, ed. Rudolfo Stavenhagen (Mexico: CISINAH, 1976), pp. 133-62.

4

PEASANT STRUGGLE, SELF-VALORIZATION, AND THE DISRUPTION OF CAPITAL

PEASANT COMMUNITY AND STRUGGLE
FOR SELF-VALORIZATION

In Chapter 1 worker self-valorization was introduced. Worker struggle is not only negative--that is, against capital--but also positive: constructive of a life separate from capital. Self-valorization implies the ability of people to reappropriate the world of use values and to escape subsumption to capital. In Mexico, peasants follow the path of self-valorization by struggling for land.

Peasants Struggle for Land versus the Wage

To be against the subsumption of labor power to capital is the phrase that captures the essence of the Mexican peasant movements. It is one of the principal reasons why they struggle for land and not for wages. Seeking land and refusing the wage is a crucial point we will now consider before continuing with the discussion of peasant community.

Warman has understood all peasant movements in Mexico to have what he calls a radical character. The common element reclaimed is space; more space to mobilize resources; space for autonomy in politics and production. Peasants want to manipulate resources outside of capitalist relations (the ultimate goal of struggle, not always the immediate) and relate to each other on the basis of reciprocal and redistributive exchange.[1] Peasants seek land, control over inputs, management of production, and political control over their own communities. In the process,

not only do they reaffirm their autonomy from capital in
their communities, but they refuse to be subsumed under
capital. Sufficient land enables peasants to resist direct
capitalist control--if they can survive without the wage
they can refuse imposed work, even that work producing
labor power for the reserve army to the degree that they
become unavailable to capital.[2] Peasants choose land as
the goal of struggle because the latent reserve army in
the countryside has swelled to such monstrous proportions,
from population increase and from peasants with insufficient
land resources, that there are few hopes of gaining any
wage increases from capital. A few statistics will clarify.
Teresa Rendón reported that the growth of labor used in
agriculture has grown in the following fashion: 1940-50,
2.5 percent per year; 1950-60, 2.3 percent per year;
1960-73, 1.45 per cent per year.[3] Armando Bartra found
that from 1940 to 1970, industry and services absorbed
only three out of every ten new rural workers.[4] Both
CIOAC and Punto Crítico agree that out of the 7.3 million
peasants in the labor force, 5 million cannot find a sufficient wage to sustain themselves.[5] According to a study
by BANRURAL, over 90,000 peasants left each month during
1979 to search for work in the United States.[6]

Let us briefly describe the situation the peasant
faces when trying to get a waged job in the countryside.
First, there is not enough work to go around. Second, it
is badly paid, with the most degrading working conditions.
In 1978, peasant leader Margarito Hernandez of the Huasteca
Hidalgüense pointed out that landless peasants go without
work for months at a time. When they do find a job it is
paid at only 20 to 25 pesos a day when the official minimum salary is 72.50 pesos. He said they are now invading lands because "salario minimo no hay." Eckart
Boege, a sociologist at UNAM, found in Hidalgo that peasants struggle for land--not fair or higher wages. Peasants
know that they cannot demand the minimum wage because
the patrón will just send a truck to another town to pick
up more workers. They have obviously found the struggle
for land more effective than one over wages. As one
peasant stated, "They only give a worker money which is
not enough to buy food."[8]

In Zamora Michoacán, Ernest Feder graphically described the labor market the peasants faced. The employers of temporary labor for the strawberry harvest control
the supply of workers by deliberately provoking the arrival

of swarms of workers à la Grapes of Wrath. They send recruiters in trucks each year to the surrounding communities and to communities as far away as Morelos. Jorge Morett interviewed a local jornalero in Zamora who revealed that strawberry growers seeking to maintain the lowest of salaries announce on the radio within a wide zone surrounding Zamora that employers in the area urgently need workers.[9]

Each day the potential peasant workers wait in a group for the employers or managers to choose the number of workers they will hire for the day. Feder estimates that for every worker chosen there are 10 to 20 more who do not get hired. The peasants chosen to work cannot even ask where they are going or what their salary will be. To those who ask questions, the managers reply, "Today there is no work for you." The peasants say, "So we don't die of hunger, we ask nothing."[10] Feder adds that the area designated in Zamora for contracting labor is always heavily guarded by soldiers with machine guns.[11]

In Chiapas the situation for peasants forced to seek the wage during the coffee harvest is even more difficult. The coffee finceros, with the protection and help of the Mexican immigration authorities, illegally import over 20,000 Guatemalans who are willing to work for pathetic wages, since their situation in Guatemala is even worse. Because there is already an overabundance of labor in Chiapas, the Guatemalans guarantee that wages will be held to the absolute minimum.[12] The peasants in these regions of Chiapas have organized and are struggling for land as their best alternative. Even so, the situation is perhaps the gravest in all of Mexico.[13]

Perhaps the best evidence of the extent of the reserve army in the Mexican countryside are the 2.5 million undocumented workers in the United States. Many are reported to be peasants forced to leave because of insufficient land resources and no available waged work.[14]

Because of the peasants' goal of autonomy from capitalist exploitation coupled with the present futility of organizing against the wage, the struggles for land and the complementary struggles over credit, local political control, and prices of products have reached monumental proportions involving almost every state of Mexico.[15]

Peasant Community

The peasants are insisting through active struggle that the community can be a basis for development. Critics label such struggle and development as anarchic or backward and not viable. What they really mean is that peasant community struggle and change is not viable for them—for members of the capitalist class who want to direct and control development, reaping benefits along the way. Capital's goal is to destroy the efficacy of the peasant community as an agent for change, thus destroying any threat to itself that may come from the autonomy of peasant struggle. Capital disdains peasant self-directed development and seeks to control the development process by transforming the people into individual production units removed from the community. If capital is unable to utilize all the peasants severed from their community in productive work, it writes them off as hopelessly doomed to a life of margination: marginal to capital and the resources the community offers for struggle. This is why, historically, capital has attacked the peasant community in Mexico. Today, capital's response to the peasant mobilizations has been vigorous aggression against their resources (communal lands) and their integrity as pueblos (communities).

Peasants are largely unconcerned with the capitalist debates over the viability of what they are doing, and are mobilizing, organizing, and forming a society as far removed from capital as they can manage. Peasants are using their solidarity and experience derived from the pueblo to effect this change.

What follows will illustrate how peasants use their community institutions for struggle. These examples from the Mexican peasant reality support my characterization of peasant struggle: they do not prove that every situation in Mexico fits the analysis. I base my analysis on today's reality in the countryside as portrayed by the press, field workers in anthropology and sociology, and writings by the campesinistas. I do not consider or review the existing literature on rural community.[16]

Henri Lefevre gives one definition of rural peasant community: "The rural peasant community is a form of social groupings which organizes according to determined historical modes in the confluences of families attached to the land."[17] Lefevre continues to explain community:

> The rural community is not a productive
> force; nor mode of production; nor is it re-
> duced to a mechanical solidarity of individ-
> ual elements; it is not defined by property
> relations because there are also collective
> endeavors which vary greatly in their type
> and strength. The rural community is not
> stagnant; not a remnant of the past; not an
> anachronism. Far from that the community
> can be reborn on a modern basis constantly
> evolving as it strategically solves these
> problems. The community organizations are
> used as a means to solve the problems thus
> transforming the community itself.[18]

The Mazatecan Indian word for pueblo, narxhí–nandhá,
best describes the dynamics of a community:

> It is a compound word. Narxhí means rock;
> Nandhá means water. The idea of a solid
> rock symbolizes the solidarity of the pueblo.
> Its stability and strength. The pueblo lasts
> forever. The idea of water indicates the
> constant transformation of water, its move-
> ment, its fresh and constant renovation. . . .
> The pueblo is never over, it is firm like a
> rock and it is renewed constantly like the
> water.[19]

The fact that rural communities have persisted under the
most unlikely geographical and historical circumstances
points to their dynamism, their constant reproduction, and
transformation.[20]

Although everyone recognizes the heterogeneity in
Mexico, discussing the regional differences is not my purpose here.[21] Nor do I want to categorize the various
community organizations into indigenous, pre-Columbian,
colonial, or postrevolutionary. We take today's communities and their internal organizations as given. Finally,
differences between Indian and peasant communities are
secondary for me because I see no real class division
between the two. Although the cultural and ethnic organizations may differ substantially between the indigenous
communities and the peasant communities, these differences
only reflect the rich cultural differences among the peoples

and regions of Mexico, differences within the working class, not between classes. Both Indians and campesinos draw on the resources of their respective communities to participate (sometimes jointly) in organizations for struggle and class movements. Esteva argues that the majority of Indians are peasants, since the collective form of social existence, that is, the sense of community, is characteristic of both.[22] In addition to the sense of community that indigenas and campesinos share, Indians and peasants alike organize and struggle against capital, eliminating any need for a class boundary between the two.

The solidarity of community is embodied in three main rural structures in Mexico--the ejido, the comunidad indígena, and the pueblo. Leaving aside the long history of each,[23] I will summarize these forms and how they promote group participation and experience for struggle.

Ejidos and communities (comunidades) have the same internal organs of decision: (1) the general assembly of ejidos is formed by all the ejidatarios, of comunidades by all the comuneros; (2) the comisariado ejidal are the officers of the ejido elected (in theory) by the ejiditarios in the general assembly. The comisariado de bienes comunales, the authority in the Indian community, is also formally elected by the comuneros.[24] But the status and power of the comisariado de bienes comunales depend on its relation with the traditional (nonlegal) authorities of the Indian community, the cargos.[25] Over three fourths of the rural population of Mexico are either ejidatarios or comuneros.[26]

In the east of Morelos, Warman found that the ejido, irrespective of the organization of production, was the central organization in the lives of the majority of the peasants. Besides the productive activities, which will be discussed later, peasants organize themselves in a myriad of ways (from total parcelization of the land--through the formation of grupos solidarios of various sizes and characteristics who work together for specific productive or commercial tasks--to complete collectivization). Among the tasks managed communally by the ejidatarios in Morelos are the allocation of available water (which sometimes transcends the boundaries of the ejido, including the participation of minifundistas); the fencing of lands to keep cattle out; the decision as to which fields are to lay fallow; and even the determination of the date of the corn harvest.[27] The ejidal organization thus contributes to the peasants' democratic experience in running their own affairs. At the same time, because the ejido can be used to manipulate and exploit the ejidatarios through corruption of the comisariado ejidal, political control of the ejido becomes the subject of sometimes determined and violent struggles.[28]

The pueblos are generally thought of as towns where both ejidatarios, comuneros, and private minifundistas live. The pueblos are subject to the politics of the municipio in which they are found. Some of the pueblos, as in Oaxaca, coincide exactly with the municipio. Others are more closely associated with a particular large ejido or group of neighboring ejidos or are comunidades indígenas. Warman has said that it is the social relations between the inhabitants of the pueblo that bind them into a community: "Land, family, fiestas, luck, sympathy, activism, affection, are criteria for the reciprocal relations among peasants," which instill in them the feeling of community to be del pueblo, del barrio, or de nuestra gente.[29] Guillermo de la Peña concurs with Warman, saying cooperation is the rule among people in the community with their social relations characterized by familial relations, godparents, neighbors, and participation in fiestas. He also cites the use of these relations for exchange of information on prices, jobs, etc.[30] Warman goes on to explain how the people who live in a pueblo interact closely and respond to one another's needs as a group.[31] First of all, familial relationships or domestic social and cultural activities consolidate a network of preferred relations. These activities include fiestas associated with compadrazgo, baptisms, weddings, birthdays, and also such fiestas as Día de los Muertos, Semana Santa, or the Pizca. The fiestas are essential to the rural pueblo life. They provide entertainment (drink, dance, talk, love) and they also provide a framework for transferring information from one group to another, which leads to the circulation of political strategies and alliances for struggles.[32]

Community as Basis for Struggle

In this section we will examine various community political and social structures such as the municipio, (faenas--unwaged community work), and religious cargos, all of which contribute to peasant organization. Then a specific case of a community--a pueblo and how it united in struggle--will be presented. Finally, circulation of the struggle between communities will be illustrated.

Municipio

Formal political activities in the municipio also contribute to peasant activism and organization. Since the municipio is usually governed by the local rural bourgeoisie such as merchants, money lenders, ranchers or caciques, the struggle for political control becomes particularly important for peasants.

For example, the municipio officials and the juntas (elected locally in assemblies for various tasks) administer the faenas or communal unwaged labor to construct public works. The unwaged labor is recruited forcibly under penalty of fines. The peasants' struggle to control the local juntas and especially the office of presidente municipal. They want to make decisions about what public works are built with their unwaged labor and even more importantly where. Peasants see very clearly why drinking water is only present in the center of town or in specific streets or electric energy is brought to the local stores and not to their houses. One should recognize that the structure of the municipio and its dependence on federal and state government financing for the construction of new works or maintenance of old ones[33] was created by the government as an agent for direct federal intervention into the internal affairs of the rural communities.[34] Nevertheless, considerable autonomy and self-development have been achieved by struggling to control the municipio politically. Struggles to control the office of presidente municipal have figured prominently as complementary and contemporaneous with land struggles.

In the pueblo of Matxoja, municipio of Tila Chiapas, peasants (probably Indians) have been petitioning off and on for the last 30 years to extend their ejido into the lands of a local large landlord. Until recently the secretary of agrarian reform (SRA) gave no response. Then, when at last the executive decision to grant the ejidal extension was about to take place, the landlord divided the land into small plots using prestanombres of all his family to escape expropriation. However, the peasants continued to pressure the SRA until an official order arrived stating that the landlord and his family must abandon the land.

At that point, the landlord applied for an _amparo_ from the district judge in Tuxtla Gutierrez. The judge, convinced by the peasants' case, refused to give the landowner the amparo, sending him another order to release the land to the peasants. The order, however, was not enforced. The peasants realized that the landlord would not leave unless forced. They also knew that no help would be forthcoming from the SRA because "lo que vale ante las autoridades de la SRA es el dinero" (what matters to the authorities of the SRA is money). Consequently, the peasants began to participate in a complementary struggle over the presidencia municipal, which could help them get possession of the land without resorting to arms and thus stimulating repression by the army. The pueblo of Tila organized for three years to get control of the office of the presidente municipal. In 1979, they elected a peasant to that office. More than 45,000 peasants united to force the removal of the previous, unwanted, presidente. Then, with the support of the new campesino presidente, the agrarian struggle of Matxoja and other communities in the municipio of Tila could be aided more vigorously.[35]

Cooperative Labor

Another community structure that is sometimes present during peasant organization and struggle is cooperative labor. Romer mentions four forms of cooperative labor that are still present among indigenous communities in Mexico. These include: (1) reciprocal and mutal help within the family and the extended family; (2) collective work by _barrio_, _paraje_, or annex of a community; (3) communal work that is designated by _tequio_.[36] To this list, Julio Moguel adds (4) faena--communal work among two or three communities that commonly benefits all.[37] Romer, distinguishing between peasant and indigenous communities, claims that these forms of cooperative labor have for the most part disappeared in peasant communities and have been replaced by capitalist relations. Yet cooperative labor is found among many peasant communities, especially in Oaxaca, Morelos, Yucatán, and even Jalisco. I have earlier considered whether cooperative labor has been replaced with capitalist relations. Chapter 3 argued that most peasants hiring other peasants to work on their land do so to survive, not to accumulate. Finally, the disappearance or survival of cooperative labor is only one aspect of peasant struggle. Peasants with completely individualized production participate in other social and cultural community organizations associated with the ejido, pueblo, or cargos, which also provide the experience and tradition useful for class activities.

On the other hand, the following example shows where cooperative labor has influenced the success of their agrarian struggle. On the coast of Jalisco around the municipio of Tomatlán, several forms of cooperative labor sprang up during struggle. Newcomers to the region, the peasants had no existing community or tradition of tequio on which to base their struggle. They simply created and built up the sense of pueblo we have been talking about, once again illustrating the dynamism of the community. Peasants struggling for the legalization into ejidos of the lands they had worked as peónes or medieros established (1) exchange of labor (prestamo de días) and of means of production (yunta, semillas); (2) exchange of products between family units; (3) communal work for mutual benefit of the communities; (4) quotas of solidarity in money or products for the defense of the land. The quotas were used as a fund to support the families who were most directly involved in the agrarian struggle. Further, the peasants realized that struggling as individual communities has its limitations, especially when the landlords reacted repressively against the peasants occupying the land. In 1973, peasants of the communities El Criadero, La Gloria, Najuapa, Comunidad Tomatlán, and El Tequesquite formed the Unión Ejidal de la Costa de Jalisco. The unión was effective in gaining control of the land solicited, and in some cases the newly acquired land was officially legalized.[38] The immediate successes have not dampened the struggle. In 1980, the unión publicizing their struggles sent an open letter to the president, published in the national newspaper Uno Mas Uno.[39] The peasants refused to make forced purchases from the BANRURAL of irrigation equipment that would put each ejido in debt to the government by 100 million pesos. The peasants knew that the equipment was overpriced.[40] They knew that no crop could pay back such a debt. It is clear that the unión realized that the investments were a way for the government to curtail the independence of the ejidos by getting them into a long-term debt situation that would legitimize direct government intervention into production to insure repayment of the debt. One of the most important struggles

of the unión has been to get direct control over credit,
thus eliminating as much as possible government intervention in production decisions.41

In addition, the unión has continued the struggle
for land involving other communities, such as the ejido of
Nuevo Nahaupa. Presently, they are struggling for the
extension of the ejidos Tequesquite, San Rafael, Cruz de
Loreto, and Gargantillo, which they only recently won!42
The unión has participated in other struggles in neighboring zones of Jalisco. With its help, ejidatarios of the
ejido Alfredo Bonfil and El Bonete have begun to resist the
aggression of the landlord Armando Camacho, who, with
the help of rural police, invaded 220 hectares belonging to
both ejidos. After this aggression, the ejidatarios, supported and aided by the unión, are on guard day and
night to prevent any further invasions by the landlord.
In the meantime, the unión president and the presidente
municipal (office now controlled by the peasants) publicize
the issue and seek solutions to the conflict.43

Faena--Unwaged Communal Work

Another form of cooperative labor found among communities (usually Indian) is called faena, or unwaged
community work done by members of the community for communal benefit. In the following example we will see how
faenas done by comuneros resulted in mobilization and organization. The comuneros throughout the state of Michoacán have a reputation for being highly organized and
cooperative with one another's struggles. Later in the
chapter I will trace with some detail a particular struggle
that highlights the effectiveness of their organization and
strategy as well as the viciousness of the enemies they
face. But for now I will illustrate only one incident of
peasant communal labor and organization for struggle.
Beginning in 1972, peasants from nine communities (Poma-
cuarán, Urapicho, Nurio, Aranza, Cocucho, Corupo, Ahuirán,
Arato, San Felipe) of the municipios Uruapan, Paracho,
and Charapan cooperated to lay fresh water pipes, which
would benefit all of the cooperating communities. In 1980,
the water finally arrived, benefiting only those in Paracho
and Charapan. In February 1980 the comuneros called an
assembly in the city of Santan Ziros, attended by 3,000
persons. They decided to close the valves of the water
pumps located in that city. The Indians said, "A glass

of water for everybody or none for anybody." The comuneros maintained guards to see that the water was not turned on until satisfaction was gained for all communities. I do not know the result of this particular struggle. However, the group action led to the formation of a permanent organization called the Comité de Pueblos.[44]

Religious Cargos

It was mentioned previously that the Indian communities had a system of religious cargos.[45] Although these cargo positions are cultural or ethnic in origin, their purposes are not restricted to religious or cultural events.

In an Indian community in Chiapas, the pueblo named a candidate for presidente municipal. Unable to register their candidate independently, they proposed him to the PRI, only to be rejected. The PRI selected their own candidate, manipulated the elections, and placed their puppet in office. The consejo de ancianos (a traditional Indian organization associated with the cargos) elaborated a strategy to gain control of their municipio. They invented four additional cargos whose jobs in practice were those of the presidente municipal. The consejo named the authentic candidate chosen democratically by the community to one of the cargos. Finally, the consejo invited the governor of the state of Chiapas, whose official policy was, of course, to respect the culture and customs of the Indians, to come to the fiestas of the pueblo and personally confirm the cargos on the four candidates. The governor did not attend but sent a deputy to preside over the ceremony. The ceremony was conducted in the native Indian language, so the deputy had no idea of what was going on. He unwittingly signed the power over to the Indians that the community had chosen. A few days later, the imposed puppet president, humiliated and insulted, resigned.[46]

Another example of a religious organization used for struggle is found in the highlands of Morelos. Although Morelos was completely different from the highlands of Chiapas in every respect, the organization La Adoración Nocturna began as a religious group formed by a priest. Eventually, La Adoración began to buy fertilizer, provide transportation, and sell the tomato crop in the Merced. In this manner, a religious community organization aided the peasants in avoiding high prices and fees charged by the owners of trucks and sellers of fertilizer.[47]

The Pueblo and Struggle

The next two examples show how the communities or the pueblo have acted as a unified body to battle against attacks on their ejidal and communal land.

A recent field study of a subsistence Indian community in Yucatán provides us with a good example of how community solidarity is crucial for struggle. In Chemax, Yucatán, Eric Villanueva proposed that the following features have produced a profound democratic sentiment essential for the self-management of the community: (1) peasants own parceled ejidal lands and communal land; (2) peasants produce for their own subsistence; (3) there exists cooperation in the labor of the milpa; (4) peasants have similar cultural, linguistic, and ethnic characteristics; (5) the slash-burn agricultural methods need large expanses of land and must be managed carefully so as not to upset the delicate cycle; and (6) each year there is a general assembly where petitions for land use are received and lands are assigned to various ejidatarios. After the agricultural cycle, the land is returned to the common fund.[48]

In 1971, the community was attacked by ganaderos who fraudulently gained control of 300 hectares of the best ejidal land. The peasants responded by fomenting a legalistic struggle proving to the official bank that none of the 26 ganaderos was a member of the ejido or of the community. Finally, in 1974, the bank responded to the peasant demands and removed the ganaderos' cattle and fences. At the end of 1975, a new presidente municipal was elected (fraudulently?) who supported the ganaderos more firmly. Once again the ganaderos invaded the ejidal lands. This time the peasants chose a more effective strategy for struggle. Less than one month later, the peasants simply tied up and jailed the presidente municipal in the municipal jail. It was necessary for the state police to rescue him. Intimidated by the peasants' organization and action, the presidente ordered the ganaderos to leave the ejidal lands in question.[49]

Since 1975, the peasant community of Tlalnepantla, Morelos, has been struggling to retain its communal lands. Cacique Arnulfo Medina attempted to steal the land and break it up into smaller plots for sale. Despite severe opposition from the agrarian reform authorities of Morelos and their own comisariado ejidal, who is manipulated by the cacique, the peasants have managed to retain and

cultivate the disputed lands while struggling for legal recognition. A peasant from the community of Tlalnepantla
narrated the history of this struggle at the Primer Encuentro Nacional de Organizaciones Campesinas Independientes.[50] In his own words, "In November of 1975 there
was a problem in the pueblo of Tlalnepantla, this problem
we confronted it and we began to resist because the pueblo
called an assembly. . . ." Later, during the legal hear-
ing between the agrarian authorities, the peasants, and
the cacique, the lawyer for the cacique who claimed the
land asked, "Who is the person that solicits these communal
lands?" The peasants answered, "There are no persons;
it is a pueblo and we have a written document as a
basis. . . ."[51] The peasant clearly reveals in his testimony that it was the pueblo acting together that had made
possible the return of their communal lands.

The Circulation of Struggle among Communities

Finally, the community spreads solidarity and support from one locale to another. In other words, the community itself serves to circulate the struggle, which makes
it a powerful organization for social transformation.

The examples of El Trapiche and Santa Gertrudis
Oaxaca (both communities have a long history of struggle)[52] illustrate how two peasant communities participated
and supported each other's struggles. The two groups of
peasants keep themselves informed of mutual problems and
plans by sending representatives to the respective general
assemblies. In one such assembly at El Trapiche the following exchange took place, as recorded by Julio Moguel:

> A peasant from Santa Gertrudis: We are
> here because we are united and we accom-
> pany the group of El Trapiche; because we
> came when they invaded the land. When
> this began we came in brigades, because
> the federal soldiers came, wanting to humili-
> ate them and for this reason the pueblo of
> Santa Gertrudis were here every night so
> that nothing would happen. On other occa-
> sions, we came to help get them animated
> to work, we came to accompany them. They
> also accompany us and cooperate with us.

A peasant from El Trapiche: We support them because they have problems because
their production is not sufficient because
their lands are few that they work in common. Also because these lands are situated
in places where there are no rivers. . . .
Then we work with them. Here [El Trapiche]
we have much animal forage. They have a
dairy so we give them hay for their cows.
We participate with them in their problems.
They have many problems because there are
many caciques.[53]

Essentially, the peasant from Santa Gertrudis traveled to El Trapiche seeking support and aid for his community. The pueblo of Santa Gertrudis had struggled to
recuperate its lands stolen by illegal sale some 30 years
ago by a corrupt comisariado ejidal.[54] Finally, the
ejidatarios organized and won the elections for comisariado
ejidal in 1970. They began a long, arduous struggle, cul-
minating in a demonstration on Oaxaca City.[55] They occupied the palacio of the state governor, refusing to leave
until promised a fair ejidal census supervised by the
pueblo. They were successful and recovered a good part
of their lands in 1972. But the lands were insufficient.
They continued the struggle in 1975, seeking aid from the
neighboring community, El Trapiche, which had also waged
a successful struggle through reciprocal community support.

The Jaramillistas in Morelos provide us with another
example of how peasant struggle circulates via communities.[56] The Jaramillistas movement was a series of struggles in the state of Morelos led by Ruben Jaramilla from
the early 1940s until his assassination by the state in
1962.[57] After having exhausted the legal channels for
struggle over the problems of the ejidatarios cañeros and
over the demands by unlanded peasants for land, Jaramillo
took to arms. On one occasion, Jaramillo organized over
5,000 peasants without land to invade 40,000 hectares on
the plains of Michapa and El Guarín in Morelos. These
lands were given to the peasants from 1922 to 1929 but
never distributed to the peasants for cultivation. A rich
ganadero had possession of the peasants' lands. The government accused Jaramillo of invading ejidal lands to
justify (falsely) his subsequent persecution and assassina-

tion.[58] The following peasant testimony is one example of support that Jaramillo received from the community.

> She [the mother of the peasant telling the story] thought that Ruben's struggle was O.K. [esta bien]. She made as much effort as possible to help him [Ruben] that was the way it was. My mother had a female pig and Ruben sends a compañero. That day she said to me, "What will we do . . . your father does nothing. But there is nothing else, the pig must go." My mother sells her pig and sends the money to Ruben. He was close by in the hills. He sends another messenger to ask for food. My mother sent him tortillas, cans of sardines, chiles, eggs, etc.[59]

We must begin to recognize that the peasant community is not a static, backward, archaic institution but a dynamic structure that embodies solidarity and organization. The fact that peasants are already highly organized within their communities is a resource for struggle often overlooked by those advocating traditional organizations such as unions or parties.

For peasants in the Mexican countryside, the integrity of the peasant community, the pueblo, is where they can begin to create space for their own self-valorizing activities, not capital's. The productive autonomy of the land and the solidarity of the community gives them the power to resist the wage and subsumption to capital. Of course, divisions and hierarchies remain within many peasant communities. Even more communities are disintegrating as the capitalist onslaught succeeds in taking away their land, their water, reducing their income through commercial exploitation, forcing them to migrate, and so on. But we are not studying peasant loss and defeat but the positive aspects of peasant struggle. We know that peasants all over Mexico are struggling to resist capitalist attack on their communities. The battle is raging in the countryside over control of the resources. The organization of the peasant community and its political, economic, and social structures are essential to the successful outcome of that struggle.

PEASANT STRUGGLE DISRUPTS CAPITAL:
EXAMPLES THROUGHOUT MEXICO

The first section discussed how peasants organize in their communities, use their political and social organizations to retain what is rightfully theirs, carve out space for activities that define and identify their communities as peasant, and refuse to be subsumed to capital. Peasants act as a class-for-itself. In this section, the working-class nature of the peasantry will be further discussed by looking at contemporary peasant struggles. To do this exhaustively is an impossible task for any one investigation, given the level of upheaval in the Mexican countryside. This is probably why frequently there are studies on one community, one peasant organization, or one region. As for overviews, Armando Bartra's article, "Seis Años de Lucha Campesina," is an excellent beginning, capturing the breadth, extent, and depth of contemporary peasant struggle throughout Mexico.

In what follows the proposition that peasants form a class-for-itself will be illustrated with a cross-sectional selection of the wide variety of peasant struggles. We will see how peasants are unified in their communities, struggle against the capitalist system that exploits them, and often disrupt capital.

Chiapas: Indígenas or Campesinos Indígenas

Taking examples from the municipios indígenas of Chiapas, we can readily ascertain that in many communities, Indians demand land, invade land, and when repressed, reorganize and publicize their struggle in Tuxtla Gutierrez or as far as the Distrito Federal. The fact that they have specific relations of production that may not be immediately identified as capitalist relations does not leave them outside of capital in some other (precapitalist, feudal, whatever) mode of production. What is shown here is that the indígenas in Chiapas are organized in a struggle to maintain or acquire land resources. We also see that the particular social and political structure of Chiapas presents one of the most formidable and oppressive situations for the peasant working class in Mexico.

Simojovel has been described as one of the more traditional municipios.[60] But as recently as May 1980 over 15,000 campesinos indígenas marched to demand an immediate solution to their agrarian demands.[61]   This is only the most recent event in a long history.   In 1977, peasants from Simojovel formed 13 ejidos from invaded lands.   The army removed the peasants, arresting 300 on July 11, 1977.[62]   Four years before, in August 1973, in another remote zone of Chiapas, Armando Bartra reports that peónes acasillados organized and occupied 80 hectares of their "patrón's" hacienda, Vista Hermosa.[63]

Some Indians (not acasillados) have been more violent in their struggle against the haciendas.   In May 1974 more than 1,000 Indians from Chamula and San Andrés Larrainzar assaulted the fincas in the neighboring municipio of del Bosque, killing six hacendados.   The intervention of the army did not stop the peasants from seeking outside publicity and support.   In October 1974, they went to Tuxtla Gutierrez for a mass demonstration denouncing existing haciendas and latifundias in Chiapas.   Our same so-called isolated Indians managed to go as far as the Distrito Federal in February 1975 to denounce the assault on their ejidal and communal lands.

Such peasant struggle in Chiapas has threatened local capitalist agricultural accumulation.   It is exactly because the stakes are high in this battle over resources that peasant mobilization in Chiapas has provoked severe repression.   While military maneuvers in the area include direct repression of the peasant communities, there is a look-the-other-way attitude on the part of the government toward the private armies of the hacendados.   The severe repression is itself a measure of the disruptive impact of the peasant struggles in Chiapas.   The battle has intensified precisely because peasant efforts at obtaining land and keeping it against the will of the local agricultural hacendados and ganaderos have intensified.   Although I am in no position to make a projection about the outcome of peasant struggle in Chiapas, it has probably reached a point where stepped-up violence against the peasantry is likely.   Whether this will intimidate peasant mobilization or spur it on, one can only conjecture.

In 1976, there were 73 land invasions, including invasions of large capitalist properties in the municipio of Villa Flores alone.[64]   Since then, Indian leaders including Tzotziles, Tzeltales, Tojolabales, Zoques, and Choles from Villa Flores and other municipios (Ocosingo, Teopisca, Las Margaritas, Soyatitan, La Concordia, and Yajalon) have denounced the retaliatory violence they have suffered in their communities at the hands of <u>guardias blancas</u>.[65] They had been soliciting lands legally for the previous 12 years with no official response. The only answer was an attempt to intimidate them. On September 9, 1979, during a general assembly held in Villa de las Rosas, state police broke in and assassinated a leader of the peasants, Elpidio Vazquez.[66]

Apparently, the repression by the army and guardias blancas extends to the southeast of Chiapas as well. In 1979, the presence of the army increased substantially with the installation of a military base near Comitán de Dominguez. The 72 ejidos and 27 communities surrounding the military zone are terrorized by the army, which is said to have over 2,000 soldiers trained in guerrilla warfare. Government and PRI leaders of Tuxtla who refused to be identified to reporters of the <u>Uno Mas Uno</u> said the army was sent to the southeast of Chiapas to intimidate the Indian population, who had begun to mobilize against the large capitalist coffee growers and cattle ranchers.[67]

The repression, however, has not prevented peasants in the coffee-growing municipios surrounding Soconusco from creating an independent organization, Bloque Campesino de Chiapas. Seven thousand peasants were reported to be mobilized after soliciting in vain the illegally held haciendas.[68]

The presence of the army is felt elsewhere in Chiapas. Early in 1980, peasants from Amatenango del Valle and Venustiano Carranza occupied local fincas only to be removed violently by the army. The removal of the peasants included deaths, public beatings, and torture in the public park of Venustiano Carranza.[69]

As of July 1980, peasant land invasions had become so frequent that the army was sent into the following municipios: Tila, Amatenango del Valle, San Caralampio, Venustiano Carranza, Yajalón, Villa de las Rosas, Bolonchán, Citalá, Chilon.[70] Because the Indians in Chiapas are sometimes in possession of lands richly endowed with natural resources, the fight for control of the resources takes other forms in addition to direct repression of communities. Under the guise of colonization projects promoted by the INI and SRA, the government has tried to relocate Indians into new centers of population in order to incorporate them into "productive activities." In other words, the government seeks to integrate the peasants into waged capitalist production. In reality, what this has meant, according to the Indians of Ocosingo, is that they must work all day for the government as waged workers for only 40 pesos. They are forced to abandon their ejidal lands and lose any autonomy they once had. This was the description of the "Centro de Población Indígena, Frontera Echeverría." What is at stake are ejidal lands given to them by presidential decree in 1937 now found to be rich in valuable hardwoods.[71]

The Indians of Ocosingo have refused to abandon their lands. They are resisting the large lumber companies of Tuxtla that, in collaboration with the SRA, are attempting to steal (literally cut trees without paying the ejidatarios) the hardwood forest resources. Given the peasant resistance, the SRA later offered the ejidatarios 1,000 pesos for each large tree and 500 pesos for the smaller ones. Convinced that the peasants will either sell cheap or be convinced to relocate, the government has begun to build a road for logging trucks or trucks for uprooted peasants to be colonized elsewhere or if necessary for mobilization of the army. It was reported that the Indian communities are forced to work on the roads for no wages. Those communities refusing to participate are treated harshly by the army. While traveling to and from their communities, the peasants are subjected to routine searches of their person, confiscation of personal effects and money, and even beatings.[72]

Faced with capitalist pressure on their lands and resources, 51 communities of Ocosingo have organized a unión ejidal whose goals include the preservation of the natural resources of the Lacandono forests, of their ethnicity, the promotion of alliances with other communities in defense of common interests, the elimination of intermediaries, and the breaking down of the geographical isolation of their struggle by publicizing their situation nationally.[73]

A different group of indígenas in the municipio Ocosingo began soliciting lands from the capitalist property Rancho Cacao in 1972. In 1975, they occupied the land, removing the acreage from commercial capitalist production. They worked the land for their own consumption. After three years of peasant production of use values on capitalist lands, the army brutally evicted the peasants, burning their houses. At the moment, the peasants are defeated and are living on the lands of a neighboring pueblo,

Taniperlas. This pueblo, in support of its evicted neighbors, took them in temporarily. These indígenas have
still not given up. They have sought to publicize their
case and even tried to see the governor of the state of
Chiapas. The pressure has been sufficient to provoke the
government to offer lands elsewhere.[74]

Chiapas provides one scene of the battle between
peasants who want the resources (land) for self-valorization
and the capitalist landlords who want the lands for endless accumulation. Needless to say, the situation the
peasants confront in Chiapas is one of the worst. The re-
moteness, the lack of sufficient outside support, and the
presence of a huge reserve army of Guatemalans make it
easy for capitalists to resist peasant demands, repress
leaders and rebellious communities by refusing to hire
Chiapanecos who struggle, starving them out, forcing them
to migrate, or backing them into the corner of armed
struggle, which at this point would be a massacre.[75]

Nevertheless, it is clear that their ethnicity, their
linguistic and cultural differences from the rest of Mexico,
has not impeded their organization or willingness to struggle. The reason the balance of class power is so over-
whelmingly on the capitalist side comes not from the so-
called backwardness of the Indian but from the geographic
and social isolation of the groups in Chiapas, which facil-
itates oppression. If the peasants in struggle can break
out of their isolation and circulate their struggle, bringing
into Chiapas support and help from other groups, the
balance of class power may improve.

Peasants and PEMEX

The vast new oil reserves found in the states of
Campéche, Tabasco, Chiapas, and Hidalgo are good news
for capital, but devastating to the peasants who work
those lands surrounding the oil fields. The ecological loss
to the agricultural fields, contamination to the water, not
to mention the out-and-out expropriation of the land itself
has roused the peasants into overt struggle.[76] In February 1979, peasants occupied land and blocked roads
around six of the most productive oil wells in Tabasco and
Chiapas for 47 days.[77] Peasants caused losses estimated
by PEMEX at over 300 million pesos, momentarily disrupting capitalist accumulation. Since then capital has had

to incur the expense of maintaining the army in all the oil-producing zones coinciding with angry peasants, draining money from potential capitalist investment.[78]

The peasants have continued to threaten sabotage to oil wells, forcing PEMEX to pay 60 million pesos in "compensation" (promised but not yet delivered); to begin effective reduction in the indices of contamination; and to continue requiring army protection. Clearly, all these responses have the impact of damaging capitalist accumulation.[79]

Peasants in the Huasteca Hidalgüense have used their community organizations to confront the invasion of PEMEX. They fear losing the autonomy of their community. They fear being forced to migrate in search of work as their plot of land is expropriated with little or no compensation.[80] For those peasants whose lands surround the petroleum-producing zones but are not expropriated, they must face the contamination of water and land and the inflation in the prices of consumer goods that has been shown to accompany PEMEX expansion.[81]

The 27 communities of peasants organized into Unión Regional de Ejidos y Comunidades de la Huasteca Hidalgüense have devised a plan to avoid contributing to the capitalist gains associated with the oil expansion. They hope to exchange products between different communities and ejidos, avoiding as much as possible the purchase of inflated subsistence goods. Benito Hernandez, leader of the Unión Regional, said "peasants in the Huasteca who earn an average of 50 pesos a day cannot and will not participate in the inflation accompanying PEMEX's invasion."[82] The government realizes the potential disruptive effect on capitalist accumulation that the peasant community and their organizations have. Since December 1979, it has sent in the army to gather information on community life for a so-called Censo Nacional Campesino.[83]

The Huasteca Hidalgüense and the Fight over Land

The agrarian struggle for control of the Huasteca Hidalgüense is complex, serious, and well publicized in Mexico.[84] It is a very complicated situation since several leftist parties are competing for support among the peasants, more often than not dividing them, while other groups of peasants organize independently. We know that peasant struggle in the Huasteca has contributed to declines in capitalist production. In July 1979, the SRA announced that peasant invasions of land in the Huasteca Hidalgüense were so prevalent that production of cattle (ganadería) fell 80 percent.[85] The ganaderos have repeatedly warned the government that if the army does not intervene directly in these agrarian disputes they will arm themselves. They have.

Repression has been marked with the murder of hundreds of campesinos; many others have disappeared or are in jail. No one denies that most of the communities of the Huasteca are enduring daily threats and repression at the hands of guardias blancas and the army. To trace the history here in detail would be enlightening but highly time-consuming and still incomplete due to lack of data. The case is mentioned because it illustrates the essence of peasant struggle in Mexico. The small capitalist class who controls the land, mostly stolen ejidal or communal lands of the Huasteca Hidalgüense,[86] are fighting the peasants for the land. The capitalist ranchers have warned they will not give up one hectare of land put to productive capitalist use. They also enjoy surplus value extracted from the Indians forced (through loss of lands) to work 12-hour days for 50 pesos.[87] Were the peasants to recover their lands, the ranchers and growers would lose that source of surplus value from cheap wages used for capital accumulation. As in Chiapas, we have an organized but not unified peasantry fighting for space for themselves as a class--space that otherwise is put to capitalist use.

Peasants Struggle for Control of Their Production and Products

Chapter 3 showed how peasants lose to capital through commercial relations. It did not much matter whether it was public capital in its many forms, such as BANRURAL, CONASUPO, or the sugar monopoly, or private capital, such as the large commercial capitalists, intermediaries, or productive capitalists entering into contracts with peasants or ejidatarios.

Peasants, organized on the basis of their communities or ejidos, are struggling to regain control over the productive and commercial processes. This reduces profits for capitalist accumulation and thus furthers the disruption of capital. Some illustrative examples of peasants resisting real subsumption to capital by getting back self-control over production from BANRURAL will be presented. One of the initial steps at throwing off direct bank control is to control the allocation of the credit itself.

In June 1975, the Unión de Ejidos Emiliano Zapata in the eastern part of Morelos, consisting of 18 ejidos, decided to invade the offices of BANRURAL, forcing negotiations (on their terms) for credit. Occupying the local offices for three days, the peasants did not leave until assured that the central authorities of the bank would deal with them directly in their own local community. High officials from Mexico City in the SRA and BANRURAL as well as state officials from Cuernavaca, Morelos, were forced to travel to the pueblo Jonacatepec for discussions, an event that was, needless to say, unusual. The ejidatarios were explicit in what they wanted: (1) the unión would be in charge of buying and selling of inputs; (2) the bank would authorize cash as credit, not commodities; (3) the credit would be allocated to the respective ejidatarios by agreement in the general assemblies; (4) the commercialization would be taken care of by the secretaríos auxiliarios de comercialización of the ejidos and not by the bank.[88]

The results were dramatic. In 1975-76, the unión, the bank, and a buyer for the principal commercial crop, sorghum, agreed that the guaranteed price must be respected and all of the crop must be purchased regardless of quantity or quality. Previously, each producer had to negotiate independently with the buyers, always receiving a price less than the guaranteed official price.[89] The government, worried that the peasants would realize just how powerful a unión of ejidos could be, began to buy sorghum in 1977, guaranteeing the official price and holding open the granaries to show these peasants that it was the government solving their problems, not the unión. The government then began a campaign to sabotage the unifying efforts of the unión de ejidos. They circulated spies in the countryside saying that the leaders of the unión were sacando plata, robbing the member ejidatarios. Bank officials would tell member ejidos that if they worked with the unión they would not be given credit.[90]

Despite the slander from BANRURAL, which was truly afraid of the unión coordinating other commercial struggles, in 1978 the unión managed to get the concession for fer-

tilizer for the entire region with the Empresa de Guanos y
Fertilizantes. This was a significant gain for the ejidatarios, who previously had to pay exorbitant prices for
the fertilizer to the sorghum buyers.[91]

In late 1979 or early 1980 the unión negotiated a
contract for the sale of the entire onion crop for member
ejidos. Evidently, the buyer named in the contract did
not pay for the delivered goods, causing severe problems
for the ejidatarios and the unión. The fraud against the
unión has contributed to its decline.[92] Nevertheless, the
SRA and BANRURAL were ready to step in and promote their
own organization to negotiate collective sorghum prices for
the ejidatarios. The SRA formed the Comité Regional de
Comercialización de Sorgo, consisting of representatives
from each ejido. Although the negotiations with the local
trilladora industry and other private buyers, such as the
processors of balanced animal feeds, have been successful,
the comité has linked the ejidatarios once again even
closer to the BANRURAL and SRA. Even the number of
hectares devoted to basic crops such as corn and beans
have been reduced, damaging the ejidos' autonomy and
making them more dependent on the government-sponsored
organization for advantageous contracts of sale of the commercial crop in order to live.[93]

Whether the Unión de Ejidos Emiliano Zapata continues to decline or whether the ejidatarios take over the
comité and use it for their own instrument in struggle, as
they have been known to do, or whether the comité continues to be subject to the close supervision and control of
the SRA and BANRURAL for contracts for maquila and sale
of products remains to be seen.

Peasants Directly Appropriate Resources and Income from Capital

Peasants do not always pay back their agricultural
loans to the official bank. In fact, CIDE (Centro de Investigaciones Agrarias) reported that only 29.3 percent of
all loans to small peasants were recovered in the late
1960s.[94] CIDE noted that peasants would sell the inputs
given them as credit and then default on the loan. They
would ask for loans year after year, eluding payment.[95]
More recently, the BANRURAL reports that for the agricultural cycle of 1979 only 33 percent of all loans for culti-

vation of maize were recovered.[96]   The peasants actually
acquire income divorced from productivity--a direct attack
on the surplus value extracted for capitalist use.   This is
another form of struggle that disrupts capitalist accumulation.

The henequeneros of Yucatán directly appropriated
income from capital unrelated to productivity for a number
of years until the restructuring of the henequen producers
in 1978.   During that time, Warman reports that over 150
million pesos a year were given to the henequeneros, unrelated to productivity.[97]   The peasants insisted on their
cash advances.   If the advances were not forthcoming,
they would take the offices, destroy the files with the
records of debts, wreak havoc until the army restored
peace, and then resume the cash payments.[98]   In September
1976, 6,000 ejidatarios henequeneros took the government
offices and the Palacio de Gobierno of Mérida, demanding
more and increased advances.[99]   In fact, Bartra reports
that because these peasants know they are really salaried
workers for the bank, they struggled for the aguinaldo
(one month's additional salary as a Christmas bonus).   The
bank, of course, refused, claiming that the henequeneros
were landowning ejidatarios involved in a commercial contract and not directly working for it.[100]

In the period preceding the bank's reorganization
of henequen credit, the bank's losses in henequen production were attributed to the high costs of production and
low productivity.[101]   Of course, in addition to high costs
and low productivity, losses were also attributed to a fall
in world demand and subsequent plummeting of prices.   In
1977, the cost to produce a kilo of henequen was 15.51
pesos and its market value only 6.46 pesos.   However, the
fall in the world demand and prices of henequen could not
explain why the more CORDEMEX or the Banco Crédito Rural
Peninsular invested, the lower was productivity.   Class
struggle in the form of peasant direct appropriation of income unrelated to productivity does explain this.[102]

The ejidatarios tabacaleros also struggle for more
income not related to work.   They have disrupted the post-
World War II capitalist mechanism of raising the rate of
relative surplus value via more productivity.   For example,
the peasant producers always ask for credit (cash advances) for tasks not performed.   They ask for money to
hire waged workers for an entire week when in reality the
additional outside help is only required for one day.   The

peasants use the extra money for direct consumption or for other productive activities of their own use outside of capital's direction.[103]   Peasants also report that more work days and workers (themselves) were required for any given task than in reality, increasing their income.[104]   Besides the extra money they drain from the enterprise, the tabacaleros often disrupt the careful industry planning by TABAMEX and the cigarette companies by planting more hectares of tobacco than approved in the contract.   The peasants get the tobacco seedlings from private nurseries, planteros libres, not controlled by TABAMEX, disturbing the careful quality control of the tobacco plants.[105]

The peasants, knowing full well that they work for TABAMEX and are not simply two businesses engaging in commerce, formed a Unión Sindicato Nacional Benito Juarez in 1977.   They organized a simultaneous occupation of the central building of TABAMEX in Distrito Federal and others in Vera Cruz, Puebla, and Nayarít.   Their demands were for higher prices of tobacco on top of current costs of production.   That is, they wanted a higher income but not higher productivity.   The director of TABAMEX has not recognized the syndicate because "there is no labor relation between the two parties . . . [it is] strictly commercial."[106]   The police were sent to remove the peasants from the offices.

Cañeros and the Disruption of Capital

Struggles by sugar-cane-growing peasants (cañeros) illustrate my basic point that peasants can and do rupture capitalist accumulation.   Here are some instances of cañeros contributing to such rupture.   Struggles by the cañeros ejidatarios are considerably complex.   In some parts of the country you have ejidatarios struggling to stop producing cane, others struggling to be included within the designated cane-producing zone.   You have, on the one hand, cañeros divided from the cane cutters (cortadores), where the first group truly exploits the other, or you find instances where the two groups have overcome these divisions and recomposed the class for further struggle.   It is truly a complicated situation, which I do not pretend to have understood completely.   Sugar cane and the relation of its producers, cutters, and buyers, being the oldest agricultural industry in Mexico, is a thesis in itself.

The small peasant sugar cane producers have disrupted the capitalist sugar industry by curtailing deliveries of cane on a number of occasions. The peasants organize around the unfair conditions of sale to the mill (ingenio) soliciting and in some instances receiving the dramatic alliance and support of the ingenio workers. Most of these work stoppages are so threatening to capital in real economic loss that the army is called in to overtly repress the peasants. Bartra narrates the struggle that enveloped over 100 ejidos surrounding the ingenio of San Cristóbal in Vera Cruz. Although deliveries of cane were suspended by the ejidatarios, large landowners continued to deliver cane to the ingenio. Thousands of peasant producers, with the support of the cane cutters, stormed the ingenio on December 31, 1972, to shut it down. On January 9, 1973, the army forced the peasants to retreat, allowing cane to be delivered by the large landowners and allowing the ingenio to continue functioning. The workers of the ingenio supported the struggle of the ejidatarios and refused to work until finally the enterprise put their jobs on the line. Faced with the reserve army, they were forced back to work.[107]

In 1980, the ejidatarios cañeros of the Ejido Puruaran in Michoacán regained control of the comisariado ejidal. Previously, the comisario had always arranged with the owners of the ingenio the worst possible prices of cane for the ejidatarios. The ejidatarios, robbed with the help and compliance of the imposed comisario, proposed and elected their own candidate. The ejidatarios, organized and unified, forced the municipal authorities to recognize the validity of the new comisario. This very small but concrete action on the part of the peasants was a successful and positive step toward putting a stop to the drain of value from peasant production to capitalist accumulation.[108]

The preceding illustrates how peasants disrupt accumulation by invading and taking over capitalist lands, interrupting oil production, and creating instability and uncertainty in the countryside--leading to lower production and fewer investments; controlling the commercialization of their crops and the purchasing of inputs, cutting into the BANRURAL's and other institutions' profits and control over production; directly appropriating resources and income from capital; and stopping deliveries of raw material to capitalist enterprises, pressing for better prices. In all, these peasants organize, based on their community ties and traditions, forming a class-for-itself.

THE DYNAMICS OF THREE CONTEMPORARY CASES

Complementing the cross-sectional view of peasant struggles given in the preceding section, three sets of specific struggles tracked over several years will be presented. By looking at the development of the struggles through time (data allowing), we can go a step beyond illustrating analytical points; we can begin to analyze the struggles themselves. To analyze a struggle one must look at its content, direction, motivation, and circulation. With this temporal approach the issue of strategy can be addressed and the development of peasant power vis-à-vis capital can be evaluated.

Despite the long histories of each struggle, the analysis that follows is subject to certain limitations. The discussion is limited to events taking place during the 1970s. Furthermore, I have no intellectual reason for choosing or not choosing any particular struggle for narration. The main criterion is availability of information. Finally, I do not pretend that these struggles are typical of peasant struggles in Mexico. Actually, there is no "typical" peasant struggle. They are as varied in their development, peculiarities, and degrees of success as the peoples and countryside of Mexico. Indeed, the peasants themselves by their struggles, are actively refusing to be homogenized, to be stripped of their individuality, their customs, their traditions, their community. However, there are a few characteristics common to many struggles, allowing me to make some general comments on the contemporary rural conflicts in Mexico.

Coalición de Ejidos Colectivos de los Valles de Yaqui y Mayo (Sonora)

On November 19, 1976, the president of Mexico expropriated 42,000 hectares of irrigated cropland and 62,000 hectares of pastureland in the Yaqui Valley of Sonora for distribution to some 8,000 peasants.[109] Such an event was unprecedented since the 1910 agrarian revolution and provoked considerable comment on the part of the Mexican analysts. One article in the prestigious Mexican journal of political economy, Cuadernos Políticos, said the expropriation was the result of internal bickering; a move to destroy the independence and power of one segment of the capitalist class.[110] It was also said that Echeverría, president of Mexico at the time, was one of those leaders who recognized that with the only alternative being severe repression, conditions had to be altered in the countryside to gain time to reorganize capital to overcome the crisis of the early 1970s.[111] One thing is certain: the expropriation was not a benevolent gift to the peasants by the "populist" President Echeverría, as Sanderson suggests in a recent book on Sonora.[112] The remarkable expropriation was rather the result of a long, protracted struggle on the part of the peasants in northwest Mexico.

Without delving too deeply into the particulars of land ownership and agricultural production in the Yaqui Valley prior to the peasant takeover, we should note that there was a significant population of campesinos without land and without sufficient work to survive. The land was tied up in latifundios multifamiliares, where the owner puts sections of land in the name of his relatives or friends but exploits them as one unit of production.[113] The ejidatarios, through a number of mechanisms, had lost control over the land (principally by renting it to one large grower, then working sporadically as waged workers--sometimes on their own land). In 1973, it was found that 42,000 hectares of the Yaqui and Mayo valleys were rented. As much as 25 or 30 years ago, peasants had migrated to the northwest in search of work, forming a waged agricultural proletariat. Conditions for waged work and the capitalist labor market became so disadvantageous for these peasants (they call themselves "campesinos sin tierra y sin trabajo") that they turned to the struggle for land.

In the middle 1970s, there was a dramatic reduction of acreage planted in the labor-intensive crop, cotton, due to the substitution of sorghum, wheat, and ranching. Gustavo Gordillo is correct that this implied a drastic reduction in agricultural employment and a grave deterioration in the living conditions of the jornaleros at the time of the intense mobilization of the landless peasants in the area.[114] But (and Gordillo ignores this point) peasants organized for land and not better working condi-

tions or for job guarantees. To this demand, the substitution of labor-intensive crops could not provide an answer, as Gordillo suggests. The peasants sought land not
only because there was no wage but because land could
free them from the unstable, grueling life of a day field-
worker for large growers. Land represented an alternative
for self-development.

Moreover, among the peasants soliciting the coveted
land were "peasants" who had long ago lost or abandoned
an unproductive, minuscule plot to go to the cities to become taxicab drivers, cobblers, petty bureaucrats, or construction workers.[115] This particular group had waged
jobs. But those jobs were low on the wage hierarchy, and
they preferred to struggle for that potential autonomy from
the wage and from capital the land offers. This is clearly
a case of "recampesinización." To the negative spur to
struggle created by the lack of a wage resulting from
changes in the cropping pattern, we must add the positive
desires for land and autonomy as motives.

The jornaleros or campesinos sin tierra in Sonora
grouped into committees to take the necessary steps to
solicit land from the government. In October 1975, after
years of waiting, one particular case became the rallying
point of the entire regional movement of Sonora. Four
hundred members of the Comité de San Ignacio Rio Muerto
voted in a general assembly to invade and occupy 100
hectares.[116] The governor of the state, not realizing the
waves he would create, ordered the state judicial police to
remove the peasants from the famous Bloque 407. The result was the murder in cold blood of 10 peasants, including the leader, and jailings of 30 others. The idea was
apparently to murder the leaders and frighten other campesinos sin tierra away from invading other capitalist lands.
However, due to the peasants' incredible ability to seek
outside support, this repression was well publicized across
the Mexican nation. The effect was immediate. The government, accused of murdering peasants, had to remove the
governor from office (whether this was only an excuse to
get rid of a troublesome political foe does not concern us--
even if this could be proven). Under the continued pressure of publicity, the federal government also sent high
agrarian officials for an investigation, and actually expropriated 4,387 hectares of the Yaqui Valley for the 433
survivors of San Ignacio Rio Muerto.[117]

The peasant struggle associated with San Ignacio Rio Muerto was only a small part of the peasant movement in Sonora and the northwest. There were many different groups active in the early to mid-1970s. Some organized independently into the Frente Campesino Independiente. They repeatedly invaded lands, only to be evicted time and again. The activities of the Frente contributed significantly to mounting regional and national pressure on the state. There were smaller groups of peasants who had armed themselves in defense of newly invaded lands. In short, the movement spread rapidly to challenge the capitalist ownership and exploitation of hundreds of thousands of hectares of land.[118] The government was also trying to regain lost prestige by showing how effective the Confederación Nacional Campesina (CNC) could be in supporting peasant movements and actually delivering the hard-sought-after land. However, the land expropriated the following year and given to 8,000 peasants was some of the richest land in Mexico, with an estimated value of over 30,000 pesos (1976) per hectare.

Although concentrated and highly active, the peasant movement was not unified. The government was successful in pitting the peasants associated with the CNC against those completely independent. As a result the movement did not explode throughout the region or throughout Mexico.

Immediately following the expropriation and distribution, the government stepped up efforts to expand control and direct the peasant struggle in the Yaqui Valley, especially the control of the new ejidos. The government centrales campesinos, CNC, CAM, CCI, and UGOCM, without consulting their presumed constituency (those who received the land distributions), signed an agreement that said that the four organizations allied under the name Pacto de Ocampo would convince the peasants (1) to pay the previous owners of the land for expenses incurred at the beginning of the previous agricultural cycle; (2) to accept within their new ejidos the peónes acasillados of the expropriated latifundios who had not supported their struggle; and (3) that they would not use the works of infrastructure built by the previous owners on the expropriated lands. The peasants were given credit, water, and technical assistance from the BANRURAL, SARH, and SRA for the first cycle of crops. Of course, as already amply demonstrated in Chapter 3, with this credit, insurance, and assistance also comes control, fees, loss of decisions, and loss of money (income). The sought-after autonomy that the land would provide remained unattained. In fact, the BANRURAL withheld 11 million pesos from the peasants to supposedly begin paying back the previous owners for their expenses on the land.[119]

In 1977, the peasants responded to these efforts by the government to reorient, control, and dilute their success in struggle by forming an organization at once autonomous of and independent of their government: the Coalición de Ejidos Colectivos de los Valles del Yaqui y Mayo.[120] What follows is a brief history of the struggles of that organization for self-control and a better life by constantly fighting for autonomy from the government's role in capitalist accumulation. We will see how these struggles interfere with capitalist accumulation. The struggles of the coalición are a spectacular example of how the acquisition of land, although in this case intended by the government to pacify the peasants, has led to the opposite effect. The land became a springboard for further struggle.

The ejidatarios realized immediately that there was a large gap between the amount of money paid to the national crop insurance company, ANAGSA, and the actual indemnity they received when disaster struck their crops. At the end of the 1978 cycle, a portion of their crops was lost due to natural causes (siniestros). After waiting an inordinate amount of time to collect damages, they received only 1.5 million pesos. The peasants knew that they had paid over 21 million pesos that year to the insurance company and that somebody else was using and investing their money for purposes unrelated to their general welfare.[121] The peasants in the coalición proceeded to withdraw their 21 million pesos from ANAGSA and to form their own Fondo Común to provide insurance coverage should the crops fail. With the Fondo Común they now have better crop coverage and have also been able to contract their own technical personnel, thus removing one more objectionable tie to the government. BANRURAL opposed the project at first, but had to accept it because the Fondo Común actually insured the crops better than ANAGSA.

In early 1979, the coalición began plans to form their own unión de crédito to completely free themselves from the control of the bank. This project was vigorously opposed by BANRURAL since a tremendous amount of capital and control would be removed from the bank by peasants seeking to use it in their own way for their own benefit. The permission was finally granted from the Secretary of Hacienda and Public Credit two years later.[122] The effect on other ejidos of the coalición's success in self-financing could be significant.

During this period, the peasants also attacked another channel of bank control over production--commercialization of the crops. Tired of the imposition of the bank's choice of buyers, such as CONASUPO, which does not always pay the best prices, the peasants from the coalición formed a department of commercialization in August 1980. It has a dual purpose: to purchase inputs such as seeds, fertilizer, and insecticides and to arrange for the sale of their crops. The department consists of three ejidatarios who have the responsibility to inform themselves and thus the other member ejidos of market conditions for the various crops. Their first experience involved the sale of the soya crop at the end of September 1980. They invited local industries to a meeting to negotiate a price. The negotiations were successful: they sold their crop at 8,500 pesos per ton, to be paid within 24 hours of delivery of the crop. It is clear that the ejidatarios selling directly to the market certainly interfered with BANRURAL's accumulation of capital at the peasants' expense. BANRURAL began threatening these enterprises with legal action if they insisted on buying directly from the ejidatarios. The bank claimed it had the only legal right to sell their crop. The peasants just "didn't understand financial matters."[123]

Another way the department of commercialization earned income for the ejidatarios otherwise lost to BANRURAL was by arranging to have the raw cotton processed, selling not only the fiber but the seed and the borra (lint or fuzz) as well. Previously they sold just the raw cotton. BANRURAL sold the by-products itself, earning extra income off the peasants' crop. Further, the ejidos also saved because their own department did not charge a fee per ton of crop sold, like BANRURAL. They added to their income approximately 1,100,000 pesos per year.[124]

The department buys inputs for the member ejidos that choose to use its services. (The various ejidos of the coalición choose individually to participate in the department of commercialization or stay with BANRURAL.) By arranging for direct purchase of wheat, corn, and soya seeds, a total of 6,240,800 pesos was saved, which is the

difference between the price per ton of seed the bank
quoted and what the ejidatarios were able to obtain themselves.   Fertilizer was also obtained directly from
FERTIMEX.   Besides the saving of 617,500 pesos, they
could ensure that the fertilizers were in the hands of the
ejidatarios at the right time so as not to delay the sowing
of the crops.   Certainly a problem for the ejidatarios was
the bank's inability to provide necessary inputs on time.
These delays and mixups often caused them to lose valuable growing time.[125]

The ejidatarios have more plans to continue closing
the doors to capitalist control of their production and surplus.   They hope to produce their own fertilizers and insecticides.[126]   FERTIMEX or Du Pont will not be too happy
if other peasants are drawn into the coalición's scheme
and exchange takes place for mutual benefit and not one-
sided gain.   They also are trying to gain control over the
distribution of water to their ejidos by having the users
of each district democratically elect the members of the
water boards instead of accepting the SARH appointments.
At present, the water boards that distribute water to the
users are controlled by the large landowners in the area,
who favor the privately owned capitalist farms over the
ejidos.[127]

The previous "owners" of the expropriated lands
have not taken the loss, and potential increased losses,
quietly.   In November 1976, a capitalist "strike" was orchestrated by large growers of the northwest who stopped
cultivating 250,000 hectares of land to protest the expropriations.[128]   Support was gained for the striking growers
when over 1,000 businesses from the industrial and commercial sectors of some 11 states closed their doors.[129]   In
a dramatic action of class solidarity, the entire business
sector of Sonora shut down and threatened to stop paying
taxes to the federal government.[130]   These tactics had
little effect.   The government could not back down because
the peasants now in possession of the land would not hesi-
tate to defend their new resources with their lives.   There
had been too much bad publicity; too much blood on the
hands of the government.   Instead, the state remained on
the path of pacification and conciliation, even though this
was proving to be ineffectual.

The "owners" then changed strategies, challenging
the validity of the presidential expropriations through the
courts.   As of October 1979, they had sought 49 amparos

against 57 ejidos. However, the coalición began a legal appeal with the Supreme Court to restrain the restitution of the lands to the old latifundistas. The peasants have repeatedly responded that they will not leave the land under any circumstances.[131] The coalición's lawyer, Medina Arroya, publicly called for all peasants in the country to be alert against such aggressions on peasant land. "If necessary we will have a unified response," he warned, should further steps be taken to remove the peasants.[132]

The peasants responded to this attack on their newly acquired lands by again seeking outside support and publicity. Instead of opening up divisions where each ejido would fend for itself, the attack provoked more unity. The peasant group announced they were not going to give up one hectare of land. In October 1979, the coalición sent representatives to the Primer Encuentro Nacional de Organizaciones Campesinas Independientes in Milpa Alta. The threat that the amparos posed to the peasants was discussed among campesinos from all over Mexico.[133] Since then, the peasants not only have retained all of the land but also successfully pressured the government into paying indemnity to the previous "owners" in order to minimize future land tenure disputes.

However, in spring 1980 there were more attempts to divide the ejidatarios. Three comisariados ejidales out of 76 member ejidos from the coalición decided that the directors of the Fondo Común had acted fraudulently. The coalición hired the accounting firm of Gomez Morgin, Meljem and Associates to audit the accounts. The dissenting group hired another firm from Ciudad Obregon to review the audit. Both the audit and the review revealed no irregularities in the handling of the funds. Since the manager of the northwest branch of the BANRURAL was supporting the new directors for the Fondo Común proposed by the dissenting 50 ejidatarios, many of the peasants of the coalición felt that the BANRURAL artificially created suspicions to create divisions among the ejidatarios.[134]

Other attacks on the ejidos colectivos have included efforts to force the ejidatarios to accept more than 10,000 landless campesinos in southern Sonora on their ejidos. The ejidatarios' refusal is not to be interpreted as not caring about the struggle of other peasants. On the contrary, they continue to support other peasant struggles for land. They recognize that there are over 25,000 peasants

in southern Sonora without land. They also see that the
solution is not to reduce their strength and power by diluting their hard-fought-for resources among themselves and
10,000 more peasants. The coalición sees the answer in
expropriating more capitalist properties. It is known that
over 40,000 hectares in Sonora are still tied up in lati-
fundía.135

When the coalición sent representatives to the Primer
Encuentro in Milpa Alta, it announced that

> It is time to close ranks between the ejida-
> tarios and solicitors of land . . . because
> it is not possible to continue tolerating the
> arbitrariness of the SRA. . . . The Coali-
> ción wants to cooperate with independent
> organizations in actions that can resolve
> common problems and contribute to the unity
> and to the struggle for the formation of a
> National Peasant Organization. . . .136

Also in 1978, the coalición organized an Encuentro
Obrero Campesino in the Yaqui Valley to celebrate the third
anniversary of the expropriation as well as to hold meetings and discussions among peasants from all over Mex-
ico.137 The details of these meetings were not publicized
for obvious reasons, since concrete plans and actions were
discussed. That the coalición recognizes the need for the
struggle to circulate is obvious. It has declared its in-
tent to establish alliances with other peasant groups politically and also economically. It intends to exchange
commercial goods and agricultural inputs with other peasant groups, accomplishing two things: gouging into capital's space and helping other groups raise their standard
of living by losing less to the commercial and industrial
circuit of capital. We also know that the coalición expressed its support and aid to the comuneros of Santa Fé,
Michoacán, in their particular struggle, discussed in the
next section.

The goals of struggle go beyond the productive
sphere. The coalición wants a branch of the Universidad
de Chapingo to be located in the Yaqui Valley. It wants
agricultural and social experts trained within its own region, where some local control would be possible. Whereas
previously with the wage the peasants did not have enough
to eat and so they fought for land, now the terrain of

struggle has shifted to better houses and education. They even want <u>more</u> land to build urban zones so as not to take good, arable land out of cultivation to build the towns.138

The Coalición de Ejidos Colectivos is an exceptional case of peasant struggle in Mexico. Where the peasants go with their riches and better life can, of course, only be answered in time. It is still possible that they could embark on a road to capitalist accumulation and begin investing to give themselves more work (self-exploitation) or put others to work (exploitation) for profit. The record thus far indicates rather that they are on a course of saying no to capital. They are trying to direct their own production and social activities as well as improve their lives. As one peasant from San Ignacio Rio Muerto said, "We are better off than before. Today we have ejidatarios with cars and houses; before with the wage we didn't have enough to eat."139 For the moment it seems that the peasants will likely continue within the terrain of self-valorization. Historically, this struggle illustrates clearly several points:

1. Peasant struggle ruptures capitalist accumulation.
2. Peasants seek autonomy from capital.
3. The struggle does not always stop when the immediate goal is achieved.
4. The struggle circulates to other sectors of the peasant working class.
5. Peasants use one form of organization when likely to succeed, i.e., government controlled <u>centrales</u>, only to change strategies when needed, i.e., to autonomous organizations.
6. Peasants in this case clearly form a class-for-itself.

Los Comuneros de Santa Fé de la Laguna (Michoacán)

Peasant struggles in the state of Michoacán are as old as the culture and traditions of the Indians who inhabit it. Prior to the Spanish Conquest, Purepecha Indians possessed lands in common throughout Michoacán. Since then the communal lands have constantly been in dispute. In Santa Fé de la Laguna, the colonial administration recognized their communal lands in 1542. A document dated 1631 (on file in the archives of Santa Fé) acknowledges that the Purepechas are the rightful owners of these lands.[140] Although the struggle summarized here concerns only one community, Santa Fé, it is very typical of conflicts among landowners, ranchers, and comuneros throughout the state of Michoacán.

Conflicts in Santa Fé de la Laguna have been raging between large landowners, ganaderos, and the comuneros for the past 30 years. These conflicts in Santa Fé grew into active confrontation in November 1979.

Previously, indiscriminate and illegal lumbering by mestizos from the neighboring commercial and ranching center of Quiroga had stripped the community of most of its forests. Consequently, in addition to their subsistence farming, the Indians from Santa Fé supplemented their income and way of life by making and selling pottery (alfarero) from clay found on their lands. More recently, their neighbors in Quiroga began to destroy what lands they had left by introducing cattle. In the summer of 1979, the Indians solicited aid from the secretary of agrarian reform to formulate a legal agreement between the ganaderos of Quiroga and the community of Santa Fé such that the former would pay a nominal fee for the use of the pastures for their cattle.[141] Although the agreement was not economically in their favor, the Indians accepted, knowing that it could provide a legal basis for further struggle, which they knew was inevitable. The ganaderos promptly broke the agreement and continued to pasture cattle on the community's land. Subsequently, in November 1979, the comuneros called a general assembly to decide as a community what action to take. They decided after discussion that they would confiscate the 64 cows, forcing the ganaderos to pay for the previous months.

While carrying out their decision, the comuneros were ambushed by armed guardias blancas hired by the ganaderos. Two comuneros were killed and ten others wounded. The participating Indians were jailed but the arrested ganaderos were immediately released! However, the comuneros held the captured cattle.[142]

Because the Indians were imprisoned for defending their own lands, for defending their lives on their own lands; because they were accused of crimes instead of the ganaderos, who were indeed the aggressors; because this was just one more incident in the long history of confrontations, there followed a rapid mobilization of the already-organized community.

The comuneros of Santa Fé have always been organized democratically. The town decisions are made by popular assemblies. The main authority is the consejo de barrios, which is made up of 16 representatives (2 from each of the 8 barrios), the presidente de bienes comunales, and the jefe de tenencia.[143]   Given the prior existence and experience of self-government, the comuneros did not waste any time in using their community resources for action. The next day, November 18, 1979, commissions were formed to rotate the tasks of feeding and caring for the captured cattle. On November 19, the comuneros set up a permanent camp (sit-in) in front of the state capital in Morelia, pressuring for resolution of their demands: (1) liberty for the prisoners; (2) indemnity for the widows of murdered comuneros; (3) medical attention for the wounded; and (4) final return and possession of their lands. In addition, they refused to return the cattle until paid fair price for their keep as well as guarantees that the ganaderos would no longer invade their lands.[144] The governor refused to talk with the comuneros or concede to any demands. The ganaderos likewise refused to pay for the pasturage of the cows. The comuneros proceeded to intensify their pressure, first on the community and regional levels and then on the national level.

These Indians of Santa Fé began holding daily assemblies. The entire community, some 4,000 people, became one way or another actively involved in the struggle. In support of the permanent campamento in front of the state capital, they formed committees to bring food, gather firewood, catch fish, and provide guards for the protection and provision of those in the sit-in. Other committees were formed to diffuse information to the press, to leaflet the communities, and to inform and seek neighboring support.

Indians from the surrounding communities of Zirahuen, Curio, Taracatio, Ichan, and Tingambato, informed of the struggle, came to the aid of the comuneros of Santa Fé by helping with the campamento.[145]   Within five days, on November 23, a march and meeting in Morelia involved over 3,000 people from some 14 surrounding communities, illustrating the degree of circulation on the regional level. Two days later, these communities participated in another meeting and march in Pátzcuaro, where the imprisoned comuneros were held.

Santa Fé is also a member of the regional organization Unión de Comuneros Emiliano Zapata. The unión has a very active and militant lawyer, Efrén Capiz, whose career has been dedicated to defending and aiding the struggle of the indígenas campesinas of Michoacán. A digression is necessary about the lawyer Capiz. His role was crucial to the eventual outcome of the struggle. However, he could by no means have been so effective without the unity and sustained pressure from the communities themselves. The peasants' strength lies in their community and their organizations. But the comuneros recognized that a very effective tactic in struggle would be the help of a lawyer whose solidarity in struggle was guaranteed.

Capiz was born in Nahuatz, Michoacán, in the heart of the Purepecha zone. As a child and young person, he worked as a campesino in the fields; later he became a sandal maker (guarachero), a baker, a shepherd, and a jornalero. According to his own statements, he worked sunup to sundown to earn enough corn to eat: "I know what it is to be peasant and an Indian." At the age of 21 he finally entered primary school. Eventually he received degrees in law and philosophy and returned to his native state and the countryside. The support from the Indians and their concern for his safety (always threatened because of his active role in struggle) is enough to convince anyone that he is authentically a partner in struggle. Actually, during the heat of the conflict between Santa Fé and Quiroga he was protected by the Indians, who actually saved his life when one attempt was made to kidnap him, allegedly by agents of the SRA during a visit to one of those offices.[146]

The Unión de Comuneros and Capiz began to circulate the struggle of the community of Santa Fé on a national and even international level. Even before the ambush took place, Capiz, representing the Unión de Comuneros, attended the Primer Encuentro at Milpa Alta in October 1979, and informed peasants from all over Mexico of the aggression being suffered by the comuneros of Michoacán.[147] The unión held interviews and talks with the Commission of Human Rights of the United Nations.[148] Information was disseminated to the national press. Uno Mas Uno published information daily that publicized throughout the nation the struggle of the tiny Indian community in the mountains of Michoacán.

Knowing the significance of national recognition and support for their struggle, the comuneros of Santa Fé sent a delegation to the national centennial celebration of the birth of Emiliano Zapata in Morelos. Recognizing the value of support from other peasant communities, the CNPA, the national coordinating organization (whose membership includes some 60 independent peasant organizations), offered active solidarity.[149]

By December 5, the government tried to convince the Indians that the struggle to recover their lands was useless. They were threatened with the prolonged incarceration of the prisoners if they did not abandon their sit-in on the streets in front of the state capital. Another tactic the government took was to publicize within the national press that the comuneros were "innocent and infantile" but badly advised by outsiders, Communists or Marxists, implying that the lawyer Capiz was a militant for the Communist Party.[150] Capiz and the Mexican Communist Party set the record straight. But red-baiting is a tactic that the government uses often to destroy public support for grass-roots movements like that of Santa Fé.

On November 20, 1979, in a show of support for the comuneros, students organized a music festival in Pátzcuaro to disseminate information about the struggle and also to collect food and money for the comuneros. In another effort to gain publicity for the comuneros, on November 30, 1979, they commandeered the public buses in Morelia, forcing the suspension of service for that day.[151] In an attack on student support for the peasants, the secretary of education threatened to cut off scholarships and close courses in the ethnolinguistic section of CISINAH (the graduate school of the national school of anthropology and history) in Morelia if they continued to actively support the struggle of the comuneros of Santa Fé.

The shopkeepers and intermediaries (comerciantes) of Quiroga showed their class support for the ganaderos by lowering the prices paid to the Indians of Santa Fé for the clay pots. Previously, the comerciantes purchased 12 pots for 20 pesos. In response to the struggle, they lowered the price to 8 pesos for 12 pots, or suspended purchases altogether.[152] The peasants responded to this price-cutting strategy by setting up their own market on December 8 and 9 in Morelia to sell their pots, craft items, and food directly to the public. The <u>tianguis</u> (market) not only raised money, sidestepping the intermediaries, but involved more of the community in the struggle.

On December 4, the ganaderos of Quiroga, represented by the presidente of the municipio, began to capitulate. They offered 25 pesos a day per cow for their return. The comuneros demanded 70 pesos, indemnity for the widows, and a new agreement promising no more invasions on their land.[153] When no agreement was reached, the comuneros declared that the captured cows were on a hunger strike! The ganaderos quickly offered 50 pesos per cow per day, agreed to pay indemnity to the widows, and signed a new agreement. In a general assembly in Santa Fé, the settlement was discussed and accepted. Money and cattle were exchanged in the presence of two state agrarian delegates. However, no long-term solution about the lands or the prisoners was reached.

On December 19 a commission of Purepechas traveled to the Distrito Federal to meet with the general director of the Instituto Nacional Indigenista and with the subsecretary of agrarian reform. They sought a definitive solution over the constantly disputed lands and an official investigation into the treatment and due process of the prisoners.[154] In the early part of December, they also participated in the meetings and marches over the issue of amnesty for political prisoners from the countryside in the Second Forum against Repression. Throughout these meetings, interventions were made in favor of and dedicated to the comuneros of Santa Fé.

Finally, after 32 days of permanent occupation of the streets in front of the state capital, the governor spoke with the Indians on December 20. The governor said that all of their demands would be met favorably within four months. Immediate settlement was not possible because he must "save the face of the principal of authority." The settlement was conditional on the Indians abandoning their campamento in front of the governor's palace within 24 hours.[155]

In defiance of the governor and to further circulate the struggle, the comuneros announced the date of an Encuentro Campesino for the Unión de Comuneros de Emiliano Zapata to be held in Santa Fé on January 19 and 20, 1980. The purpose would be to evaluate their struggle, circulate the experiences and knowledge to other communities, and take stock of their present situation. Apparently, the announcement of the Encuentro and the possible volatile situation provoked the early release of the wounded comuneros from custody.[156]   In addition, the secretary of agrarian reform was forced to legalize new boundaries in favor of the comuneros.

Because the comuneros were organized and unified on the community level and the regional level, their efforts at circulating their struggle on the national level were effective.   There is no doubt that the experiences and knowledge gained from this particular incident will have profound impact on the organization of peasants within the region.   The regional organization, Unión de Comuneros Emiliano Zapata, has been strengthened now. It supports and aids more communities.   If the base had not been so strong and unified or as closely articulated with other peasant groups outside of Michoacán,[157] the pressure would probably never have been sufficient to force the governor to release the prisoners as promised and achieve new legal boundaries from the SRA in July 1980.

Many times, sufficient pressure and mobilization can force the government into apparently conceding to some demands, but without the continued presence of a well-integrated organization with a solid community base, the concessions can sit on the shelf and never be carried out.[158]   In the case of Santa Fé, the comuneros effectively recovered 1,500 hectares of communal lands invaded by the ranchers of Quiroga.   On July 30, 1980, surveyors from SRA and representatives from the subsecretary of communal goods placed the new boundary markers while over 3,000 Indians spread along the five-kilometer boundary oversaw the project.   The Indians recovered, for their own use, not only their land but several of the ranchers' investments, which included a high school, a football field, more than 150 houses, new subdivisions in the midst of development, orchards, and planted fields.   Significant to this tangible result of years of struggle was the fact that hundreds of comuneros from other communities nearby (Cheranistico, Uren, Ahuiran, Tarejro, and Lajas del Bosque) were also present during the boundary marking, manifesting their support for the comuneros of Santa Fé de la Laguna.[159]

Another result of the struggle was the granting of 75,000 pesos of "gratifications" to the widows of the murdered comuneros. Of course, the governor refused to call it indemnity because that would be admitting guilt. It also seems that the ganaderos were never punished in any manner. But this was one of the first times that a crime against peasants defending their land and their way of life did not go completely unnoticed. One peasant clearly analyzed the situation by noting that "75,000 pesos can never pay the life of a man. But what is important is for the first time the crime did not remain totally exonerated."160

This struggle is significant because it illustrates that Indians struggle just as effectively as mestizos. It shows beautifully how a local, potentially isolated struggle circulated from the local to regional to national levels, bringing about its successful conclusion. Traditional divisions within the class were broken down and a higher political class composition obtained as housewives, students, urban workers, day laborers, and culturally different peasants (as from Sonora) joined and supported the comuneros of Santa Fé. The content of the struggle was not unlike most of those in Mexico--a fight over the control of the land and resources for self-use as opposed to capitalist use. These peasants, by gaining control over land previously lost to capital and by taking over capitalist investment, showed dramatically how peasant struggle can disrupt accumulation. We see, as pointed out earlier in this chapter, how peasants use their community organizations to maintain and strengthen a way of life that is not necessarily within capitalist plans for society. They have effectively opposed the establishment of a mobile society of independent units of labor power to reaffirm their ties to the community and therefore their potential power and strength.

Campamento Tierra y Libertad (San Luis Potosí)

This set of struggles shows that not all peasant struggles are as successful or as clear-cut about their strategy as those of the coalición or the comuneros of Santa Fé. Including the struggles from the Huasteca Potosina will aid us in putting the peasant movement of Mexico in perspective.

The region of Mexico known as the Huasteca includes the extreme southeast of Tamaulipas, the east of San Luis Potosí (SLP), the northeast of Hidalgo, the extreme northeast of Puebla, and all of the north of Vera Cruz. The Campamento Tierra y Libertad (CTL) has concentrated its activities among peasant communities in the Huasteca Potosina (the northwest and west of the Huasteca in general), although it has spread into northern Vera Cruz as well.

For over 35 years, the peasants of the Huasteca Potosina legally petitioned for extensions to their ejidos and for new centros de población. Through government channels, they also solicited the breaking up of illegal latifundios, the best known being those of Gonzalo N. Santos, Robles Martinez, Gastón Santos Púe, Robert Blagg, and Malcom Niven.

In June 1973, the peasants of the ejido Los Otates, tired of waiting for the solicited lands, invaded the latifundio known as ex-Hacienda de la Mata. The ejidatarios, mainly sons of ejidatarios (con derechos a salvo), constructed thatch lean-tos on the invaded lands, which became known as the Campamento Tierra y Libertad. The army arrived two days later and forcefully removed the peasants. They then regrouped and reorganized the campamento on the ejido Los Otates. The army surrounded the ejido for an entire week, searching for the leaders of the invasion and in general creating a climate of terror for the peasants. However, the military occupation of the zone did not discourage the peasants from going to the various pueblos and ejidos of the zone in search of support and additional peasants who would participate in the struggle.[161] The peasants who founded the CTL printed up a manifesto in flyer form which they distributed throughout the zone surrounding Ciudad Valles. They held a meeting in Ciudad Valles to publicize the land issue, their organization, and their determination to resolve their demands for land. By the end of June 1973, more than 20 groups of solicitors of land from surrounding ejidos became affiliated with the CTL.

In an interview with reporters of Solidaridad, peasants from the CTL described their organization: "The CTL is an organization of independent peasants formed by various groups; the majority are those soliciting lands and others who seek additional land. The goal of the CTL is to get justice for the peasant."[162] The CTL is not one unified group as with the coalición in Sonora or the community of Santa Fé in Michoacán. It is composed (as of 1979) of about 80 individual groups from various communities throughout the Huasteca Potosina. Each group (officially a comité de solicitantes) has from 50 to 600 members.[163]   The individual groups try to keep in contact with one another by sending representatives to their respective assemblies and through their common link in the campamento.   The campamento is run by a consejo de representantes since the assassination of their founder and leader, Chebo Garcia, in June 1976.[164]   Apparently, each community sends a representative to the consejo, which then makes decisions collectively.[165]   The decentralized democratic organization with no apparent leader has given a feeling of security to the peasants.   They feel that since there is not one person that "they" can single out to kill, their organization is less vulnerable.[166]   Another advantage is more direct participation and direction of the political activities by the individual groups.   According to the peasant members of CTL, "the invasions of lands in 1978 were not led by the same people . . . the leaders are always different."[167]   With more participation on the grass-roots level, the risk of having the government coopt or corrupt one or two peasants knowledgeable about the struggle and the legal proceedings is minimized.

The organization is unique, but it appears to suffer from a lack of unity.   Individual communities "affiliated" with the CTL have had little success invading lands.   In fact, as we shall see, repression is the order of the day, and the government ignores the demands of these peasants. The support and solidarity among communities often exists more on paper and in the minds of the consejo de representantes of the CTL than in actuality.   This is in contrast to Michoacán, where thousands of peasants from surrounding communities directly participated in the struggle.   The strength and power of the coalición is also absent.

Most of the peasants, with meager holdings of poor land in the Huasteca Potosina, work as jornaleros for the surrounding latifundistas.   It is significant that they have chosen the struggle for land as opposed to the struggle for traditional worker demands, such as job guarantees or higher wages.   We have detailed information from Tanlajás in the heart of the Huasteca Potosina as to why the jornaleros have chosen to struggle for land.   According to Augustín Avila, in direct interviews with peasants from Tanlajás SLP, the jornaleros tried to start a labor union in 1973.   They had heard over the radio that peasants should receive the minimum wage of 25 pesos a day as opposed to the 10 to 13 they were receiving.   After a series of letter writing during 1973 and part of 1974, the group received instructions from the CTM on how to officially form a union recognized by the CTM. More peasants grew confident and joined the small group, which grew to 110 people. The large landowners who employed the jornaleros in the area reacted to the union by menacing its members with violence and threats of lynching. The patrónes announced that they would not pay the minimum wage. They rounded up a group of peasant union members and took them to the judicial police station in Ciudad Valles to intimidate them. They were released, but only after being detained for one day for no reason. The police advised them that for their own good they should forget about forming a union.[168]

There were other obstacles besides the threats. The landowners began investing in capital goods to do the work of the dissatisfied workers (the secret of the tendency of the organic composition to rise is no secret here--clearly the class struggle). In addition, there was a clear wage hierarchy between the mestizos and the Huastecan-speaking Indians, especially in Tanlajás. The Indians earn half the salary of the mestizos for the same work. This division imposed by capital and based on identifiable cultural and linguistic differences was successful in keeping the class divided over the wage issue at that time.

The peasants from Tanlajás heard of the land invasions all over Mexico and specifically the efforts of the Campamento Tierra y Libertad in nearby Aquismón. The peasants from the tiny union reassessed their situation and began to struggle for land. They joined the CTL, seeking to rectify their isolated situation and hoping to benefit from the strength that a regional organization could offer. The land issue helped break down some of the divisions among the peasant workers. Indians joined mestizos in the struggle for land. During the fifth anniversary of the CTL on June 18, 1978, Huastecan-speaking Indian members of the CTL (municipio unknown) were quoted by reporters as stating the need to unify and confront the government and caciques.[169] In addition, the Huastecan-speaking community, San Pedro, in the municipio San Antonio, has also joined the CTL and the struggle for land.[170]

Alongside its legal solicitations for land, the CTL was involved with a number of land invasions during the 1970s, summarized below:

June 18, 1973	Peasants from the ejidos Los Otates and Las Crucitas, Municipios Aquismón and Valles, invaded property of Malcolm Niven. Driven off the lands by the federal army, they retreated to the ejido Los Otates to form the campamento, vowing to continue the struggle.
April 15, 1974	Campesinos from Ejido Puente del Carmen, Municipio Rio Verde SLP, invaded 61 hectares of irrigated land, property of Ildefonso Turrubiates.
May 6, 1974	Seven hundred peasants from Municipio Ciudad del Maíz invaded latifundio "Maitines," property of Robert Blagg.
May 28, 1974	The groups of solicitantes with derechos a salvo invaded the latifundio "Españita" in Municipio Ciudad Valles, property of the family of Robles Martinez.
July 18, 1974	The solicitantes of Otates and Crucitas from Municipios Aquismón and Valles again took physical possession of the lands of Malcolm Niven.
September 17, 1975	Peasants from Huasteca, Municipio Carrillo Puerto Vera Cruz, invaded lands of the deceased Gil Vorvonio, which they had been soliciting legally for decades.
March 23, 1977	One hundred peasants gained possession of the eighth floor of the SRA, demanding lands legally theirs by presidential order but still not distributed.
August 11, 1977	Peasants from the Nuevo Centro de Población Ejidal Gral. Emiliano Zapata invaded the land "El Estribo" in Municipio Ciudad de Maíz SLP.
October 24, 1977	Peasants from Tampate, Municipio Aquismón SLP, removed landowners

and comerciantes who had invaded their community many years ago.

April 10, 1978   Peasants from the communities La Lima, La Subida, Benito Juarez, Otates, La Caldera, and San Pedro invaded solicited lands simultaneously.

The peasants affiliated with the CTL were successful in gaining presidential resolutions in their favor for the solicited lands for ejidos Otates, Maitines, Puente del Carmen, and Las Crucitas. Peasants who invaded "El Estribo" were removed days later. They never got the desired land. One week after the invasions by peasants from La Lima, La Subida, La Caldera, Benito Juarez, and San Pedro, in 1978, the peasants agreed to leave after given promises by agrarian reform authorities to resolve their agrarian demands.[171] Subsequently, we know that the promises were only promises used to momentarily contain the struggle. In the specific case of La Caldera, by September 1979 nothing had been resolved. In fact, repression has been stepped up on the part of the landowners of the area threatened by the peasant mobilization. On July 23, 1979, an ejidatario from La Caldera was stopped by landowners and ranchers, Cesáreo Gomez and Leoncio Palacios of the Asociación de Ganaderos. They offered him 20,000 pesos for the names of the leaders of the group. When the peasant refused they asked him if he wanted a ride to the town Aquismón, which he also refused. One day later, this ejidatario, Julio Marcial, was found murdered. On July 25, Diego Lugas was found murdered in a nearby ejido, Tanchanaco Aquismón. Both were ejidatarios from La Caldera.[172]

Although the peasants now possess the desired lands in Huasteca Carrillo Puerto, Vera Cruz, a victory in itself, they have been constantly harassed since the original invasion in September 1975. In late 1975 their crops were destroyed by cattle introduced into planted fields by the rancher Molinas and others associated with the Unión Ganadera of Vera Cruz.[173] On February 29, 1979, 13 peasants were kidnapped for ten days. Seven of the 13 were jailed on prefabricated crimes for over seven months in Córdova Vera Cruz. These were efforts to break the strength of the group of peasants who had struggled for the lands in Huasteca.[174] In late August 1979, they were finally released.[175]

The peasants invading the lands of "Espanita" were forcibly removed almost immediately following the occupation. It is significant that these lands, property of the latifundista Robles Martinez, were confiscated by the government in August 1978.[176] Apparently, they were earmarked for peasants loyal to the CNC--peasants who had not agitated for the lands to be redistributed. The peasants from the CTL, those who had done the organizing and work of bringing pressure to bear on the government, were punished by receiving nothing.

Even more discouraging, six years after the presidential resolution awarding 1,920 hectares of the latifundio belonging to Malcom Niven to the ejidatarios of Otates, the peasants still do not have possession of the land. These are the very peasants whose energy was spent organizing the CTL and struggling for Niven's lands. Niven was awarded an amparo through the courts, which, as we have seen in other struggles, prevents the execution of any presidential order until fully investigated through the courts.[177] This means indefinitely. It seems that the strategy used thus far has been unsuccessful in convincing the government to resolve the situation.

To understand why peasant struggles in the Huasteca Potosina have had mixed results requires considerable educated guessing. One can point out what may appear as weaknesses in the class or divergences in strategy from the two other, more successful struggles. Also what is needed is a closer examination of capital's side and the state's role.

In immediate response to the initial mobilization and land invasions, the government sent the army to patrol the zone, creating a tense environment. The army searched the ejido Otates four times looking for the leaders of the movement. Finally, in 1976, although never officially investigated, it appeared that the government played a supportive role in the assassination of Chebo Garcia by guardias blancas employed by latifundistas. Police have threatened CTL members, saying that if they continue to be active in the organization they will be thrown in jail. The rumor was circulated throughout the Huasteca that orders were out to apprehend all members of the CTL. This was designed to create a climate of fear.[178] Periodic jailings of activists for no legal reason have been common.[179] (Those from Vera Cruz, the jailings of Miguel

Martinez and Maclovio Hernandez for 18 months for no legal reason, are examples.)

 Direct repression by the latifundistas via guardias
blancas is not unlike what occurs in many other regions of
Mexico, already discussed in this chapter. In the Huasteca, the menace of lynching is very real in the peasants'
minds today.[180] How much lynching actually goes on today in the Huasteca Potosina I do not know. But it is
clear that when caciques like Gonzalo Santos and his hired
guardias blancas dominated the region with a free hand,
lynching of peasants was not uncommon. Santos was reported to have said, "the Jarrilla tree looks more beautiful
when its branches are decorated with bodies of Huastecan
peasants."[181] (In the Huasteca, the Jarrilla tree is known
as arbol bonito, "beautiful tree.")

 The repression suffered by the campesinos of the
CTL has been justified publicly by announcing over the
radio and in the press that the CTL was linked to a guerrilla terrorist organization. The defamatory campaigns
were started in 1973, soon after the first invasion, to
discourage other peasants from joining the movement. The
state government of San Luis Potosí tried to link the CTL
to the kidnapping of a millionaire in the Huasteca and accused it of having a direct connection with Lucio Cabañas,
the leader (now assassinated) of an armed guerrilla army
in Guerrero.[182] After the assassination of Chebo Garcia
in 1976, the government again began unfairly accusing the
CTL of terrorism. By linking the name of the CTL to the
terrorist organization "Liga 23 de Septiembre," they tried
to justify to local public opinion why none of the assas-
sins were apprehended.[183] The governor of SLP, Guillermo
Fonseca, went so far as to declare to the national press
that the CTL was preparing a plan to destabilize his
state.[184] As already mentioned, red-baiting is a tactic
often used by the government to justify its own terrorism,
jailings, harassment, and other efforts to break up peasant
movements and protect land illegally tied up in capitalist
agricultural enterprises.

 The government of José Lopez Portillo applied the
Echeverría tactic of distributing infamous latifundios to
loyal peasants associated with the CNC as a reward for
docility. The land distribution was a way of rewarding
the quiet peasants and punishing the militants of the CTL.
Whereas in Sonora this strategy backfired because the

peasants were not so tranquil or trusting of the government, only cagey in selecting their strategy of struggle,
in the Huasteca the government tactic has been fairly
effective.

On August 17, 1978, Lopez Portillo announced that
latifundios in the states of Sinaloa, Vera Cruz, Tamaulipas,
and San Luis Potosí would be expropriated and distributed
to peasants before the end of 1978.[185] The secretary of
agrarian reform stated that "only by distributing the
lands held illegally to the peasants could we bring peace
to the countryside--the peace that the nation requires to
produce enough necessities to be self-sufficient."[186] The
fact that San Luis Potosí would be the first state affected
indicates that the peasant struggle of the CTL in the
Huasteca had aroused public attention. Nevertheless, the
designated recipients of the latifundio "El Gargaleote,"
property of Gastón Santos Púe, son of Gonzalo N. Santos,
were peasants affiliated with CNC.[187] These peasants had
never directly participated in struggle. The end result is
that the government had intended to control more peasants
by encouraging their loyalty to the government-controlled
centrales CNC, CCI, etc. The government wanted it clear
that "independent" peasant movements such as the CTL
would not be successful.

Two years after the distribution of "El Gargaleote"
to 133 ejidatarios and their families, they still live in
straw huts, without running water (or purified drinking
water at all), and are in debt to the BANRURAL for 39.6
million pesos for ten years. Originally, the government
had plans to irrigate 1,720 hectares of the peasants' new
land. But as of April 1980, only 612 hectares were
planted in maize, sorghum, and beans. These peasants,
although awarded land, live in poverty. They do not
complain, confident that the government will resolve their
problems, finish the new houses (supplied by the government but left half-constructed), and irrigate the land.[188]

One of the reasons that the government has been
successful in diluting the strength of the peasant struggle
in the Huasteca Potosina is the continued presence of divisions within the class. There are too many complacent
peasants coopted by the government and too many individual communities and ejidos struggling in an "independent"
but unsupported manner. Further, the groups soliciting
land both legally and via invasions are small in number.

These are individual groups of a few hundred peasants, never in the thousands, as occurred in Sonora. Further, the struggle does not involve an entire well-integrated regional community, as in Santa Fé Michoacán. Groups or ejidos struggle as in the municipios of Tanlajás or San Antonio, but the entire pueblo is not directly involved or truly supportive. Divisions within a community, such as townspeople and small comerciantes versus the ejidatarios or minifundistas or jornaleros have not been overcome. Although progress has been made in breaking down the principal division between mestizos and Huastecan Indians, this probably remains the most outstanding obstacle.[189]

The obstacles presented above should not be attributed solely to the weakness of the peasant class. Geographical disadvantages have dampened the potential strength of the struggle as well. The Huasteca Potosina is subtropical and mountainous. Some areas are impassable during the rainy season. It takes days of hiking to reach small pueblos in the Sierra Madre Oriental, as in the municipio of Aquismón. Others can be reached only by four-wheel-drive vehicle.[190] Many of the pueblos are separated from one another by mountains, jungle, and foot trails. Others in the lowlands are more accessible.

The good, arable lands are located in various valleys and are almost exclusively controlled by latifundistas. There are no large expanses of land, as in Sonora, easily identifiable, easily reached, and easily singled out for struggle.

Finally, the level of national support for the struggles of the CTL has been limited. Contingents of peasants from the CTL did come to Mexico City in the early 1970s to protest, to occupy the eighth floor of the agrarian reform building, and to solicit support. The campaign in Distrito Federal was not as effective as that of Santa Fé. The CTL, supported by the leftist press, never had the widespread national coverage of the coalición or the comuneros of Santa Fé. Further, the joining with other, more powerful, peasant organizations and struggles has been limited to the participation of representatives from the Unión Campesino Independiente in Puebla, the Frente Popular de Zacatecas, and the Comité de Campesinos Estudiantes del Istmo in Oaxaca in the CTL's demonstrations in Ciudad Valles and the previously mentioned occupation of the agrarian reform offices in Mexico City in October 1975.[191]

Despite all of this, it is too soon to throw flowers on the grave of the CTL. Peasant struggles change as new experiences are gained and new knowledge of other struggles acquired. These peasants have made a beginning toward autonomously organizing and struggling for land. We can only hope that progress and strength will be gained despite their weakness at the moment.

TOWARD AN UNDERSTANDING OF CONTEMPORARY PEASANT STRUGGLE IN MEXICO

Peasants struggle according to their particular relation with capital. Diversity is the norm in strategy and organization. Peasant actions range from actually taking up arms to legal battles in the courts.

Many communities have organized into different types of groups in attempts to modify the government and private structures that impede their own development. They have formed negotiating groups (grupos de gestión), grupos solidarios, sectors (sectores), unions (uniónes), credit societies, and consumer coops or marketing groups. The results of a field survey of over 94 communities in 1981 showed that such forms of peasant self-organization and struggle had permitted most of these communities to enjoy better living conditions and more control over their resources and productive processes. They have been able to retain more economic surplus to generate their own process of development. There is significant evidence that the via campesina, or peasant self-directed struggle and development, is taking place in Mexico.[192]

On the other hand, as noted throughout this chapter, other peasant communities are still struggling to acquire land or more land or to get back what was robbed from them. Organizing and creating strategy for their struggle, peasants have learned to form large commissions to confront the government when making their demands for land. In this way leaders are more difficult to single out, buy off, coopt, or assassinate. Peasants have tried to stay informed of the particulars of their struggle when engaging in transactions with the government. In the event that a peasant handling some key aspect is murdered, he can be replaced. Peasants have learned through experience in dealing with the government that it is best to lobby for several communities at once, maintaining pressure until each community's problems are resolved. The government has tried to separate petitions, pitting peasant against peasant. Another tactic that has been effective in gaining support for land petitions has been to conduct mass marches or demonstrations in the cities.

When pressure and legalistic strategies lose their effectiveness, peasants will often surround lands but not actually occupy them. Nevertheless, when the political moment is appropriate for an invasion, the peasants will begin to cultivate and live on the land. On the other hand, premature invasions have led to massacre.[193] Peasants have adapted strategy to take land for cultivation, but entering the desired land only when necessary to tend the fields. Sometimes peasants have taken lands and, when removed by force, allowed the "owner" to sow the crops. Later, carefully, so as not to provoke reprisal, they secretly harvest the lands themselves. Other times peasants may vow to stay on the lands continuously, day and night, defending themselves with arms.[194]

Strategy formed by the peasantry has included more than just tactics for land invasions; it included the formation of peasant organizations to unify their communities and circulate their struggle to other sectors of the peasant and working class. Their organizations range from small local asociaciones to a national coordinating committee called the Coordinadora Nacional de Plan de Ayala (CNPA), which boasts membership of some 60 local and regional peasant organizations. Although there are many large peasant organizations in Mexico, varying in influence and constituency, the CNPA is interesting because of the way it was originally formed and the direction in which it is heading.

On August 8, 1979, hundreds of peasants participated in the official ceremony commemorating the hundredth anniversary of the birth of Emiliano Zapata. During the final speeches of the event, held in Cuautla Morelos, peasants expressed their disgust for the agrarian politics of President López Portillo and the secretary of agrarian reform, Antonio Toledo Corro, who were present. The peasants prevented Corro from delivering his speech, yelling in unison: "Death to the bad government," "Long live Emiliano Zapata." This was wholly unpredicted by the government, since the peasants invited were not reputed to be hostile.

Peasant groups gathered in Cuautla for the celebration agreed to meet again to discuss their problems and experiences. A time and place was agreed upon. The result of the First National Encounter of Independent Peasant Organizations held at Milpa Alta D.F. on October 12-14, 1979, was the creation of the CNPA, a national coordination organization which would help promote and unite independent peasant struggles.[195]   By late November 1980, CNPA had sponsored three National Encounters for Independent Peasant Organizations. The national conferences offer a forum for peasants all over Mexico to share experiences, failures, and successes. The encounters have helped circulate the struggle and break down isolation, which is so often the trump card for landlords and state agencies repressing peasants. CNPA has also attempted to begin coordinating efforts of several peasant organizations and to lobby with agrarian reform. It has supported and strengthened local organizations and increased their participation on the national level by sponsoring regional encounters in Michoacán, the highlands of Puebla, Morelos, Nuevo León, the Huasteca, La Laguna, Tuxtepéc, Oaxaca, and Chiapas.[196]   We already saw the very active role CNPA played in the struggle of the comuneros of Santa Fé de la Laguna Michoacán.

I have no crystal ball to predict the future path of CNPA and the coordination of the hundreds of peasant communities struggling for land and their concept of life. No one can say that CNPA will not be taken over by an elite clique, losing touch with the peasant grass-roots movement. Or who is to say tht it will not fade away, failing to continue its efforts to coordinate peasant groups and promote peasant class recomposition and circulation of their struggle. For now, I mention CNPA to show that peasants do formulate strategy at more than just the local level, that peasants do organize politically.

Peasants recognize the need for unity and linkages with each other, which the peasant discussion at the Primer Encuentro shows.[197]   Reviewing the peasant statements from the conferences at the Primer Encuentro, one cannot help but conclude that many peasants throughout Mexico know exactly who their enemy is and what mechanisms of exploitation are used against them. They have clearly identified the linkages between the state and large landowners. "The truth is that I understand that in all parts of the Mexican Republic are the same problems" (peasant

from Tlanepantla, Morelos). Peasants who came to the
Encuentro met with peasants often culturally and ethnically
distinct from distant parts of Mexico. This Encuentro indicated that peasants are not backward, isolated, or
frightened but underlined to share their problems with each
other. They know that linking the struggles is the only
answer.

"It gives me pleasure to see here representatives
from so many organizations, it is a satisfaction and at the
same time an admiration for ourselves [sic]. It is a won-
der for me because it is the first time that I find myself
in a group of peasants from [all over] the Mexican Republic" (peasant from Ejido Emiliano Zapata Unión de Ejidos
en Lucha Campesina, Chiapas). In intervention after intervention, it was clear that peasants were fully cognizant
of the need for unification and a strong peasant organization.

> We propose above all in this assembly that
> things don't remain in the air but as a
> first step we obtain information and second,
> we coordinate or arrive at some agreements
> to continue towards triumph that doesn't
> stop in words but to construct an organiza-
> tion not only in name but as part of the
> concrete struggle (peasant from Zinapám,
> Municipio Santiago Tuxtla, Vera Cruz).

Peasants reject outside manipulation or direction.[198]
The Coalición de Ejidos Colectivos de los Valles Yaqui y
Mayo attended the conference, where they insisted (from
their own experience) that independence from the government-controlled peasant organizations was essential for
success. Independence from political parties was also
brought up by peasants.

> We all know that there exist different polit-
> ical parties that only use us to comply
> with their objectives. They do not look for
> a solution to our problems; they only look
> for a bureaucratic position. . . . I think
> that where we must look for organization
> and solution to the problems that plague
> us is among ourselves (peasant from Villa
> Gonzalez, Municipio de Abasolo Tamaulipas).

Peasants participating in the Primer Encuentro vocalized their disapproval of students trying to dominate the conference. Evidently university students from the UNAM thought they were helping the peasants by writing the conclusions for one session of the conference, "Analysis of the Agrarian Politics of the State." The peasants rejected the "help," arguing that the conclusions were written with the vocabulary and bias of students, not peasants.

> I oppose the approval of these texts that contain a series of words that are not from peasants. . . . I recommend that all those who want to better conditions in the countryside to ally with the peasants but first let us unify ourselves and later we will listen to the university students. We respect and invite them to work with us here at Milpa Alta but I ask them if they would let us, the peasants, go to their student assemblies in the University and speak for the students (peasant from Milpa Alta D.F.).

In another session of the Encuentro, entitled "The Struggle for Land," a delegate from the Communist Party youth group called Central Independiente de Obreros Agrícolas y Campesinas (CIOAC) gave quite a long rhetorical speech seeking membership for the organization. The peasants in the assembly were not convinced by the delegate. They asked where were the peasants that belong to their organization? Why was not a peasant delegate sent to the conference? The peasants ended up throwing him off the panel, unconvinced that CIOAC was a real peasant organization.[199]

On the other hand, when help that furthers their struggle is offered from outside parties, peasants accept. They are not rigid about their autonomous position, only careful not to lose control of the direction of their movement. For example, Juchitán, Oaxaca, a community with a long history of struggle for land, became affiliated with a regional organization in Oaxaca called the COCEI (Coalición Campesinos Estudiantes del Istmo). They had tried unsuccessfully in the past (1974 and 1977) to democratically elect candidates to municipal offices. The elections were fraudulently won by the official PRI candidate and sustained by military occupation of the town. In November

1980, the peasants of Juchitán once again tried to elect their candidates to office. This time the pueblo of Juchitán and COCEI accepted a temporary alliance with the Communist Party (PCM) for election purposes. The electoral law of Mexico states that all ballots and slates of candidates be presented by registered political parties. Since COCEI is an independent regional organization not registered nationally, their candidates, even if elected, could be prevented from holding office. But the PCM was registered nationally and allowed COCEI to use its name.

As it turned out, the elections were again fraudulently manipulated by PRI supporters, who voted five to ten times, having been given ID cards valid for several precincts. Some 3,000 to 6,000 peasants, confident they had really won, occupied the municipal offices of Juchitán, protesting the fraud. The secretary of interior affairs (secretaría de gobernación) was forced by the mass demonstration to recognize "irregularities" in the election and proposed that it be null and void. The COCEI was very clear about the kind of support received from the Communist Party. The alliance was understood to be temporary for the election only. The candidates and the plan de gobierno (political platform) were chosen and written by COCEI. This is a clear case where support was offered and accepted from a national organization but the peasants retained the leadership of the struggle and their autonomy.[200]

Peasants in their many struggles in Mexico have achieved some degree of class recomposition. In the Encuentros held nationally, peasants from very different cultural and ethnic backgrounds have met together to find that their struggles were common struggles. We have seen where predominantly Indian groups have been able to link up with the mestizo peasant groups elsewhere (the comuneros from Michoacán). Peasants who have land and peasants who do not are in some areas able to support and aid each other.

But divisions among the peasant working class remain. For example, the unity of peasant groups and associations is often threatened by the emergence of a caudillo or opportunistic leader who takes advantage of the organization and struggle to better himself at the expense of the others. Armando Bartra narrated a case in Zimatlán Oaxaca where the success of obtaining lands for the community was ruined by the leader, who gave himself

and his friends more and better land, almost excluding
the rest of the pueblo, who had struggled as well. The
caudillo maintained his position by rewarding a small following and then intimidating, threatening, or beating up
any others who protested.[201]

There certainly exist cases where peasant associations are at first successful in their struggle and then
begin to exploit other peasants, imposing work and accumulating at the expense of poorer peasants. Such cases
portray the process of differentiation of the peasantry.
These richer peasants have become petit bourgeois. Although I do not deny the existence of either divisions or
defeats, I have emphasized the other side, where peasants
have succeeded in overcoming divisions.[202]

On the other hand, peasant movements dominated by
a corrupt peasant have overthrown his influence and recomposed the class to a higher level of organization and
struggle. Bartra discusses a group of comuneros in
Nayarít who solicited restitution and title to communal
lands taken by landowners in the late 1960s and early
1970s. The leader, who dominated the group until the
peasant invasions were repressed by the army, was bought
off by the landowners. He abandoned the group to defeat.
However, a few years later, the comuneros reconstituted
the unión, this time with a strong democratic base--no
caudillo. They were able to continue the struggle for
their lands confident that no one individual could be
bought off.[203]

Finally, peasants are organized in their communities on various levels and in a number of forms. The individual organizations run the gamut from small communities to entire ejidos, unions of several ejidos, regional
unions, and national coordinating organizations. At this
time the peasants are not unified regionally or nationally.
There is no doubt that the peasantry is cognizant of the
need to unify into a single front. But they insist on
maintaining their integrity as individual communities. It
is a trade-off that must be worked out by the peasants
and other sectors of the working class.

Peasant goals are to have land, to increase output,
and to continue and improve a peasant way of life. From
what I have learned from three years of investigation in
Mexico, I do not think that peasants on the whole seek to
accumulate for accumulation's sake--expanding the scale
of production and imposing work on others for their benefit.

Nowhere is that clearer than in Michoacán. A community in Michoacán (Santa Clara) not only has successfully maintained its communal lands and forests but has also saved enough to build a shop complete with power equipment. The shop is used by the Indian artisans to create copper craft items and household utensils. This type of creative activity is enjoyed by the comuneros. In addition, it brings needed income for consumption goods.

Production in their copper shop is not intended to lead to even more production--more profit--expansion. It is intended to satisfy their needs as they define them. In fact, they have set a goal of working only 200 days a year in the shop even though they stand to earn 500 pesos (1981 pesos) a day there. The shop is for enjoyment and satisfaction, not for maximizing profits. These comuneros are clearly within the terrain of self-valorization, not capitalist accumulation. On one occasion, Gustavo Esteva personally visited these peasants and found the shop, with all its modern equipment, idle. He inquired as to the whereabouts of the comuneros. A peasant replied that they were in the forests enjoying themselves (diviertiendose). When would they return? When they want to come back-- a week or two or three.[204]

NOTES

1. Arturo Warman, Y Venimos a Contradecir: Los Campesinos de Morelos y el Estado Nacional (Mexico: CISINAH, Ediciones de la Casa Chata, 1976), p. 287.

2. See discussion on reserve army, peasants, and reproduction of labor power in Chapter 3.

3. Teresa Rendón, "Desarrollo Agrícola y Absorción de Mano de Obra en Mexico," Narxhí-Nandhá (May 1977): 26-35.

4. Armando Bartra, "Seis Años de Lucha Campesina," Investigación Económica 3 (July-September 1977):73.

5. Punto Crítico, February 1980, p. 38, and CIOAC representative quoted in Memoria del Primer Encuentro Nacional de Organizaciones Campesinas Independientes, Proceedings of Peasant Conference held in Milpa Alta, D.F., October 12-14, 1979 (Mexico: Universidad Autonomía de Guerrero, 1979).

6. Punto Crítico, February 1980, p. 38.

7. Punto Crítico, August 1978, p. 25.

8. Eckart Boege, "Acerca de la Organización Laboral y Política de los Trabajadores Asalariados del Campo," Revista Mexicana de Sociología (July–September 1977):930.

9. Jorge Morett, "El Proletariado Agrícola en la Region de Zamora Michoacán," Cuadernos Agrarios 6 (May 1978):100.

10. Ernest Feder, El Imperialismo Fresa (Mexico: Editorial Campesina, 1977), p. 112.

11. Ibid., p. 110.

12. See statements by peasants from the peasant organization Bloque Campesino del Estado de Chipas in Primer Encuentro, pp. 75–77.

13. We will discuss Chipas and peasant struggle when we look at disruption of capital later in the chapter.

14. Study by CNC on the agricultural crisis (1978), quoted in Uno Mas Uno, May 20, 1980.

15. See Armando Bartra, "Seis Años," for an excellent summary of peasant struggles, giving a good idea of just how pervasive they are.

16. See bibliography of Marta Romer, "La Comunidad Rural," October 1980. Unpublished.

17. Henri Lefevre, quoted by Gustavo Esteva in "Lo Indígena y lo Campesino: Supervivencia del Pasado o Simiente del Proyecto Futuro," I.N.I. 30 Años Después, special issue of Mexico Indígena (December 1978):269.

18. Ibid.

19. Quoted from the cover of Narxhí-Nandhá, Journal of Peasant Economy.

20. Esteva, "Lo Indígena y lo Campesino," p. 269.

21. Social anthropologists have dedicated the better part of this century to documenting and describing the heterogeneous Indian and peasant communities in Mexico. To suggest a bibliography here would be a project well beyond the scope of this work.

22. Esteva, "Lo Indígena y lo Campesino," pp. 265–67.

23. See John Womack, Zapata and the Mexican Revolution (Chicago: University of Chicago Press, 1969), for what happened to the communidades before the revolution in 1910. See also the chapter on ejidos for a synopsis of the agrarian reform and reconstitution of the ejidos in Centro de Investigaciónes Agrarias, Estructura Agraria y Desarrollo Agrícola en México (Mexico: Fondo de Cultura Económica, 1974).

24. For a description of the new laws governing ejidos and the duties of the comisariados, see Gustavo Gordillo, "Estado y Sistema Ejidal," Cuadernos Políticos 21 (July–September 1979):23.

25. Cargos are discussed more fully in subsequent pages.

26. Esteva, La Batalla, p. 153.

27. Warman, Y Venimos, p. 316.

28. See David Ronfeldt, Atencingo: The Politics of Agrarian Struggle in a Mexico Ejido (Stanford: Stanford University Press, 1973), for a good account of struggles by ejidatarios to democratically control their internal affairs.

29. Warman, Y Venimos, p. 324.

30. Guillermo de la Peña, Herederos de Promesas Agricultura: Política y Ritual en los Altos de Morelos (Ediciónes de la Casa Chata, 1981), p. 118.

31. Gordillo also mentions the ability to respond as a "bloque" even when certain individual interests may be perturbed by the group action. Gordillo, "Estado y Sistema Ejida," p. 17.

32. Warman, Y Venimos, p. 323.

33. The formula is one-third federal, one-third state, one-third local for financing of construction. All labor is local and unwaged. Warman, Y Venimos, p. 319.

34. For example, we know in concrete cases that the presidente municipal can call in troops to maintain order or to remove peasants from their own lands or support local ganaderos or finceros who invade peasant lands.

35. Testimony of peasant from Matxoja, Tila Chiapas, quoted in Primer Encuentro, p. 85.

36. Marta Romer, "La Comunidad Rural," p. 34.

37. Lorena Paz Paredes and Julio Moguel, Santa Gertrudis: Testimonios de una Lucha Campesina (Mexico: ERA, 1979), p. 103.

38. Miguel Szekely, "La Organización Colectiva para la Producción Rural," Comercio Exterior 27 (December 1977): 1475-83.

39. "Carta Abierta al Presidente Lic. José Lopez Portillo," Uno Mas Uno, February 1980.

40. It is common knowledge that the government inflates the price of goods to its clients by as much as 50 percent.

41. Szekely, "La Organización Colectiva," p. 1483.

42. Unión de Ejidos de la Costa de Jalisco, quoted in Uno Mas Uno, February 7, 1980.

43. Uno Mas Uno, February 11, 1980.

44. Punto Crítico, March 1980, p. 25.

45. See Evon Vogt, The Zincantecos of Mexico (New York: Holt, Rinehart and Winston, 1970), pp. 19–24, for an explanation.

46. Armando Bartra, Notas Sobre la Cuestión Campesina (México 1970–1976) (Mexico: Editorial Macehual, 1979), pp. 83–84.

47. Guillermo de la Peña, Herederos de Promesas, p. 118.

48. Eric Villanueva Mukul, "La Lucha de la Comunidad de Chemax," Yucatán História y Economía (September–October 1978):33–51.

49. Ibid., p. 45.

50. Memoria del Primer Encuentro Nacional de Organizaciones Campesinas Independientes (Mexico: Universidad Autonoma de Guerrero, 1979), 103–5.

51. Primer Encuentro, pp. 103–5.

52. See Paz Paredes and Moguel, Santa Gertrudis.

53. Ibid., pp. 88–89.

54. Ibid., p. 104.

55. Summarized in ibid., p. 105.

56. Ruben Jaramillo, leader of the Jaramillistas, is somewhat of a modern hero to the peasantry. He organized and led peasants in struggle for over 20 years. See Renato Ravelo, Los Jaramillistas (Mexico: Editorial Nuestro Tiempo, 1978); Ruben Jaramillo and Froylan C. Manjarrez, Autobiografía y Asesinato (Mexico: Editorial Nuestro Tiempo, 1967); and Francisco Gómez Jara, El Movimiento Campesino en México (Mexico: Editorial Campesina, 1970), pp. 203–5.

57. I am not saying that peasant struggles in Morelos stopped in 1962. Far from it; today some of the largest mobilizations are in Morelos, as I shall point out later in the chapter.

58. Gómez Jara, El Movimiento, pp. 204–5.

59. Ravelo, Los Jaramillistas, p. 96.

60. Mercedes Olivera, "Sobre la Explotación y Opresión de las Mujeres 'Acasilladas en Chiapas," Cuadernos Agrarios 9 (September 1979):46.

61. Punto Crítico, June 1980.

62. Punto Crítico, February 1978, p. 30.

63. Bartra, "Seis Años," p. 166.

64. Antonio Garcia de León, "Mapachismo y Poder Político en el Campo Chiapaneco: 1914–1977," Cuadernos Agrarios 5 (September 1977):64–65.

65. Uno Mas Uno, August 8, 1979.
66. Uno Mas Uno, September 20, 1979.
67. Uno Mas Uno, August 7, 1979.
68. Ricardo del Muro, Uno Mas Uno, October 12, 1979.
69. Punto Crítico, April 25, 1980. Information is sketchy about the zones in Chiapas virtually occupied by the army. I was told by a professor of anthropology that he was told by the army not to enter Venustiano Carranza for a field investigation. The professor took the army at their word and left. Interview with [name withheld for obvious reasons], November 1980.
70. Punto Crítico, July 1980, p. 4.
71. Punto Crítico, September 25, 1979, p. 24.
72. Ibid., p. 25.
73. Ibid.
74. Punto Crítico, May 1978, pp. 22-23.
75. See my newspaper file on Golonchán.
76. See Guillermo Bonfil, "Los Indios y el Petróleo," Uno Mas Uno, July 29, 1979.
77. Uno Mas Uno, February 20, 1979.
78. Uno Mas Uno, February 21, 1979.
79. Uno Mas Uno, February 14, 1980.
80. Uno Mas Uno, July 30, 1979.
81. "Inflation has been permanent. There is no local control over prices of basic consumer goods. Subsistence goods are subject to constant increase and speculation." SAHOP, "La Explotación Petrolera y su Impacto en las Comunidades Rurales de Vera Cruz," quoted in Uno Mas Uno, July 30, 1979.
82. Uno Mas Uno, July 31, 1980.
83. Uno Mas Uno, March 17, 1980.
84. For more detail on the peasant insurrections and government repression in Hidalgo, see the following articles in Uno Mas Uno: "Secuestran y Encarcelan Campesinos en la Huasteca Hidalgüense," May 19, 1979; "Libertad a Benito Hernandez," May 23, 1979; "Alto a la Represión en la Huasteca Hidalgüense," May 24, 1979; "Asesinaron a Marta Hernandez Lider de CAM en Huejutla," May 24, 1979; "Denuncian Represiónes Campesinos de la Huasteca Hidalgüense," May 25, 1979; "Encarcelan a 3 Campesinos por Supuesto Robo en Hidalgo," June 1, 1979; Arturo Warman, "Huejutla Hidalgo: Los Sin Razón," June 3, 1979; and Carmen Lira, "Represión a Indígenas en la Huasteca: State of Siege en 11 Municipios," June 4, 1979.

85. Sol de Mexico, July 17, 1979.
86. José Martinez, Uno Mas Uno, March 4, 1980.
87. Ibid.
88. Enrique Astorga and Clarisa Hardy, Organización Lucha y Dependencia: La Unión de Ejidas Emiliano
Zapata (Mexico: Editorial Nueva Imagen, 1978), pp. 162-65.
89. Ibid., p. 168.
90. Ibid., p. 177.
91. Ibid., p. 183.
92. Fondo de Cultura Campesina, "Informe de
Trabajo de Campo y del Estudio Teórico del Sector Rural,"
Spring 1981. Unpublished field study.
93. Ibid.
94. CIDE, Estructura Agraria y Desarrollo Agrícola
en Mexico, p. 857.
95. Ibid., pp. 786, 819, 823.
96. BANRURAL, "Programa de Participación Inmediata
del Sector Agropecurio en el Sistema Alimentario Mexicano,"
April 1980. Unpublished.
97. Arturo Warman, Los Campesinos Hijos Predilectos
del Regimen (Mexico: Editorial Nuestro Tiempo, 1972), p.
83.
98. Ibid.
99. Bartra, "Seis Años," p. 181.
100. Ibid., p. 160.
101. José Gamboa, "El Crédito en el Proceso de Restructuración de la Zona Henequenera Yucateca," Estudios
Políticos 4 (July-September 1978):58.
102. It was common knowledge that the ejidatarios
would swell the payrolls of the bank with children, old
people, dead people, anyone they could, to get more money.
These acts were of course unrelated to productivity. Ibid.,
p. 66.
103. Jesús Jaurequi et al., TABAMEX, Un Caso de
Integración Vertical de la Agricultura (Mexico: Editorial
Nueva Imagen, 1980), p. 146.
104. Ibid., p. 167.
105. Ibid., p. 170.
106. Manuel Aguilera, director of TABAMEX, quoted
in Narxhí-Nandhá 4/5 (June 1977):68-69.
107. Bartra, "Seis Años," p. 181.
108. Unión de Comuneros Emiliano Zapata, "El
Comunero," Michoacán, 1980. Mimeograph.
109. Diario del Yaqui, Ciudad Obregon, Sonora,
September 18, 1979.

110. Rubén Jiminez Ricardez, "Movimiento Campesino en Sonora," Cuadernos Políticos 7 (January-March 1976):77.

111. José Ayala, "La Devaluación Antecedentes Económicos y Políticos," Cuadernos Políticos 11 (January-March 1977):37-38.

112. Steven E. Sanderson, Agrarian Populism and the Mexican State: The Struggle for Land in Sonora (Berkeley: University of California Press, 1981).

113. Jiminez Ricardez, "Movimiento Campesino en Sonora," p. 68.

114. Gustavo Gordillo, Uno Mas Uno, April 16, 1979.

115. Uno Mas Uno, November 24, 1979.

116. Jiminez Ricardez, "Movimiento Campesino en Sonora," p. 70.

117. Ibid., p. 77.

118. My impressions from reviewing all the issues of El Imparcial, the daily newspaper from Hermosillo Sonora, November 2, 1976 to November 29, 1976.

119. Gustavo Gordillo, Uno Mas Uno, April 16, 1979.

120. Ibid.

121. Gustavo Gordillo, Uno Mas Uno, May 4, 1980.

122. Communication with Gustavo Esteva, May 19, 1981.

123. Coalición de Ejidos de los Valles del Yaqui y Mayo, En Defensa del Ejido (Mexico: Centro de Estudios Económicos y Sociales del Tercer Mundo, A.C., 1982), p. 42.

124. Ibid., p. 33.

125. Ibid., p. 42.

126. Uno Mas Uno, November 27, 1979.

127. Uno Mas Uno, April 16, 1979.

128. El Imparcial, Hermosillo, Sonora, November 24, 1976.

129. Camara Nacional de Comercio, quoted in El Imparcial, Hermosillo, Sonora, November 25, 1976.

130. Ibid.

131. Uno Mas Uno, September 26, 1979.

132. Uno Mas Uno, October 9, 1979.

133. Primer Encuentro, p. 116.

134. Gustavo Gordillo, "Lucha de los Ejidos Colectivos," Uno Mas Uno, May 4, 1980.

135. Uno Mas Uno, November 21, 1979.

136. Primer Encuentro, p. 132.

137. Uno Mas Uno, November 21, 1979.

138. Uno Mas Uno, November 25, 1979.

139. Ibid.

140. Gustavo Esteva, "Los Comuneros de Santa Fé," La Cultura en Mexico, supplement of Siempre! 945 (April 30, 1980):II-IV. For more history on Santa Fé, see statements by Efrén Capiz in Uno Mas Uno, December 23, 1979.

141. Esteva, "Los Comuneros de Santa Fé," p. 2.

142. Ibid.

143. Uno Mas Uno, December 13, 1979.

144. Uno Mas Uno, December 9, 1979.

145. Esteva, "Los Comuneros de Santa Fé," p. 4.

146. Uno Mas Uno, December 19, 1979.

147. Primer Encuentro, p. 80.

148. Uno Mas Uno, November 23, 1979.

149. Esteva, "Los Comuneros de Santa Fé," p. 4.

150. Uno Mas Uno, December 2, 1979.

151. Uno Mas Uno, November 30, 1979.

152. Uno Mas Uno, December 5, 1979.

153. The situation in Michoacán today is very reminiscent of the one faced by the peasants in Ireland in the mid-nineteenth century. The landowners, as discussed in Chapter 1, displaced the peasants with cattle, robbing them of their lands and therefore their lives.

154. Uno Mas Uno, December 19, 1979.

155. Esteva, "Los Comuneros de Santa Fé," p. 5.

156. Ibid.

157. The Coalición de Ejidos Colectivos de los Valles Yaqui y Mayo, aware of the struggle in Michoacán, also made public announcements of solidarity.

158. See the following section on the struggle in San Luis Potisí.

159. Uno Mas Uno, July 31, 1980.

160. Campesino from Santa Fé, interviewed by Esteva and quoted in "Los Comuneros de Santa Fé," p. 5.

161. Punto Crítico, July 1976, p. 19.

162. "Solo Organizados Se Puede Hacer Algo," Solidaridad 185 (August 1978):35.

163. Interview with Augustín Avila, March 1978, Colegio de Mexico, who conducted fieldwork with the CTL from 1976 to 1978.

164. Punto Crítico, August 9, 1976.

165. Punto Crítico, April 15, 1977.

166. "Solo Organizados Se Puede Hacer Algo," p. 36.

167. Ibid.

168. Interviews with Augustín Avila, March 1978, at the Colegio de Mexico.

169. Punto Crítico, July 1978.

170. Punto Crítico, July 1976, p. 21.

171. Punto Crítico, May 1978.

172. Voces del Campo 1 (September 1979):10–11.

173. Ibid., p. 13.

174. Primer Congreso Nacional Sobre Problemas Agrarios, Chilpancingo Guerrero, March 2–17, 1979. Mimeograph.

175. Voces del Campo, p. 13.

176. Excelsior, August 18, 1978.

177. Ricardo del Muro, Uno Mas Uno, April 18, 1980.

178. Punto Crítico, July 9, 1976, p. 26.

179. Ibid.

180. Interviews with Augustín Avila, March 1978.

181. Punto Crítico, July 1976, p. 13.

182. Punto Crítico, June and July 1973.

183. Punto Crítico, August 9, 1976.

184. Excelsior, August 18, 1978.

185. Ibid.

186. Ibid.

187. El Universal, August 19, 1978.

188. Ricardo del Muro, interviews with peasants of Nuevo Ahaucatitla, San Luis Potosí, Uno Mas Uno, April 17, 1980.

189. Anthropologists working in the area, such as Brian Stross from the University of Texas, have long noted the hostility between ethnic groups in the Huasteca Potosina.

190. Personal experience in the Huasteca on and off in the years of 1971 to 1974.

191. Punto Crítico, July 1976, p. 17.

192. Fondo de Cultura Campesina, "Informe del Trabajo de Campo y del Estudio Teórico del Sector Rural" (Mexico, 1981). Unpublished.

193. Some Tzeltzal Indian peasants in Chiapas were badly advised and manipulated by the Partido Socialista de los Trabajadores (PST). The PST proposed that the peasants invade the finca Golonchán when the terrain of struggle had not been properly analyzed or prepared. The result was a massacre by police, federal soldiers, and finceros of 12 peasants, wounding some 19 others. Uno Mas Uno, June 14, 1980; July 4, 1980.

194. Bartra, Notas Sobre, p. 78.

195. Punto Crítico, February 1980, p. 40.

196. Punto Crítico, December 1980, p. 22.

197. As far as I know this was the only Encuentro recorded in its entirety. The transcript was lent to me. It

is not readily available. In fact, I spoke with the organization responsible for recording and typing the sessions (CLETA) to try and obtain a copy. They were not willing to sell or give me a copy.

198. Of course, peasants are manipulated by outsiders in some communities, but the most successful struggles are generally autonomous.

199. Primer Encuentro, pp. 108–10.

200. Punto Crítico, December 1980, pp. 3–5.

201. Bartra, Notas Sobre, p. 80.

202. I would hope that someone will investigate, from the viewpoint of the peasants, their defeats. Information about failure is just as useful for strategy as information about success.

203. Bartra, Notas Sobre, p. 77.

204. Interview with Gustavo Esteva, November 1981.

5

CONCLUSION

> The peasant movement despite its intensity
> achieved in the last years still is separated
> from workers' struggle. That is the root
> of its weakness and of the danger that it
> disperses in outbreaks more or less violent
> but without an organized structure nor
> political line to give it coherence.[1]

Statements like these still abound in Mexico within
the press, the academic community, and among some leftist
political parties.[2] This attitude condemns peasant struggles to failure because they are not led by the urban proletariat or infused with rhetoric from political parties.
This position is drawn from the orthodox Marxist perspective, summarized in Chapter 1. One of the principal moti-
vations for this work was to expose where these ideas
originated, how they translate into policy affecting the
peasantry, and to analyze them within the social capital
perspective, which is more useful in analyzing the contemporary Mexican peasant reality.

In the review of the orthodox Marxist literature,
several propositions were challenged in light of Mexican
reality. We discussed proletarianization, concluding that
in Mexico it has not completely occurred everywhere.
There is some doubt that it is a one-way process (from
peasant to proletariat). There exists a tendency for ex-
peasants (supposed proletarians) to try and go back to the
land to reaffirm their peasant status and livelihood. The
issue of a peasant mode of production and the whole set of
arguments surrounding articulation of modes of production
was criticized for ignoring peasant class struggle and for

diverting needed analytical energy away from the study of peasant class actions toward endless categorization of production structures and theories of transition.

In the review of the literature, the wage category and ownership of the means of production (like land) were shown to be used by some Marxists to deny working-class status of the peasantry. It is necessary to see behind the myriad production structures that confuse students into labeling the peasantry as precapitalist, semiproletariat, or petit bourgeois. Peasants work for capital.

Unwaged peasants work for capital, reproducing labor power in the home and on the land to be used when needed in the reserve army. The reserve army functions today in Mexico in many ways that differ from Marx's times. The substitution effect of the reserve army works through a hierarchy of wages. The peasant reserve affects only the lowest rungs and has limited impact, if any, further up the hierarchy. The reserve effect is much less important today than in times of extensive capitalist expansion with low organic composition of capital. Linkages exist among unwaged peasant production, the reproduction of labor power, and the circuits of capital.[3] In addition to the function of producing labor power for the reserve army, unwaged peasants work for capital in building infrastructures or providing services.

Where peasants apparently relate with merchant capital only within the sphere of exchange, capitalist-worker relationships exist within the sphere of production, hidden by the sale of commodities. Other peasants involved in contracts with private or public industrial and commercial capital are actually in a modern-day putting-out system, supplying raw materials and food in exchange for subsistence goods. Each year their contract locks them into an arrangement in order to survive in which they must cultivate and sell crops to the commercial or industrial institution advancing the credit. Not only is the credit used for productive inputs, it is often used for consumption. The credit is really a wage for work done for the capitalist. Furthermore, the bank, industry, or public agency providing the credit interferes directly in the production process. Behind the petit bourgeois mask lies the peasants' true working-class character, despite the lack of a wage or the presence of credits. The fundamental conclusion drawn from this examination of peasant reality in Mexico is that the peasantry forms a sector of the working class-in-itself.

Mao recognized that the peasantry (including his category of semiproletariat) formed a class-in-itself. Mao realized that peasants rebelled against their oppressed situation. Even Engels reported their explosive nature. But none of the Marxist thinkers, including today's structuralists or mode-of-production analysts, would admit that the peasantry forms part of a working class-for-itself. All remained faithful to Lenin's writings, according to which the peasantry must be taught, led, and educated by the urban industrial proletariat—still the working class. The characterization of the peasantry presented here clashes with the orthodox Marxist tradition, which portrayed peasant production and society as individual and isolated, with no bonds of community, no political organization. Chapter 4 introduced some of the cohesive, unifying aspects of the peasant community in Mexico. Different forms of communal or cooperative labor still persist today. We looked at some of the social, political, and cultural organizations that can bind the peasantry into a community—a community capable of uniting in struggle. Further, concrete evidence from contemporary peasant struggles was presented in Chapter 4, illustrating that peasants in Mexico form a sector of the working class-for-itself.

Peasants are struggling against capital. Their struggle is revolutionary because they want to extract themselves from exchange-value and to create space for their own self-valorizing activities instead of capitalist-valorizing activities. Peasants are already beginning to organize society themselves. They do not look to "socialists" or workers to direct the process or to tell them what to do. Conversely, workers do not need peasants interfering with their struggle, either. The type of society they may organize, peasant society, may not conform to what socialists envision. But is that to say it is petit bourgeois or not revolutionary? Does it mean that if peasants do not follow a socialist blueprint for organization then we should refuse to admit the constructive potential of their movement? An alliance between urban workers and peasant workers is essential, but upon what grounds and at what costs to the respective movements? This certainly opens up ground for further analysis of the linkages between conventional worker struggles and those of the peasantry. Although peasants strive to achieve autonomy or independence from government financial institutions (BANRURAL, ANAGSA), government political organizations (CNC, CCI, or PRI), or other social groups (students, leftist parties) that seek to dominate and manage, peasants know there must be linkages with the struggles of other sectors of the working class to be effective. They also know they must struggle for unification within the peasant sector.

Some peasant communities are struggling to maintain and preserve their society (see Chapter 4). These peasants have embarked on paths of self-development alternative to traditional concepts of development. The Ejidos Colectivos de los Valles Yaqui y Mayo provide us a spectacular example of a community on a course of autonomy from capital despite constant capitalist attack. They are creating space for peasant self-development. The problem with evaluating or discussing the vía campesina is time. Without the perspective of time we cannot even broach the subject of what the peasants envision. Peasants are only in the preliminary stages of social revolution: trying to regain the means of production (or hold onto them), to take the resources away from capital, and to organize and produce themselves. It is difficult if not impossible to predict what will come of the vía campesina. However, just because the scene of peasant self-valorization has not been completely revealed is no justification for denying a priori the possibility of that revelation. We know that as struggle continues, peasants gain experience, knowledge, and ideas. The struggle itself transforms and changes them, preparing the path for postcapitalist development.

NOTES

1. Punto Crítico, January 1979, p. 46.
2. See "La Tesis Políticas del P.C.M." (Partido Comunista Mexicano), Machete, November 1980, pp. 44-45.
3. See the first section of Chapter 4.

BIBLIOGRAPHY

Althusser, Louis, and Etienne Balibar. Reading Capital. London: New Left Books, 1977.

Astorga, Enrique, and Clarisa Hardy. Organización Lucha y Dependencia: La Unión de Ejidos Emiliano Zapata. Mexico: Editorial Nueva Imagen, 1978.

Autonomía Post Political Politics, vol. 3. New York: Semiotext (e) Inc., 1980.

Ayala, José. "La Devaluación Antecedentes Económicos y Políticos." Cuadernos Políticos 11 (January-March 1977).

Baldi, Guido. "Theses on Mass Worker and Social Capital." Radical America 6 (May-June 1972):3-21.

BANRURAL. "Programa de Participación Inmediata del Sector Agropecuario en el Sistema Alimentario Mexicano." Mexico, April 1980. Mimeograph.

Barjau, Luís. "Yucatán Trabajo y Explotación Económica." In Capitalismo y Campesinado en México. Edited by Rodolfo Stavenhagen, pp. 163-96. Mexico: CISINAH, 1976.

Bartra, Armando. La Explotación del Trabajo Campesino por el Capital. Mexico: Editorial Macehual, 1979.

_____. Notas Sobre la Cuestión Campesina (Mexico 1970-1976). Mexico: Editorial Macehual, 1979.

_____. "Seis Años de Lucha Campesina." Investigación Económica 3 (July-September 1977):157-209.

Bartra, Roger. Estructura Agraria y Clases Sociales en Mexico. Mexico: Ediciones ERA, 1974.

Bell, Peter. "Notes on the History of the Perspective." New York, n.d. Mimeograph.

Blackstock, Paul W., and Bert F. Hoselitz, eds. The Russian Menace to Europe: A Collection of Articles, Speeches, Letters and News Dispatches. By Karl Marx and Friedrich Engels. Glencoe, Ill.: Free Press, 1952.

Boege, Eckart. "Acerca de la Organización Laboral y Política de los Trabajadores Asalariados del Campo." Revista Mexicana de Sociología (July–September 1977).

Bologna, Sergio. "The Tribe of Moles: Class Composition and the Party System in Italy." In Working Class Autonomy and the Crisis, pp. 67–91. London: Red Notes and CSE Books, 1979.

Centro de Investigaciones Agrarias. Estructura Agraria y Desarrollo Agrícola en México. Mexico: Fondo de Cultura Económica, 1974.

Cleaver, Harry. "Food, Famine and the International Crisis." Zerowork 2 (Fall 1977):7–70.

_____. "The Internationalization of Capital and the Mode of Production in Agriculture." Economic and Political Weekly, March 27, 1976, pp. A2–16.

_____. "Malaria, the Politics of Public Health and the International Crisis." Review of Radical Political Economics 9 (Spring 1977):81–103.

_____. Reading Capital Politically. Austin: University of Texas Press, 1979.

Comité Promotor de Investigaciones para el Desarrollo Rural (COPIDER). Narxhí-Nandhá: Revista de Economía Campesina 1–10 (March 1977–September 1978).

Cornforth, Maurice. Historical Materialism. New York: International Publishers, 1977.

Dalla Costa, Mariarosa, and Selma James. The Power of Women and the Subversion of the Community. Bristol, England: Falling Wall Press, 1972.

de Gortari, Ludka, and José del Val. "Mujer Campesina, Parentesco y Explotación." Nueva Antropología 8 (April 1977):5-16.

de la Peña, Guillermo. Herederos de Promesas Agricultura: Política y Ritual en los Altos de Morelos. Mexico: Ediciones de la Casa Chata, 1981.

de la Peña, Sergio, et al. Polémica Sobre las Clases Sociales en el Campo Mexicano. Mexico: Editorial Macehual, Cuadernos Agrarios and Instituto de Investigaciónes Sociales, 1979.

Díaz Polanco, Hector. "Estructura de Clases y Comercialización: Un Caso Mexicano." In Marcado y Dependencia, edited by Ursula Oswald. Mexico: Editorial Nueva Imagen, 1979.

Duggett, Michael. "Marx on Peasants." The Journal of Peasant Studies 2 (January 1975):159-81.

Dunayevskaya, Raya. Marxism and Freedom. London: Pluto Press, 1975.

Engels, Friedrich. AntiDuhring. New York: International Publishers, 1970.

_____. The Peasant War in Germany, edited by Leonard Krieger. Chicago: University of Chicago Press, 1967.

_____. "Speech at the Graveside of Karl Marx." In The Marx-Engels Reader, edited by Robert Tucker, pp. 603-4. New York: Norton, 1972.

Espinosa, Gisela, and Roberto Sandoval. "Capital Industrial y Explotación Campesina en Oacalco Morelos." Cuadernos Agrarios 4 (October-December 1976):37-55.

Esteva, Gustavo. La Batalla en el Mexico Rural. Mexico: Siglo XXI, 1980.

_____. "Los Comuneros de Santa Fé." La Cultura en Mexico, supplement of Siempre! 945 (April 30, 1980): II-V.

_____. "La Economía Campesina Actual como Opción de Desarrollo." Investigación Económica 38 (January–March 1979):223–46.

_____. "La Experiencia de la Intervención Estatal Reguladora en la Comercialización Agropecuaria de 1970 a 1976." In Mercado y Dependencia, edited by Ursula Oswald, pp. 207–46. Mexico: Editorial Nueva Imagen, 1979.

_____. "Lo Indígena y lo Campesino: Supervivencia del Pasado o Simiente del Proyecto Futuro." I.N.I. 30 Añnos Después, special issue of Mexico Indigena (December 1978):260–76.

Feder, Ernest. "Campesinistas y Descampesinistas: Tres Enfoques Divergentes (No Incompatibles) Sobre la Destrucción del Campesinado." Comercio Exterior 27 (December 1977):1439–46.

_____. El Imperialismo Fresa. Mexico: Editorial Campesina, 1977.

_____. The Rape of the Peasantry. Garden City, N.Y.: Doubleday, 1971.

Fondo de Cultura Campesina. "Informe del Trabajo de Campo y del Estudio Teórico del Sector Rural." Mexico, 1981. Unpublished.

Frank, André Gunder. "Not Feudalism––Capitalism." Monthly Review (December 1963):468–78.

Gamboa, José J. "El Crédito en el Proceso de Restructuración de la Zona Henequenera Yucateca." Estudios Políticos 4 (July–September 1978):55–102.

García de León, Antonio. "Mapachismo y Poder Político en el Campo Chiapaneco: 1914–1977." Cuadernos Agrarios 5 (September 1977):57–66.

Gómez Jara, Francisco. "La Lucha por la Tierra Debe Convertirse en Lucha contra el Capital." Críticas de la Economía Política 5 (October–December 1977):110–77.

_____. El Movimiento Campesino en México. Mexico: Editorial Campesina, 1970.

Gonzalez Navarro, Moises. La Confederación Nacional Campesina. Mexico: B. Costa-Amic, 1968.

Gonzalez Pecheco, Cuauhtemoc. Organización Campesina y Lucha de Clases: La Confederación Nacional Campesina. Mexico: Instituto de Investigaciónes Económicas, UNAM, n.d.

Gordillo, Gustavo. "Estado y Sistema Ejidal." Cuadernos Políticos 21 (July–September 1979):7–24.

_____. "El Núcleo Estatal en el Medio Rural: Algunas Consideraciones Sobre el Crédito Agrícola en México." Investigaciones Económica 147 (January–March 1979): 199–221.

Gurley, John G. Challengers to Capitalism. San Francisco: San Francisco Book Company, 1976.

Guzman, Rosario. "Informe del XVIII Congreso Agrario Nacional Ordinario de la Central Campesina Independiente, 18–21 January 1981." Mexico, 1981. Unpublished.

Harnecker, Marta. Los Conceptos Elementales del Materialismo Histórico. Mexico: Siglo XXI, 1977.

Harris, Richard. "Marxism and the Agrarian Question in Latin America." Latin American Perspectives 5 (Fall 1978):2–26.

James, C. L. R. State Capitalism and World Revolution. Detroit: Facing Reality Publishing Committee, 1950.

James, Selma. Sex, Race and Class. Bristol, England: Falling Wall Press, 1975.

_____. "Wageless of the World." In All Work and No Pay: Women, Housework and the Wages Due, edited by Wendy Edmond and Suzie Fleming, pp. 25–34. Bristol, England: Falling Wall Press, 1975.

Jaramillo, Ruben, and Froylan C. Manjarrez. Autobio-
    grafía y Asesinato. Mexico: Editorial Nuestro Tiempo,
    1967.

Jauegui, Jesús, et al. TABAMEX, Un Caso de Integración
    Vertical de la Agricultura. Mexico: Editorial Nueva
    Imagen, 1980.

Jiminez Ricardez, Rubén. "Movimiento Campesino en
    Sonora." Cuadernos Políticos 7 (January–March 1976):
    67–78.

Laclau, Ernesto. "Feudalism and Capitalism in Latin
    America." New Left Review 67 (May–June 1971):19–38.

Lenin, V. I. Alliance of the Working Class and the Peas-
    antry. Moscow: Progress Publishers, 1971.

_____. The Development of Capitalism in Russia. Col-
    lected Works, vol. 3. Moscow: Progress Publishers,
    1972.

Mao Tse-Tung. Selected Works of Mao Tse-Tung, vols. 1
    and 2. Peking: Foreign Language Press, 1967.

Margolis, Jane. "El Papel de la Mujer en la Agricultura
    del Bajio." Iztapalapa 1 (1979):158–70.

Marx, Karl. Capital, vols. 1, 2, and 3. New York: In-
    ternational Publishers, 1967.

_____. Capital, vol. 1. New York: Vintage, 1977.

_____. The Class Struggles in France 1848–1850. Moscow:
    Progress Publishers, 1972.

_____. A Contribution to the Critique of Political Economy.
    New York: International Publishers, 1970.

_____. "The Eighteenth Brumaire of Louis Bonaparte."
    In The Marx-Engels Reader, edited by Robert Tucker,
    pp. 436–525. New York: Norton, 1972.

_____. "Manifesto of the Communist Party." In The
    Marx-Engels Reader, edited by Robert Tucker, pp. 335–
    62. New York: Norton, 1972.

_____. Pre-Capitalist Economic Formations. New York: International Publishers, 1964.

Marx, Karl, and Friedrich Engels. Correspondence 1846-1895: A Selection with Commentary and Notes. New York: International Publishers, 1935.

_____. The German Ideology. New York: International Publishers, 1947.

_____. Selected Works in One Volume. New York: International Publishers, 1972.

Meillassou, Claude. Mujeres, Graneros y Capitales. Mexico: Siglo XXI, 1977.

Memoria del Primer Encuentro Nacional de Organizaciones Campesinas Independientes. Proceedings of Peasant Conference held in Milpa Alta D.F., October 12-14, 1979. Mexico: Universidad Autónoma de Guerrero, 1979.

Mitrany, David. Marx Against the Peasants. London: George Weidenfeld and Nicolson Ltd., 1951.

Morett, Jorge. "El Proletariado Agrícola en la Region de Zamora." Cuadernos Agrarios 6 (May 1978):67-97.

NACLA. "Cosecha de Ira: Agroimperialismo en el Noroeste de Mexico." Cuadernos Agrarios 5 (September 1977): 87-94.

Negri, Toni. "Capitalist Domination and Working Class Sabotage." In Working Class Autonomy and the Crisis, pp. 93-117. London: Red Notes and CSE Books, 1979.

Newspapers. Information cited extensively from issues of daily newspapers from Mexico D.F.: Uno Mas Uno (1977-1981), Excelsior, El Día, El Universal, Sol de Mexico, and from Sonora: Diario del Yaqui, El Imparcial.

Olivera, Mercedes. "Sobre la Explotación y Opresión de las Mujeres Acasilladas en Chiapas." Cuadernos Agrarios 9 (September 1979):43-55.

Oswald, Ursula, ed. Mercado y Dependencia. Mexico:
Editorial Nueva Imagen, 1979.

_____. "El Monopolio de la Central de Abastos y Sus
Efectos en la Sociedad Campesina." In Mercado y
Dependencia, edited by Ursula Oswald. Mexico: Edi-
torial Nueva Imagen, 1979.

Palerm, Ángel. "Sobre la Formula M-D-M y la Articulación
del Modo Campesino de Producción al Sistema Capitalista
Dominante." Cuadernos de la Casa Chata 5 (1977):1-23.

Paré, Luisa. El Proletariado Agrícola en Mexico. Mexico:
Siglo XXI, 1977.

Paz Paredes, Lorena, and Julio Moguel. Santa Gertrudis:
Testimonios de una Lucha Campesina. Mexico: ERA,
1979.

Pearse, Andrew. "Agrarian Change: Trends in Latin
America." In Agrarian Problems and Peasant Movements in Latin America, edited by Rodolfo Stavenhagen,
pp. 11-40. Garden City, N.Y.: Doubleday, 1970.

Peña, Devon. "Las Maquiladoras: Mexican Women and
Class Struggle in the Border Industries." Aztlan 11
(Fall 1980).

Pepin-Lehalleur de Martinez, Marielle. "El Empleo de
Trabajo Ajeno por la Unidad Campesina de Producción."
In Capitalismo y Campesinado en Mexico, edited by
Rodolfo Stavenhagen, pp. 133-62. Mexico: CISINAH,
1976.

Pineda, Miguel. "La Subsunción del Trabajo Agrícola al
Capital." Thesis, Instituto Nacional de Antropología y
Historia, 1980. Mexico D.F.

Poulantzas, Nicos. Political Power and Social Classes.
London: New Left Books, 1975.

Pozas, Ricardo. Los Indios en las Clases Sociales de
Mexico. Mexico: Siglo XXI.

Punto Crítico: Revista Quincenal de Información y Análisis Político. Mexico: Editorial Antares, issues from 1976 to 1981.

Quijano, Anibal, and Francisco Weffort. Populismo, Marginalización y Dependencia. Costa Rica: Editorial Universitaria Centro Americana, 1976.

Rama, Ruth. "Empresas Transnacionales y Agricultura Mexicana: El Caso de las Procesadoras de Frutas y Legumbres." Investigación Económica 37 (January 1978):75-117.

Ravelo, Renato. Los Jaramillistas. Mexico: Editorial Nuestro Tiempo, 1978.

Rello, Fernando. "Modo de Producción y Clases Sociales." Cuadernos Políticos 2 (April-June 1976):100-5.

Rey, Pierre Philippe. Las Alianzas de Clases. Mexico: Siglo XXI, 1976.

Reynolds, Clark W. The Mexican Economy: Twentieth Century Structure and Growth. New Haven, Conn.: Yale University Press, 1970.

Romano, Phil, and Raya Dunayevskaya. The American Worker. Detroit: Facing Reality Publishing Company, 1946.

Romer, Marta. "La Comunidad Rural." Mexico, 1980. n.p.

_____. "Los Mixes de Totontepec en Comunidad, Migración y Desarrollo: Un Proceso Integrado de Cambio Social." Thesis, Instituto Nacional de Antropología y História, 1979. Mexico D.F.

Ronfeldt, David. Atencingo: The Politics of Agrarian Struggle in a Mexico Ejido. Stanford, Calif.: Stanford University Press, 1973.

Rosales Gonzalez, Margarita. Los Intermediarios Agrícolas y la Economía Campesina. Mexico: INAH, 1979.

Sanderson, Steven E. Agrarian Populism and the Mexican
State: The Struggle for Land in Sonora. Berkeley:
University of California Press, 1981.

Schejtman, Alejandro. "El Agro Mexicano y Sus Interpretes."
Nexos 4 (March 1981):37-47.

Schram, Stuart R. The Political Thought of Mao Tse-Tung.
New York: Praeger, 1976.

Secretaría de Agricultura y Recursos Hidraulicos. Dirección
General de Distritos y Unidades de Temporal. "El
Riesgo Compartido Como Medio para Acelerar el Cambio
Tecnológico en el Sector Agropecuario." Mexico, June
5, 1980. Mimeograph.

Servolín, Calude. "Aspectos Económicos de la Absorción de
la Agricultura en el Modo de Producción Capitalista."
Cuadernos Agrarios 2 (April-June 1976):105-26.

"Solo Organizados Se Puede Hacer Algo." Solidaridad 185
(August 1978):34-37.

Stalin, Joseph. Dialectical and Historical Materialism. New
York: International Publishers, 1977.

Stavenhagen, Rodolfo, ed. Agrarian Problems and Peasant
Movements in Latin America. Garden City, N.Y.:
Doubleday, 1970.

Szekely, Miguel. "El Apoyo a Procesos de Desarrollo
Autogenerado." Narxhí-Nandhá Revista de Economía
Campesina 8/9/10 (September 1978):10-17.

_____. "La Organización Colectiva para la Producción
Rural." Comercio Exterior 27 (December 1977):1471-84.

"Las Tesis Políticas del PCM." Machete: Revista Mensual
de Cultura Política 7 (November 1980):22-67.

Tronti, Mario. "Social Capital." Telos 17 (Fall 1973):
98-121.

Villanueva Mukul, Eric. "Las Condiciones Económicas y
Sociales y Políticas del Trabajador Henequenero."
Yucatán Historia y Economía 3 (September-October 1977).

196 / Contemporary Peasantry in Mexico

_____. "La Lucha de la Comunidad de Chemax." Yucatán: História y Economía 7 (September–October 1978):33–51.

Voces del Campo 5 (September 1979):n.p.

Vogt, Evon. The Zincantecos of Mexico. New York: Holt, Rinehart and Winston, 1970.

Warman, Arturo. Los Campesinos Hijos Predilectos del Regimen. Mexico: Editorial Nuestro Tiempo, 1972.

_____. "Los Campesinos y la Política." La Cultura en Mexico Suplemento de Siempre! 778 (January 12, 1977): II–IV.

_____. "Las Crisis Agrícola y Agraria en Mexico." La Cultura en Mexico Suplemento de Siempre! 798 (June 10, 1977):VII–IX.

_____. "Frente a la Crisis Política Agraria o Política Agrícola?" Comercio Exterior 28 (June 1978):681–87.

_____. Y Venimos a Contradecir: Los Campesinos de Morelos y el Estado Nacional. Mexico: CISINAH, Ediciónes de la Casa Chata, 1976.

Wheelwright, E. L., and Bruce McFarlane. The Chinese Road to Socialism. New York: Monthly Review Press, 1970.

Working Class Autonomy and the Crisis: Italian Marxist Texts of the Theory and Practice of a Class Movement—1964–1979. London: Red Notes and CSE Books, 1979.

Zerowork: Political Materials 1, 2 (1975, 1977):n.p.

INDEX

ABOUT THE AUTHOR

ANN LUCAS DE ROUFFIGNAC is a lecturer in Economics at the University of St. Thomas, Houston, Texas.

From September 1977 to September 1980, she resided in Mexico D.F., conducting research on the peasantry in Mexico. The last year she worked closely with Lic. Gustavo Esteva, Director of COPIDER (Comité Promotor de Investigación de Desarrollo Rural).

Her work has been published in Mexico in Comercio Exterior and El Día.

Dr. de Rouffignac holds a B.A. in Latin American Studies from the University of Texas at Austin and a Ph.D. in Economics (1982), also from U.T.